For Bob & Cristle,
With all kind regards!

Richard

CHERUBINO'S LEAP

CHERUBINO'S LEAP

In Search of the Enlightenment Moment

RICHARD KRAMER

THE UNIVERSITY OF CHICAGO PRESS

Chicago and London

The University of Chicago Press, Chicago 60637
The University of Chicago Press, Ltd., London
© 2016 by The University of Chicago
All rights reserved. Published 2016
Printed in the United States of America

25 24 23 22 21 20 19 18 17 16   1 2 3 4 5

ISBN-13: 978-0-226-37789-6 (cloth)
ISBN-13: 978-0-226-38408-5 (e-book)
DOI: 10.7208/chicago/9780226384085.001.0001

This book has been supported by the Gustave Reese Endowment of the
American Musicological Society, funded in part by the National Endowment
for the Humanities and the Andrew W. Mellon Foundation.

Library of Congress Cataloging-in-Publication Data
Names: Kramer, Richard, 1938– author.
Title: Cherubino's leap : in search of the Enlightenment moment / Richard Kramer.
Description: Chicago : The University of Chicago Press, 2016. |
Includes bibliographical references and index.
Identifiers: LCCN 2016019385 | ISBN 9780226377896 (cloth : alk. paper) |
ISBN 9780226384085 (e-book)
Subjects: LCSH: Music — Germany — 18th century — History and criticism. |
Music — Austria — 18th century — History and criticism. | Enlightenment. |
Music — 18th century — Philosophy and aesthetics. | Klopstock, Friedrich Gottlieb,
1724–1803 — Musical settings — History and criticism. | Music and literature —
History — 18th century.
Classification: LCC ML275.3 .K73 2016 | DDC 780.943/09033 — dc23
LC record available at https://lccn.loc.gov/2016019385

For SIEGMUND LEVARIE,

who lived every moment in this music

CONTENTS

ACKNOWLEDGMENTS

Of the many encounters that nourished the fragmentary ideas from which this book would materialize, I think first to a run of seminars at the Graduate Center of the City University of New York. "Surfing the Enlightenment," it was called, its participants taking to its fledgling ideas with fresh hearings and bold, skeptical thought, opening into new perspectives that I could hardly have anticipated. From these keen-eared students I learned more than they can know.

When it came to the actual writing, I was fortunate to have been invited to share several of its themes at various campuses and to have profited greatly from the often vigorous conversations that followed. An early version of chapter 3, on that riddling moment of silence in Emanuel Bach's Sonata in F Minor, was read at the invitation of Annette Richards for the conference "Keyboard Culture in Eighteenth-Century Berlin" at Cornell University in March 2011; and it was again at the invitation of Professor Richards that some of the ideas developed in the Klopstock chapters were offered in a keynote address at the conference "Sensation and Sensibility at the Keyboard in the Late Eighteenth Century" at Cornell in October 2014. Beethoven's engagement with Klopstock (chapter 6) was earlier explored in a keynote talk for the New Beethoven Research Group at the meetings of the American Musicological Society in Pittsburgh in November 2013. It was generous of David Levy, William Kinderman, and William Meredith to tender the invitation. A preliminary version of the chapter on Gluck's *Iphigénie en Tauride* was read at a birthday celebration for Maynard Solomon at the Juilliard School in May 2010; my thoughts are very much with Maynard as I write these lines. "Konstanze's Tears" (chapter 9) was offered at a conference honoring James Webster at Cornell University in October 2012; a still earlier version of it was read at Stony Brook University, thanks to Ryan Minor's gracious invitation to participate in a symposium on Mozart's *Entführung* one perfect afternoon in April of that year, and to my fellow co-conspirators, Adrian Daub, Sarah van der Laan, and Jessica Waldoff, from whom I learned much.

Chapter 2 first appeared in *Variations on the Canon: Essays on Music from Bach to Boulez in Honor of Charles Rosen on His Eightieth Birthday* (Rochester, NY: University of Rochester Press, 2008), and I am grateful to the Press for granting permission to publish the essay here with only minimal emendations. Those who have been moved by Rosen's incomparable writings, by the profundity of his music making, by the intensity and wit of his intellect, will understand the humility with which one endeavors to write in his honor.

That Wendy Allanbrook is no longer physically with us only deepens the regret that my Cherubino chapter could not profit from the immediacy of her incisive and embracing critique, but my indebtedness to her work (and her spirit) will, I hope, be evident behind and between the lines, and in our shared wonder at this creature whom she unforgettably recognized as "the presiding genius of the opera."[1]

And Cherubino, this *improvvisatore* of endless fascination, has been the topic of spirited conversations with the remarkable artist Friedrich Danielis, active in Vienna, Venice, and New York, whose *Leichter als Licht: Innenansichten über das Schöne* (Vienna: Löcker, 2012), in its unique, aphoristic insights into art, music, and literature, has been a constant and lively inspiration. But it is Frieder's whimsical and brilliant inked drawings evoking the mercurial Cherubino that I think of here with wonder and joy.

My indebtedness to colleagues and friends who've responded to my inquiries with advice and material support is heartfelt: to Paul Corneilson, managing editor of *Carl Philipp Emanuel Bach: The Complete Works*, who has been more than generous in furnishing copies of otherwise inaccessible source material; to Annette Richards, for her brilliant and subtle interrogation of my thought; to Robert Marshall, whose deft editing of the piece for the Rosen volume was only the latest in a lively conversation initiated in our graduate student days. To Lewis Lockwood, ever willing to dip into his seemingly inexhaustible well of knowledge, I owe an even greater debt for his sage advice and the constancy of his support over the years. Kristina Muxfeldt's meticulous reading of my work comes always with richly provocative insights that lead into brave new worlds. Ellen Rosand took precious time away from other commitments to read a lengthy chapter and share her thoughts. The publication in 2014 of Christoph Wolff's exemplary edition of Emanuel Bach's *Miscellaneous Songs* and the *Polyhymnia Portfolio* for the *Complete Works* happily inspired some late-hour reflections on Bach's extraordinary engagement with the poets of his Hamburg years. Finally, two readers for the Press led me to rethink some overly rash formulations, and saved me from further embarrassments. That their identities are held in con-

---

1. *Rhythmic Gesture in Mozart*: Le Nozze di Figaro *and* Don Giovanni (Chicago: University of Chicago Press, 1983), 98.

fidence does nothing to diminish my deep gratitude for their hard work, from which only I have profited.

For invaluable help in the acquisition of materials from their precious collections, I am indebted to Clemens Brenneis and his colleagues at the Staatsbibliothek zu Berlin; to Ulrich Leisinger, Gabriele Ramsauer, and Armin Brinzing at the Internationale Stiftung Mozarteum, Salzburg; to Frances Barulich, the Mary Flagler Cary Curator of Music Manuscripts and Printed Music at the Morgan Library and Museum, New York; to Bettina Baumgärtel, of the online Angelika Kauffmann Research Project, and Waltraud Maierhofer, University of Iowa, with whom I consulted about some drawings by Angelika Kauffmann; to Karin Ellermann, Archivarin of the Goethe- und Schiller-Archiv, and Olaf Mokansky, of the Herzogin Anna Amalia Bibliothek, both at the Klassik Stiftung Weimar; to Henni Kanstrup, the Music Collection at the Royal Library, Copenhagen; and to the librarians and their staffs at the Bayerisches Staatsbibliothek, Munich; the library of the Metropolitan Opera Company, New York; and the Bibliothèque-musée de l'Opéra, Paris. A generous award from the University Committee on Research at the City University of New York helped defray expenses for the acquisition of illustrations and the preparation of music examples. Other expenses were offset by a grant from the Otto Kinkeldey Endowment of the American Musicological Society, funded in part by the National Endowment for the Humanities and the Andrew W. Mellon Foundation.

From our first conversation over coffee in Toronto in 2014, Marta Tonegutti, the superb music editor at the University of Chicago Press, has been a devoted and even passionate advocate for this project, and for this I shall be ever in her debt. Among the helpful staff at Chicago, Evan White has been masterful in shepherding the book through its various stations at the Press and advising on every aspect of its production. I was fortunate to have been introduced to Rex Isenberg, whose elegant touch and expertise transformed my diverse music examples into handsome, legible copy; and to Marilyn Bliss, who composed the index under constraints of an unfriendly deadline and did so with consummate professional expertise.

It was Siegmund Levarie who first led me to think about music as an engagement with ideas, and it is his *Geist* that hovers over these pages. What I owe him is immeasurable. As ever, Martha Calhoun has been my true compass, holding me to course through those inevitable rough seas, sharing her expert legal advice, her musicianship, her wisdom, her unwavering support, her companionship. No author, no partner, could ask for more.

PREFACE

This is a book of snapshots. Each of them captures a moment, just as in the predigital past of recent memory we'd attempt to freeze the action of an event, that fleeting instant caught on high-speed film through a complicity of lens and shutter, the before and after left to the imagination. To put in play this *camera obscura* in search of such moments was to anticipate an action, a smile, a gesture that would reclaim for us a place and a time long after its players had vanished.

Hearing music this way is no less challenging, if not quite analogous in how the camera does its work. In our encounters with music, we listen for such moments: the smile, the gesture, the telling action that invites us into the piece and that, upon further reflection and if the music will allow, guides us into its less accessible recesses, deepening for us its befores and afters. In the Enlightenment, or that slice of it that happens in Germany and Austria in the 1770s and 1780s, these moments have special appeal. Put the other way round, the languages of art in the Enlightenment — music, literature, drama, the visual arts, even critical writing about ancient art — seem, each on their own terms, to invigorate their narratives from the stimulus of such moments: the stretched syntax in an ode by Klopstock, where meaning hinges on the precise placement of a syllable, a phoneme; the barely comprehensible dissonance at some critical turn of phrase in a sonata by Emanuel Bach; the frisson of recognition captured in an ensemble by Mozart, a *scena* by Gluck. And we eavesdrop on Lessing and Goethe, each in pursuit of the moment frozen into the marble of Laocoon.

Moses Mendelssohn had a word for it: *Überraschung*, the stunned surprise that excites the sensation of beauty. It is this *Überraschung* that we come to expect and even fear when, deep into the fourth act of Gluck's *Iphigénie en Tauride*, the executioner's knife about to do its work, these long-lost siblings, the issue of the tragic house of Atreus, finally recognize each other. The precise moment of recognition, Aristotle's *anagnorisis*, is prepared and enabled in a sequence of lesser moments, each setting off its own revelatory *Überraschung*. This singular event, it seemed to me, could be taken to stand for a condition of art in the Enlightenment, a provocation to pursue its vast implications in a range of works that would appear, on the face of it, to have little, if anything, to do with the grand Parisian stage for which Gluck conceived his *tragédie*. Here, for one, is Carl Philipp Emanuel Bach, withdraw-ing into his clavichord, composing a sonata in F minor whose moments of *Überraschung* would inspire hardly less critical wonder than Gluck's opera.

A glance at the table of contents will suggest something of the trajectory of our journey. From the chromatic moment, empowering the solitary tone that will move the music into the linguistic sphere of poetry, toward a lan-guage not of words but of feeling—a *Sprache der Empfindungen*, it would be called[1]—we are led to the poetic moment, where word takes on the elo-quence of tone. If, in the literary world of the German Enlightenment, a single genre was understood to have served as a crucible for the marriage of word and tone, this was demonstrably the ode, both in its challenge to the poet who would seek to reclaim for the German language the complex prosody and sonic resonance that it found in the ruins of ancient Greece, and to the musician who would endeavor to translate its eloquence into music, both as song and, in the figurative sense, as sonata. Again, Moses Mendels-sohn, writing in 1764: "A singular and complete sequence of the most vivid ideas, as they follow upon one another according to the rules of an inspired imagination, is an ode."[2] Nearly twenty years later, Johann Nikolaus Forkel would take Mendelssohn's lapidary formulation as the basis for a simile of ode and sonata, to which we shall return in a later chapter.

It is this touching of the nerve endings of tone and word that is explored in several chapters below, the ode tending in its language toward the sensual immediacy of musical utterance, the music coming to terms with the com-plex syntax, the prosody and accent of poetic language. Klopstock, the *spiri-tus rector* of German letters in the 1760s and 1770s, is at the center of our in-quiry, drawing composers to the perilous challenge of his poetry as moths to the flame. Drawn to the challenge were both Gluck, a man exclusively of the theater, now in Paris, now Vienna, and Emanuel Bach, seemingly oblivious of the opera stage, and close by in Hamburg: two magisterial figures whose work otherwise described alien worlds, inspiring lively encounters with the poet himself, inviting us into the vibrant Enlightenment colloquy between poet and musician.

1. By Forkel, for one. See his *Allgemeine Geschichte der Musik*, vol. 1 (Leipzig: Schwick-ert, 1788; repr. Graz: Akademische Druck-u. Verlagsanstalt, 1967), 19.

2. "Eine einzige ganze Reihe höchst lebhafter Begriffe, wie sie nach dem Gesetze einer begeisterten Einbildungskraft auf einander folgen, ist eine Ode." *Briefe, die Neueste Liter-atur betreffend*, 17. Theil, 274. Brief (Berlin: Bey Friedrich Nicolai, 1764), 150.

Finally, there is opera. On this larger stage, word and tone are amplified, the tensions and dissonance of syntax, of poetic language, of sonata magnified in *drammi per musica*. In Gluck's *tragédie en musique*, its music and drama unfolding as one, Iphigénie and Oreste live out their ancient roles in the new sensibilities of the Enlightenment, their actions limned in a music of sublime pathos. For Mozart in the 1780s, the challenges lay elsewhere. If the operas of Gluck and the sonatas of Emanuel Bach, uncompromising in their bold unorthodoxy, constituted a formidable legacy, for the younger composer these lofty models were no doubt heard as impediments toward a new theater that plays with the volatile wit of Revolutionary Europe. Chérubin, a lightning rod for much of the action in the course of Beaumarchais's *folle journée*, is himself the fitful adolescent soul of the Enlightenment. In Mozart's hands, Cherubino's quicksilver moments are caught in an evanescent music always about to vanish, most notably in the final measures of a manic, mercurial duettino with Susanna. At the edge of a precipice, figurative and literal, he exposes his raw feelings, and Mozart, as though alive in the role, takes us with him in a split second of intensely chromatic music.

At the other extreme is the disconsolate Konstanze, whose tears inspire Mozart to a music that probes deeply into their source, beyond metaphor to the roots of language. In the tragic accents of her *Traurigkeit*, she, like the Pamina in a later *Singspiel*, along with the other troubled women in Mozart's operas, resists the conventions of genre. With her, we are drawn into the vortex of a chromatic language that transfigures Bretzner's touching conceit, in search of the inner Konstanze.

How to hold fast to this music that refuses to pose motionless before the camera? The explorations that follow are so many attempts to come to terms with these indelible moments, to reconstruct the complex and often paradoxical contexts in which they dwell, often uncomfortably. At the end of the day, it is to these moments that we return again and again, reliving in them the *Überraschung* that dwells within the interstices of meaning.

––––––––––

If there were an epigraph to seduce us into this journey, I'm drawn to the ironic wit with which Charles Rosen captures the Enlightenment condition: "The mere rendering of sentiment was not dramatic enough; Orestes must be shown going mad *without his being aware of it*, Fiordiligi must desire to yield while trying to resist, Cherubino fall in love without knowing what it is that he feels."[3] Extending the inquiry, we shall ask with the Pasha what it is that provokes Konstanze's tears. As Mozart's music probes beyond this "mere rendering of sentiment" to the root of something deeper, we follow him into the subconscious matrix of the work in search of some marked moment, the irritant that sets things in motion. "Dramatic sentiment was replaced by dramatic action," Rosen concludes — a shade too neatly, perhaps, for in the Enlightenment, sentiment and action feed on one another in a perpetual play of character and plot and sensibility. It is this play and the pursuit of these marked moments that will drive much of the enterprise ahead.

---

3. Charles Rosen, *The Classical Style: Haydn, Mozart, Beethoven* (New York: W. W. Norton, expanded ed., 1997), 43. Italics are Rosen's.

PRELIMINARIES

I

THE CHROMATIC MOMENT IN
ENLIGHTENMENT THOUGHT

A PREAMBLE ON PORTRAITURE AND LANGUAGE

Titles, in their terse ideogrammatic language, have a way of enfolding their subjects in enigma. A title does its work when it seduces the reader into the mysteries of the text that it prefigures, the text itself then a kind of unraveling, an exploration of the title that provokes it. And so to the title of this chapter. "Moment," at its center of gravity, holds pride of place here and in each of the chapters that follow. Leaning on the German *Moment*, it means to convey a sense of impulse, or even motive, something of substance leaching into the temporal instant, an essence of the music caught in this momentary inflection. In its specificity, the definite article further identifies this moment with the singular event that provokes the music to its extremities. To speak of the moment as *chromatic* — if that is its claim to prominence — is to inquire into the nature of its relationship to the diatonic environment within which it is defined. Must we apprehend this relationship as frozen in the hierarchies of a tonal spectrum, or ought we to hear its elements as variables in tension between two extreme positions?

To frame the question this way is to engage the music in the dialectical dramaturgy of Enlightenment thought. Without claiming to know what *is* the Enlightenment — or more to the point, what it *was* — I shall prefer, here and in the chapters that follow, to tease out those aspects of discourse — of music, of literature, of art and its criticism — that to my mind constitute a way of thinking, of holding a world teetering in ironic imbalance, of taking pleasure in the irreconcilable tension between reason and the irrational that is at the core of the Enlightenment mind.

For Moses Mendelssohn, it is the element of surprise — *Überraschung* is his word — that, in some measure, defines Enlightenment sensibility: "Our happiness depends upon enjoyment and enjoyment depends upon the swift sentiment with which each beauty surprises our senses. Unhappy are those

3

whom reason has hardened against the onset of such a surprise."[1] By these lights, it is not the timeless contemplation of beauty that is at issue, but the moment at which our sensibilities are caught off guard. Indeed, it is not clear wherein lies this *Schönheit* that is revealed to Mendelssohn's interlocutor, how it is constituted, even whether, as a thing unto itself, it exists at all, or whether what Mendelssohn has in mind is the experience of the moment, this *Überraschung* with which the sensibilities are overcome. These lines are in fact given to the fictive Euphranor, one of the disputants in an exchange of letters titled "Ueber die Empfindungen"; his counterpart, Theocles, will have much to say in defense of reason in the course of the expansive Platonic dialogue in which these matters are examined. And if there is some question whether Mendelssohn's sensibilities are in sympathy with the one or the other, perhaps it is enough that the eloquence of Euphranor's words endows them with an appeal that Mendelssohn himself must have found difficult to dispel.

From another perspective, Johann Gottfried Herder's ever-stimulating essay toward the "Origins of Language" sharpens its focus on the moment of recognition, the moment at which language is created, but also on the very notion of thought: *"Placed in the state of reflection* [Besonnenheit] *which is inherent in him, with this reflection for the first time given full freedom of action, man created language. For what is reflection* [*Reflexion*]*? What is language?"*[2] For the Enlightenment mind, if we may take Herder's impassioned *scena* as symptomatic, it is the process of discovery that is prized. "He

1. Moses Mendelssohn, *Philosophical Writings*, tr. and ed. Daniel O. Dahlstrom (Cambridge: Cambridge University Press, 1997), 10. "Unsre Glückseligkeit hanget von dem Genusse ab, und der Genuß von der schnellen Empfindung, mit der jede Schönheit unsre Sinne überraschet. Unglücklich sind diejenigen, welche die Vernunft wider den Anfall einer solchen Ueberraschung abgehärtet hat." Mendelssohn, *Philosophische Schriften*, verbesserte Auflage, erster Theil (Berlin: Bey Christian Friedrich Voß, 1771), in Moses Mendelssohn, *Schriften zur Philosophie und Äesthetik*, vol. 1 (in *Gesammelte Schriften: Jubiläumsausgabe* ... erster Band), ed. Fritz Bamberger (Berlin: Akademie-Verlag Berlin, 1929), 238.

2. *"Der Mensch, in den Zustand von Besonnenheit gesetzt, der ihm eigen ist, und diese Besonnenheit (Reflexion) zum erstenmal frei würkend, hat Sprache erfunden. Denn was ist Reflexion? was ist Sprache?"* Johann Gottfried Herder, *Abhandlung über den Ursprung der Sprache* (1772), in Herder, *Sämtliche Werke*, ed. Bernhard Suphan (Berlin: Weidmann, 1891; repr. Hildesheim: Georg Olms, 1967), vol. 5, 34, where the passage here in italics is given in *Sperrdruck*. For a slightly different English version, see *On the Origin of Language* (*Jean-Jacques Rousseau, "Essay on the Origin of Languages"; Johann Gottfried Herder, "Essay*

manifests reflection," continues Herder, "when, confronted with the vast hovering dream of images which pass by his senses, he can collect himself into a moment of awareness" — of *Anerkennung*.[3] Of this signal moment, Herder isolates a recognition of the single distinguishing mark that would enable its expression as language: "The first act of this *Anerkenntnis* results in a clear concept." In a burst of enthusiasm, the act is celebrated: "*Wohlan*! Let us acclaim him with shouts of eureka!"[4] As with Mendelssohn on beauty, it is the frisson of recognition that Herder wants us to imagine, this fleeting moment in which the world seems to hang in the balance, that is at the core of Enlightenment thought. In like mode, both Lessing and Goethe seek out this moment in coming to an understanding of the sculpture group Laocoon, to which we shall return in a later chapter.

In conjuring the iconic images of an Enlightenment sensibility, one that springs to mind is a portrait in profile by Jean-Baptiste Greuze, a chalk drawing now at the Morgan Library in New York (shown as fig. 1.1). Its subject is Denis Diderot, age forty-seven, without wig, the exposed head a sign of the free-thinking, independent mind. Diderot thought it a more accurate representation than the famous painting by van Loo: "My children, I warn you that this is not me," he writes of the van Loo. "In the course of a single day I assumed a hundred different expressions, in accordance with the things that affected me. I was serene, sad, pensive, tender, violent, passionate, enthusiastic. I had a large forehead, penetrating eyes, rather large features, a head quite similar in character to that of an ancient orator, an easygoing nature that sometimes approached the fool, the rustic simplicity of ancient times."[5] Still better, in Diderot's view, was a portrait by "a poor devil named Garant, who," Diderot writes, "managed to trap me, just as a fool sometimes comes

on the Origin of Language"), tr. John H. Moran and Alexander Gode (Chicago and London: University of Chicago Press, 1966), 115.

3. "Er beweiset Reflexion, wenn er aus dem ganzen schwebenden Traum der Bilder, die seine Sinne vorbeistreichen, sich in ein Moment des Wachens sammlen . . ." Herder, *Sämtliche Werke*, vol. 5, 35. Moran and Gode, ibid., 114.

4. "[D]er erste Aktus dieser Anerkenntnis gibt deutlichen Begriff. . . . Wohlan! Lasset uns das eureka zurufen!" Herder, ibid., 35. Moran and Gode, ibid., 114.

5. *Diderot on Art, II: The Salon of 1767*, ed. and tr. John Goodman (New Haven, CT, and London: Yale University Press, 1995), 20. My translation differs in some respects. For the original, see Denis Diderot, *Salons, III: 1767*, ed. Jean Seznec (London: Oxford University Press, 2nd ed., 1983), 67.

Figure 1.1. Jean-Baptiste Greuze: Portrait in chalk of Denis Diderot.
New York: Pierpont Morgan Library. By kind permission.

up with a witty remark. Whoever sees my portrait by Garant, sees me. 'Ecco il vero Polichinello.'"[6] To assign to himself this burlesque rôle in the *commedia dell'arte* is of course a badge of honor, a refusal of the arrogance of the aristocracy, even if we read Diderot's self-deprecation with a whiff of skepticism. It is the sensibility of the man that Diderot wants depicted. More to our point, it is the transient sense of moment, the suggestion of character as always in motion, that Diderot finds lacking in the stiff formality of the van Loo.

The Greuze profile, with shirt opened casually at the neck, brings to mind a similar one: the curious lithograph of Joseph Haydn by Adolph Kunike (see fig. 1.2). With the exception of the bust in antique style engraved by David Weiss, this is the only representation of Haydn without wig; here, too, the shirt is loosely opened at the neck, the collar rumpled. Kunike's lithograph is riddled in contradictory messages, for it shows a man in his forties (Haydn in the 1770s or even around 1780), but imagined from a date no earlier than 1817 and perhaps as late as the 1820s.[7] Its credentials as an "authentic" view of Haydn are without merit; at best, Kunike was formulating his Haydn from some contemporary image, perhaps an engraving of 1809 made from the pencil drawing (1794) by George Dance, which Haydn himself considered to be the best likeness.[8] Kunike's rare glimpse of an unbuttoned, unwigged Haydn in rumpled house coat conjures the composer in his study, the busy detail of formal portraiture, its superficial signs of authenticity, replaced by an image of a different kind, reaching inward toward the unknowable Haydn beneath the surface. Unintentionally, it conjures Greuze's profile of Diderot.[9]

6. The artist is thought to be Jean-Baptiste Garand, and while the portrait has disappeared, Garand made a pencil drawing from it which has survived, and which was first reproduced by Herbert Dieckmann, "Description of Portait," in *Diderot Studies* 2 (1952): 6–8.

7. Adolph Friedrich Kunike (1777–1838) was awarded a license as lithographer in 1817. An image of the lithograph is reproduced in H. C. Robbins Landon, *Haydn: A Documentary Study* (New York: Rizzoli, 1981), 167.

8. For the drawing by Dance, see László Somfai, *Joseph Haydn: His Life in Contemporary Pictures* (New York: Taplinger, 1969), 148 (sketch) and 149 (dated "March 20th 1794"). For another view of the latter, see H. C. Robbins Landon, *Haydn: A Documentary Study*, 105.

9. I'm reminded once more of Diderot's touching homage to his well-worn, ink-stained dressing gown—"the badge of an author," he calls it—in "Regrets sur ma vieille robe de chambre," in *Diderot: Oeuvres complètes*, vol. 18: Arts et lettres (1767–70), ed. Jochen

Figure 1.2. Adolf Kunike: Portrait of Joseph Haydn,
lithograph print (Vienna, ca. 1817). Private collection.

Figure 1.3. Joseph Lange: Portrait in oils of Wolfgang A. Mozart. Before restoration, from a photograph made in 1946. Salzburg, Mozarteum. By kind permission.

Then there is Joseph Lange's provocatively unfinished oil of Mozart (shown as fig. 1.3) — "am Klavier," as it is called, though the keyboard remained sealed in Lange's imagination.[10] The only authenticated image of

Scholbach with Jeanne Carriat et al. (Paris: Hermann, 1984), 41–60. See the discussion in my *Unfinished Music* (New York: Oxford University Press, 2008, rev. ed., 2012), 145.

10. See *Mozart und seine Welt in zeitgenössischen Bildern/Mozart and His World in Contemporary Pictures*, initiated by Maximilian Zenger, presented by Otto Erich Deutsch, in Wolfgang Amadeus Mozart, *Neue Ausgabe sämtlicher Werke*, Serie X, Werkgruppe 32 (Kassel: Bärenreiter, 1961), 299, and plate 13. "Unvollendetes/Unfinished," Deutsch calls it, but Michael Lorenz has recently shown the original work to have been completed as a smaller portrait that was then set awkwardly into the larger canvas that we know, presumably by Lange himself, showing more of a torso and, by a stretch of the imagination, a keyboard instrument in ghostly outline. Lorenz's "Joseph Lange's Mozart Portrait" is to be found

Mozart without wig — "natürliches Haar (braun)," in Otto E. Deutsch's description of it — the painting captures the immediacy of mind, the eyes fixed with an intensity almost exaggerated, as though turned inward, focused on something not visible to us, oblivious of the painter and his audience.[11] A snapshot, this seems, of the composer caught in the solitude of the moment.

Refusing the postures of conventional portraiture, undoing its masks, these images invite us into the private places of the mind. So it is with the music of the Enlightenment. The conventions are well known, and we admire the wit and originality with which the important composers take up their challenges. But then there are those moments when the composer's ear turns inward, beneath the elegant surface of the music to some less comfortable recess, beyond convention, and very nearly inscrutable, beyond our ability to seize the moment, to grasp its significance. It is this moment — Mendelssohn's *Überraschung*, Herder's *Anerkenntnis* — that is endowed, both as a mark in the great temporal expanse of music and as a signifier of refractory meaning. The quest to locate such moments, to grasp their significance, is the itch that animates the paragraphs below and the chapters that follow, where the chromatic inflection opens onto unsuspected terrain, capturing the internal probings of the composer caught between those salient contradictions that the Enlightenment mind struggled to hold in balance, where the music reveals its human face.

THE CHROMATIC MOMENT

In the apparent bedrock of an opposition between diatonic and chromatic inheres a timeless abstraction which each generation of theorists, beginning

---

at his website, as a blog dated 19 September 2012. See also Robert Münster, "Die Mozart-Portraits des Joseph Lange," in *Mozart Studien* 19 (2010): 281–95, esp. 285–86. Our illustration, courtesy of the Fotoarchiv of the Internationale Stiftung Mozarteum, shows this state of the portrait, photographed before its restoration in 1963.

11. Wolfgang Hildesheimer sees it differently: "[W]e have no idealization of Mozart, except one painterly euphemism, probably unintentional, which is most often chosen by biographers to illustrate their hero." This is the Lange portrait, which, for Hildesheimer, is memorable only "in the protruding eyeballs." See his *Mozart*, tr. Marion Faber (New York: Farrar, Straus, Giroux, 1982), 53; the original text, in German, is *Mozart* (Frankfurt am Main: Suhrkamp Verlag, 1977), 59–60. But it is precisely in those eyes, exaggerated or not, that Lange captures an intensity of concentration true to his subject — or so we would like to believe.

in ancient Greece (and no doubt earlier and elsewhere as well), interrogates as an aspect of a more broadly conceived idea of how music goes. It is far from my purpose here to attempt anything foundational toward the defining of a theoretical problem, but rather to understand, empirically, how, in the music of the Enlightenment, the tension between these two conditions — the diatonic and the chromatic — plays itself out in a music that seems often enough an exploration of this very tension.

I

We begin in 1762, on the final page of Emanuel Bach's *Versuch über die wahre Art das Clavier zu spielen*. Tipped into the book at just this place is a handsome copper-plate engraving of a Fantasia in D, a modest piece on its surface, far less challenging than the grand Fantasia in C Minor with which Bach brought to a telling conclusion his *Probestücke*, those eighteen study pieces published with Part 1 of the *Versuch* in 1753. This lesser Fantasia, a *Probestuck* of another kind, is however significant in quite another sense, for it was offered as a final illustration at the end of a lengthy disquisition titled "Von der freyen Fantasie" — offered, in fact, in two forms: as a *Gerippe* (literally, a skeleton), a representation of the piece as figured bass, typeset on the last page of text; and, in the engraved plate, as an *Ausführung* (a performance; a realization, in that paradoxical condition somewhere between improvisation and composition).[12] (The two are shown in fig. 1.4.) The complex relationship between the two — between *Gerippe* and *Ausführung* — has been long admired, ever since Heinrich Schenker took this final chapter as the topic of his own essay toward a theory of improvisation.[13]

12. For a facsimile reprint, see Carl Philipp Emanuel Bach, *Versuch über die wahre Art, das Clavier zu spielen, Erster und zweiter Teil*, Faksimile-Nachdruck der I. Auflage, Berlin 1753 und 1762, ed. Lothar Hoffmann-Erbrecht (Leipzig: Breitkopf & Härtel, 1969). Finally, we have a scholarly edition of the work: *Versuch über die wahre Art das Clavier zu spielen* (*Carl Philipp Emanuel Bach. The Complete Works*, series 7, vols. 1–3), 3 vols., ed. Tobias Plebuch (Los Altos, CA: Packard Humanities Institute, 2011). For a review, see my "Probing the *Versuch*," in *Keyboard Perspectives* 5 (2012): 83–94. The standard English translation of Bach's text is *Essay on the True Art of Playing Keyboard Instruments*, tr. and ed. William J. Mitchell (New York: W. W. Norton, 1949).

13. Heinrich Schenker, "Die Kunst der Improvisation," in Schenker, *Das Meisterwerk in der Musik* [vol. 1] (Munich, Vienna, Berlin: Drei Masken Verlag, 1925), 11–40, esp. 21–30; English as "The Art of Improvisation," tr. Richard Kramer, in *The Masterwork in Music*,

Figure 1.4. Carl Philipp Emanuel Bach, *Versuch über die wahre Art das Clavier zu spielen*, Part 2 (Berlin, 1762), 341, and unpaginated plate.

My purpose is more modest. I want simply to root around in Bach's language, savoring his way of talking through the events of the Fantasia, seeking an entry into our larger topic. The text of the full paragraph has been given many times. Here is the core of it:

> At (1) we see the long sustaining of the harmony in the principal key at the beginning and at the end. At (2) a modulation to the fifth is advanced, where we remain for quite a while, until, at (x) the harmony proceeds to E minor. The three notes at (3), under which a slur is drawn, elucidate the preparation for the following repetition of the chord of the second, which is retaken via an inversion of the harmony. The preparation at (3) is realized through slow figures, in which the bass has been intentionally omitted. The transition from the B with the seventh chord to the following Bb with the second chord reveals an ellipsis, for a six-four chord on B or a triad on C ought really to have preceded it. At (4) the harmony appears to proceed to D minor, but instead, with the omission of the minor triad on D, the augmented fourth in the second-chord on C is taken, as if one were to modulate to G major, but G minor is taken in its place (6), whereupon, through frequent dissonant chords, the music is returned to the tonic, and the Fantasia closes with an organ point.

No talk here of anything resembling thematic substance. In a comparison of the earlier C-minor Fantasia with this one, Bach writes merely that the earlier one is "mit vieler Chromatik vermischet" (interlarded with much chromaticism) while this one consists "**mehrentheils** [emphasis Bach's] aus ganz natürlichen und gewöhnlichen Sätzen" (for the most part of quite natural and usual passages). Harmony is the main business — not, however, as a thing in itself, admired for its sonorous beauty or its shaping of phrases, but rather as a function of what might be called the chromatic moment. What matters here is the gradual and deliberate deployment of chromatic tones toward a point of greatest remove from the tonic, the advance of each tone celebrated in some new *Figur*, in turn setting off a music that approaches the condition of theme. The very first chromatic tone, the G♯ marked by Bach's numeral 2, provokes just such an event, as if liberating the music from a locked-down tonic. (The numerals are entered only in the figured-bass example, and, tellingly, not in the full-blown fantasy.) Even at the moment of its resolution,

———
vol. 1, ed. William Drabkin (Cambridge and New York: Cambridge University Press, 1994), 2–19, esp. 8–13.

the bass having moved to A, it is the G♯ that lingers, isolated high in the treble and sustained, dissonantly. Only the most austere player would resist the temptation to indulge that high G♯ with *Bebung*, that tremulous vibrating of the string that, among keyboard instruments, only the clavichord can produce. At the end of its duration, the tone is embellished with a *Doppelschlag*, pressing toward a resolution that is frustrated by the introduction of the next chromatic tone: a D♯ which at once divests the A of its function as the root of a new tonic. Now a dissonant seventh above B, it drives the music to a farthest reach in its chromatic adventure. Bach's **X** only signals what is to happen here—or rather, what *might* happen—in the *Ausführung*. Bach speaks of a modulation to E minor, and to a subsequent "ellipsis" when the bass moves from B♮ (a root) to B♭ (a seventh below a root C).[14]

It is precisely here, where the theoretical idea of the piece is at its most extreme, at the continental divide between sharp side and flat side, where the drive outward toward ever more remote fifths from the tonic is corrected, abruptly and, so to say, irrationally, at the turn toward the subdominant—in this case, and in many others, toward the minor subdominant (achieved, finally, at Bach's numeral 6): it is here, at this inscrutable moment—this ellipsis, as Bach calls it—that the music springs to life, as though in search of its meaning. Runs and arpeggiations give way to music of substance. Those big dotted chords announce the moment. An eloquent rhetoric is engaged. The deep B is sustained beneath a serpentine elaboration of the seventh chord, now in languorous eighth notes, whose curves intimate thematic shape. And here is where theory and practice are in dispute. The sustained B in the *Gerippe* can't account for all those notes that evolve from it in the *Ausführung*. Even Bach's description of the ellipsis—the theoretical gap between this deep B and the B♭ that follows—doesn't quite explain what happens here.[15] It is as though Bach pushes the music to its limit, toward a tension at the edge of coherence.

Ellipsis is a device that toys with reason, containing within its space a violation of some syntactic rule: reason and its adversary head to head. It is

14. Why Bach assigns the letter **X** to this moment, interrupting the sequence of numerals, is not clear to me. Perhaps the typesetting of the music example was already fixed when Bach realized the need to mark this moment, inserting "bey (x)" in the text at the last moment.

15. Indeed, Bach's elliptical prose inspired Schenker to a remarkable explanation of the substrata of the passage. See fig. 12 in his "Kunst der Improvisation," 29; and "Art of Improvisation," 13.

this tension, at the elliptical moment, where imagination (the improvisatory *Ausführung*) and its staid companion (the grounded structure of a figured bass, and its extension in some greater tonal design) go at each other. What is creation, Bach seems to say, if not this drive toward the edge, the control of reason holding hard against the flight of the imagination? This latter condition is eloquently amplified by Johann Georg Sulzer as a music performed "from a certain fullness of feeling and in the fire of inspiration" [aus einer gewissen Fülle der Empfindung und in dem Feuer der Begeisterung].[16] Sulzer's powerful metaphor for the unleashing of the creative act overshadows his failure to recognize the grounding of the act in the no less powerful restraint of what might be called the theoretical imperative.

To read this final illustration in the *Versuch* as a lambent mark in the unfolding of the Enlightenment tapestry would risk exaggerating its significance. On the face of it, its meaning in Bach's project is simple: to articulate the crossing of a border from rudimentary keyboard pedagogy to the improvisatory process of fantasia—*fantasieren*, a verb, an act—as requisite to mature composition.[17] We are witness to this rare glimpse into the mind of the composer even as he composes—or, more accurately, as he attempts to explain, *ex post facto*, how the improvisatory rush of the piece is to be reconciled with a timeless and unforgiving theoretical bedrock that underlies the music. But the music has its own story to tell. These chromatic moments are identified not merely in elaboration of some modulatory scheme, as equidistant modules of architectural structure. Rather, they are conceived as *dramatic* events, endowed with meaning, each celebrated, in some idiosyncratic way, thematically, rhetorically. This is what the piece is *about*.

II

It is in this sense, in its focus on the chromatic moment and the ellipsis that it provokes, that Bach's final paragraph can be said to open into the larger

16. In the article "Fantasiren; Fantasie," in *Allgemeine Theorie der Schönen Künste*. Neue vermehrte zweite Auflage (Leipzig: Weidmann, 1792–94; repr. Hildesheim: Georg Olms, 1970), vol. 2, 205.

17. "Es kann einer die Composition mit gutem Erfolge gelernet haben, und gute Proben mit der Feder ablegen, und dem ohngeacht schlecht fantasiren. Hingegen glaube ich, daß man einem im fantasiren glücklichen Kopfe allezeit mit Gewißheit einen guten Fortgang in der Composition prophezeyen kann . . ." *Versuch*, Zweyter Theil, 326; Plebuch, ed., vol. 2, 323; *Essay*, 430.

theater of Enlightenment music. One memorably daring engagement with this idea is to be encountered in the first movement of Mozart's magisterial Quintet for Strings, K. 515 (dated 19 April 1787, in the thematic catalogue of his works that Mozart had begun to keep in February 1784[18]), a moment which we shall explore more fully in the next chapter. Here, I want only to remind us of those very grand arpeggiations in C major with which the work opens, so conspicuously *diatonic*, an aura enhanced by the key itself: there is something about C major, this blankest of keys, that only sets in sharp relief the slightest chromatic infraction — and by "blank" I mean, too obviously, to play upon that aspect of chromaticism that has to do with color, for the etymology of the word is itself bound up in the concept. And so it is in this context that a detonation of the chromatic at measure 15 sets the music off in all those other directions that give meaning to the work: a simultaneity (as we once called these things) whose notes — from bottom to top: F, C♯, G, B♭, E — literally stop the music in its tracks. (See below, ex. 2.2.) We, and the players of those edgy notes, must pause as well, if figuratively, in bemused contemplation of the significance of the moment, a significance that we can only vaguely surmise, for its meaning will come clear in the leisurely expanse of time in which this story unfolds.

Two years after the composition of Mozart's quintet, a nineteen-year-old Beethoven confronted the challenge of the chromatic in a very different way. Among the keyboard music of his Bonn years are two Preludes through all the keys, composed (we are to believe) in 1789. That, at any rate, is the date, possibly in Beethoven's hand, at the top of a score otherwise in the hand of a copyist, but to which Beethoven put his signature.[19] Beethoven evidently thought well enough of these curious pieces to allow their publication in 1803. In both of them, Beethoven proceeds methodically, even pedantically, from C major through seven fifths ascending along the sharps axis, till C♯, and it is here, and <u>not</u> at the symmetrical division of the octave at F♯/G♭, that the bridge is crossed to the flat side. The crossing is enacted not without

---

18. The *Verzeichnüss aller meiner Werke*, as he titled it. The document is now at the British Library, Stefan Zweig MS 63. See *Mozart's Thematic Catalogue: A Facsimile*, Introduction and transcription by Albi Rosenthal and Alan Tyson (Ithaca, NY: Cornell University Press, 1990), fols. 10, 11.

19. The manuscript is at the Staatsbibliothek zu Berlin–Preußischer Kulturbesitz, Mus. Ms. Artaria 128. See, for one, Eveline Bartlitz, *Die Beethoven-Sammlung in der Musikabteilung der Deutschen Staatsbibliothek: Verzeichnis* (Berlin: Deutsche Staatsbibliothek, 1970), 15.

Ex. 1.1. Beethoven, Two Preludes through the Twelve Major Keys, op. 39.
A. No. 1, mm. 1–13.

some deeper recognition of the existential moment. In the first of the two preludes, as if to celebrate the achievement of C♯ major, the modulatory formula, with its busy eighths and sixteenths, is forsaken at measure 38 for an almost penitential texture and a new profile that adumbrates the theme that will govern the second prelude. The moment is sustained, and at measure 47 the music turns to C♯ *minor*, in that lean, spaced-out texture almost prophetic of the late quartets. (See ex. 1.1B.)

"Praeludium durch die 12 Dur-Tonarten" (through the twelve *major* keys), the manuscript reads, and so this turn to C♯ minor seems a furtive escape, a stolen moment from that other mode. And then, apparently to prolong the enharmonic moment, if not to obscure it, the music moves through a true Neapolitan in C♯ minor, now leading the harmony chromatically back to C (but now minor), then along the flats axis until D♭ major. But if we were about to extrapolate some theory of enharmonics from this moment, Beethoven disabuses us, for in the second Prelude, the negotiation (at measure 21) between C♯ major and D♭ major is immediate and direct (see ex. 1.2). C♯ *becomes* D♭. The keyboard player may feel as though nothing much

Ex. 1.1. Beethoven, Two Preludes through the Twelve Major Keys, op. 39.
B. No. 1, mm. 38–60.

Ex. 1.2. Beethoven, Two Preludes, op. 39, no. 2: mm. 1–29.

has happened, but the string player, if this were his music, would struggle to reconcile the discrepancy. The music is now recast in register, its texture reformulated. Briefly in five voices, three of them sustaining pedal tones on D♭, the motive is set deep, in imitative motet style, once more in homage to the moment, and perhaps in unconscious acknowledgment of the medieval durus/mollis.[20] It is as though the modulatory extravagance that in the first Prelude drove the music into the gap between C♯ and D♭ is here pointedly refused. In strict theoretical terms, the music must at this turn chart its descent through the twelve fifths that stand between C♯ and D♭. Here, in its place, is the extreme ellipsis.

III

If these two Preludes capture a young Beethoven exploring the enharmonic enigma, the modulatory trajectories of the Fantasia (Adagio) in Joseph Haydn's String Quartet in E♭ Major, op. 76, no. 6 (likely composed in 1797), sets its readers a very different challenge, and one that has been broached in earlier theoretical essays.[21] Here is a work that begins in B major (without key signature, an orthographic convention in the notation of fantasies of a certain kind) and plots its way through a number of keys, establishing a few as stations for a restatement of its opening theme, before settling for good in B major, anointed with a proper key signature, at measure 60 and through to the end at measure 112. The narrative unfolds in two large cycles: a modu-

20. Indeed, Ludwig Schiedermair was led to speak of these Preludes as bearing witness to the "Wandel . . . der sich im inneren Leben der Beethovenschen Stimmenbewegungen damals allmählich vollzog . . ." [to the mutation that then gradually came to pass in the interior life of Beethoven's voice-leading]; *Der junge Beethoven* (Leipzig: Quelle & Meyer, 1925), 356–57. Perhaps the earliest account of the Preludes is in the opening chapter of Gustav Nottebohm's *Beethovens Studien* (Leipzig and Winterthur: J. Rieter-Biedermann, 1873), 6–7.

21. For a meticulous study, heavily indebted to Heinrich Schenker, see Felix Salzer, "Haydn's Fantasia from the String Quartet, Opus 76, No. 6," in *The Music Forum*, vol. 4, ed. Felix Salzer (New York: Columbia University Press, 1976), 161–94. The movement is studied as well in László Somfai, "A Bold Enharmonic Modulatory Model in Joseph Haydn's String Quartets," in *Studies in Eighteenth-Century Music: A Tribute to Karl Geiringer on His Seventieth Birthday*, ed. H. C. Robbins Landon in collaboration with Roger E. Chapman (London: George Allen and Unwin Ltd., 1970), 370–81, esp. 375–77, where the problem is framed as a challenge to the pure intonation of string players in the tension between "fictional and real keys" (371).

latory first cycle, through measure 59, and a more conventionally stable second cycle.

It is toward the end of the first of these cycles that the chromatic moment is exercised in an enharmonic locution whose notation hints at deeper hermeneutic readings. (The entire passage is shown in ex. 1.3.) Having returned to B major at the close of a statement of the theme that had begun in B♭ major, the music continues from the cadence at measures 38–39 in reaffirmation of this sense of return, and then, in a sudden and catastrophic turn of events, breaks down on a diminished-seventh chord at measure 46, its dissonant E♮ relocated to the lowest octave, where it sounds in isolation. The music pauses here as though deep in thought, pondering the implications of its predicament. Here, it would be good to remind ourselves that for Haydn and his contemporaries, syntax is everything: the diminished seventh will be heard as a dominant ninth, where the ninth is what the Berlin theorist Johann Philipp Kirnberger would call an "inessential" [zufällige] dissonance, displacing the understood (and unsounded) root of the harmony. For Kirnberger, the true seventh of the dominant is an "essential" dissonance that resolves only with a change of root.[22] What, then, shall we hear as the displaced root of the harmony at measure 46? One plausible candidate is F♯, the F✕ in the second violin behaving as an implied G♮, the flat ninth as appoggiatura to the true root of a dominant on F♯. Our isolated E would then be heard as the essential seventh deep in the bass. And yet, its immediate context would encourage us to hear that harmony no less persuasively as a dominant on D♯, the E suspended above it delaying the arrival of a root.

The harmonies that follow at measures 47 and 48, each occupying its own measure — fermata-lengthened, as though to suspend the moment in timeless contemplation — only complicate this hearing. If the diminished seventh at measure 46 is to be heard as a dominant on F♯, its magnetic field will draw in the diminished seventh at measure 47, so that the two together will imply a succession of the roots F♯ and C♯, its bass suggesting the upward motion E through E♯ to a root-position dominant on F♯ that does not come. Within this aura, the root-position dominant seventh on E♭ that follows seems a non sequitur, effectively reversing the magnetic field so that, in retrospect,

22. For one explanation, see Johann Philipp Kirnberger, *Die wahren Grundsätze zum Gebrauch der Harmonie... als ein Zusatz zu der Kunst des reinen Satzes in der Musik* (Berlin and Königsberg: G. J. Decker and G. L. Hartung, 1773; repr. Hildesheim and New York: Georg Olms, 1970), esp. 18–21.

Ex. 1.3. Haydn, String Quartet in E♭ Major, op. 76, no. 6, second movement, mm. 39–63.

we hear the harmony at measure 47 as a dominant on Bb, its upper note a misspelling of Cb. That dissonant E♮ in the bass at measure 46 will now be re-construed as Fb, an appoggiatura that will resolve to the deep Eb at measure 48. Haydn's *con licenza* admits to the enharmonic sleight of hand in the notation, but also to the odd displacement of the Bb in the first violin to an inner voice, evidently to avoid the implication of parallel (or rather, "covered") fifths in the outer voices from measure 47 to measure 48.

In their sphinx-like notation, these three bars challenge us to hear an inflection of meaning in the music that now follows. Squarely in Ab major, this new exposition of the principal theme assumes a posture and a significance that no other statement of it can claim: here, indeed, is the last time that the theme will be heard in its full eight measures. Here, too, the outer voices are separated by two full octaves — in every other statement, the distance is an octave — so that the deep Ab feels more firmly grounded. Even the grace-note Ab in the first violin, delivering the theme into an upper register, has its baggage, having been forced into a lower register by the curious disposition of the Bb in measure 48. And so, the opening of the theme here sounds, if only momentarily, in two registers.

The apparent obfuscation around these three chords, in the fragile web of their relationship to one another, has then a true bearing on the significance of the piece, for the emergence of the theme in Ab major now resonates with a clarity that demystifies these obscure harmonies, setting itself apart from the labyrinthian modulatory track of the first cycle. It is as though the grinding progress of the piece, from its inception in B major up through these elliptical chords, has been in fitful, empirical quest to find its bearings, to locate a center. Indeed, the centrality of Ab seems only underscored in the manner in which it is abandoned. The utterly plain extension of Ab in the four bars that follow the cadence (measures 56–59) comes upon B major inadvertently, an echo of those earlier, similarly unexpected discoveries of E major and Bb major. To put it simply, the return to B major is endowed with none of the significance — dramatic, rhetorical, logical — that one might otherwise claim for the retrieval of the tonic after excursions of this extreme tonal range.

Still, the syntax of the movement is not quite so simply parsed. To the Enlightenment mind, this apparent antithesis of Ab major and B major would be apprehended less as ratio, in the language of enharmonic abstraction, than as a tension between players staged in a drama of wit and irony. Within the Adagio, Emanuel Bach's vision of ellipsis seems apropos. For it does not take a bold leap of imagination to understand the return to B major at measure 60 as a delayed response to the music beginning at measure 39 and running through the two diminished sevenths. In one sense, the stopping of time precisely here — before, that is, the intervention of the dominant seventh on E♭ — puts us at the threshold of the return that comes finally at measure 60. The missing harmony is the root-position dominant at F♯ that might have come at measure 48. In its place, we are led to this otherworldly sounding of the theme in a remote A♭.

Yet, in the larger theater of the quartet, A♭ is anything but otherworldly. This is the key in which the Adagio might well have sounded — *ought* to have sounded, if we are reading accurately the signs of its statement at measure 49. And if this is so, we are then witness to a reversal of the diatonic/chromatic circuitry. In the quartet-world of E♭ major, B major is the extreme outlier, eight fifths away on the spectrum of ascending fifths toward the sharps side.[23] The finding of A♭ is a journey inward toward the diatonic.[24]

IV

If, in the Enlightenment and beyond, music is born of an increasingly complex dialectic between two tonal spheres, each of its tonics generating its own array of over- and undertones, then the identity of one of these areas as a chromatic function of the other readily plays out in a confrontation of substance, so that it no longer seems quite adequate to speak of the one as the secondary issue (a chromatic embellishment) of a primary, diatonic basis. And yet, when the game is over, when the temporalities of this confrontation are exhausted and the piece is returned, as by convention it must be, to its tonic of origin, then (paradoxically, perhaps) we are inclined to view such relationships hierarchically, and the question then arises whether this

23. Somfai takes up this passage in his "A Bold Enharmonic Modulatory Model," 375–77.

24. We will be reminded here of the Andantino ed innocentemente in B major, the second movement of the Trio for Piano and Strings in E♭ Major (Hob. XV: 29) published in 1797, the year in which the quartet, on the best evidence, was very likely composed; see Anthony van Hoboken, *Joseph Haydn: Thematisch-bibliographisches Werkverzeichnis*, vol. 1 (Mainz: B. Schott's Söhne, 1957), 710–12. In the Andantino, the music remains in B major through thirty bars, and then, enharmonically, finds E♭ major, where it remains until the end: here, too, the outlier key is drawn back into the diatonic tonal orbit of the Trio. For the dating of the quartet, see Hoboken, *Werkverzeichnis*, vol. 1, 434.

hierarchy ought not itself to be understood dialectically. In certain pieces, the anti-tonic, the remote key, is the destination, the locus of music-making at its most inventive while the return to the tonic is conventional, even *en passant*. If this way of construing the tonal spectrum is common currency in early Romantic thought, the idea might be extended back into the Enlightenment — even to this curious Prelude of Beethoven's from 1789, and its evocation of C♯ minor. In such cases, the chromatic might be said to be where the action is, tending thereby to usurp the function of the tonic: the chromatic, that is, tends toward the diatonic, the diatonic toward the chromatic. If the tonal systems of a Haydn or a Beethoven won't allow this to happen in any complete sense, we might at least work this discomfiting idea into an understanding of their music.

MOMENTS MUSICAUX

2

THE FUGAL MOMENT

On a Few Bars in Mozart's Quintet in C Major, K. 515

"Although the C major Quintet is accepted as one of Mozart's greatest works, it is not generally recognized as perhaps the most daring of all," wrote Charles Rosen, in a discussion that few who have since thought about this work can ever put out of mind.[1] I want to pursue Rosen's claim with some observations about a few notes in the midst of the first movement of the work, where the daring, to my ears, is most deeply felt.

I

The passage that I have in mind is a famous one, but identifying the moment at which it begins — testimony, no doubt, to the seamless unfolding of thought and idea in this remarkable work — is no simple matter. At measure 170, the cello finally joins a cadencing in A minor that had begun a few bars earlier. Its deep E might at first suggest the incipit of another of those grand arpeggiations that have been setting new paragraphs in motion since the opening bars. Of course it is nothing of the kind, but rather, the incipit of a fugal subject. Here, too, the identity of this subject at its inception and its close is intentionally complicated. The subject means to recall the expansive closing bars of the exposition, music of perfect equipoise, spun out over what seems an endless pedal on the new tonic, G major. The phrasing of this closing music is not quite as simple as it may seem. The whole note at measure 131, emphatically the final note of the cadence before the closing theme, has a Janus-like aspect to it, triggering this lavish epilogue of afterbeats. Here, too, the whole note is ambivalent, for while the downbeat at measure 131 sets up the first of a series of four-bar metrical units, the new theme itself begins only at measure 132, suggesting a downbeat that cuts across the larger metrical background, oblivious of the whole-note G that sets the passage in motion (see ex. 2.1).

1. Rosen, *The Classical Style*, 268.

Ex. 2.1. Mozart, String Quintet in C Major, K. 515, first movement, mm. 129–35.

At the inception of the fugue subject, this whole note now seems to re-examine the ambivalence of its articulative function at measure 131. Its placement here at measure 170, the dominant in the resolution of the big cadence in A minor, suggests its articulation as an upbeat, pointedly reversing its function as a powerful downbeat that establishes structural closure toward the end of a very long exposition. In the chemistry of fugue subjects, such matters of articulation are intensified, fixed in a state of rhetorical certitude. That's the case here. This E at measure 170 begins life in the larger narrative of the piece, at an extreme moment of crisis, but is then immobilized, so to speak, in the highly wrought intervallic casting of a fugal subject (see ex. 2.2).

What follows is no fugal exposition in even the loosest sense, but a complex passage that drives its entries relentlessly around the circle of fifths from A minor to F minor. The chromatic saturation of the passage puts us in mind of fugue, but somewhere in the belly of the thing, where the implications of the opening of the subject are played out. To put it more schematically, the music beginning at measure 170 in the cello and second violin sets off a canon, strictly enforced through the circle of fifths in all the voices: A minor, D minor, G minor, C minor, F minor. At measures 185–90, the subject is abbreviated, the canon reconfigured: cello and violin 1 paired against violin 2 and viola 1 (viola 2 has its own independent counterpoint), bringing the music to the edge of a dominant pedal at measure 193.

The creation of a fugal subject begins here, in the reconceiving of this whole note whose function is radically altered: the whole note at measure 131 is a tonic, the whole note at measure 170 a dominant, and this of course has everything to do with its syntactical relationship to the music that follows. The cool balance of the phrase at measure 131 is now subjected to radical metamorphosis, a compression of interval and prosody, and of diction. The whole-note *Kopfton* of the subject remakes itself, for in the closing music in the exposition, it is the tone of ultimate arrival, from which the rest of the exposition is mere, but exquisite, afterbeat. Its articulation in the fugue subject is consequently problematized. The E behaves as an upbeat, in the sense dominant → tonic, and yet the implicit performance of the thing is such that the player will need to breathe between the E and its continuation, suggesting of the fugue subject not that it comprises two "motives" in the conventional sense — motivic analysis, as it is conventionally practiced, would reject a naming of the E as a motive unto itself! — but rather, that it is consumed in the idea to signify and to reconcile, as subject, two disparate musics that stand on either side of a cadential divide. This E, then, is an intensely charged note whose performance is deeply engaged in the playing out of these contraries. The extremity of the music is only intensified in the counterpoints, whose dissonances strain at the edge of comprehensibility. The resolution of the dissonant B in the second violin is made coincident not with a tonic A minor, but with its subdominant, and in six-four position. The malleable substance of the subject traffics in "difficult" intervals, finally in a diminished fourth followed by a stunning *downward* leap of a major ninth — excepting, of course, the initial statement, where the bottom string of the cello constrains it to the closer octave: in retrospect, we must imagine hearing this Bb an impossible octave lower — grating against a suspension in another voice.

What sets all this off? I return to the crux at measure 170 and its release in fugue. The music around this cadence, in its pitching of E in the highest register, will bring to mind what might be called the first crisis of the piece, at measure 15 (to which I alluded in the previous chapter). It is here that the controlled decorum of the opening of the quintet is threatened. The E high in the first violin seems to catch the players by surprise. The incessant eighth notes in the inner voices give way to the pitches of a dominant-ninth chord — the first truly chromatic notes in the piece — whose root, strongly implied, is A. In its place, the cello sounds a deep F, anticipating the resolution of the high E to D, and ignoring the powerful appeal of the other voices to provide a missing root. The effect of this F is exceptional, clinching the linear configuration plotted out by the cello at the incipits of its three arpeggiations, at C, G, and E. The F, heard for a fleeting moment to initiate yet another such arpeggiation, upsets this neat patterning.

And it is at just this moment that everything happens: an eruption of the chromatic, C♯ and Bb suggesting — but only suggesting — trajectories along the sharp, dominant axis and the flat subdominant, conjoined with a rupture

Ex. 2.2. Mozart, String Quintet, K. 515, first movement,
mm. 1–15, 150–81, and explanatory sketch of mm. 11–15.

of the rhythmic surface, where the throbbing stops and the first violin and cello touch one another for the first time. And then there is the bass, which disturbs yet more violently the larger rhythmic unfolding, or rather, reacts to the five-measure out-of-phase motion of the opening phrases. The F in the bass comes a half bar too soon, if we legitimize those chromatic inner voices with real harmonic, functional purpose. Kirnberger (for one) would have installed a deep A as fundamental bass at this point, identifying the implicit root of the harmony.[2] But then our deeper ear hears the F as just right, the upper voices as the ephemeral ones, four appoggiaturas to the true harmony, D minor in first inversion. The F continues to hold true beneath the unfolding of the harmonies above it, resolving finally to E at measure 19.

Something in our inner, theorist's ear is triggered precisely here, at measure 15, a mere instant before the actual downbeat. That is because the deep E in the bass, continuing to sound across those three bars of arpeggiation, is doubled at the extreme treble: doubled for a barely audible instant, but doubled nonetheless, and thereby stakes a modest but compelling claim for root-ness. The phrasing—the narrative—won't allow that claim to take root just yet. But then, the central crisis of the development is brought on precisely in response to this moment: again, the harmony unfolds around C major (see measure 164) and the first violin turns its figure to the high E. When it does, the throbbing stops once again, and E is isolated for three full measures, finally doubled deep in the bass, the root of a big dominant and the incipit of a chromatically bent fugue subject. The graphing in ex. 2.2 suggests how this goes.

The attack at the downbeat of measure 15 is highly charged. The opening bars of the development pick up precisely at its dissonant pitches—a diminished seventh with powerful implications of a dominant ninth on A. In a sense, the entire first part of the development might be understood as a rehearsal of the issues surrounding the enigma of measure 15. The first violin reaches up to its high E at measure 168, and the other instruments, as though recalling measure 15, again break off their chattering, endorsing the E as the root of a dominant seventh that is sustained for three chromatically infused bars, finally supported by the deep E in the cello whose deft placement is endowed as the first note of the fugue subject.

Fugue, in its studied disquisition on a subject, takes on another layer of

2. The issue is explored, contemporary readings of the diminished seventh defeated, in Kirnberger, *Die wahren Grundsätze zum Gebrauch der Harmonie,* esp. 18–19 ff.

meaning—signifies, beyond the self-referential world internal to fugue—when it is staged as a scene in the unfolding of the larger drama of sonata. The subject of this disquisition, itself a transformation of theme, seems to bring its own consciousness of theme to some deeper place, as though in exploration of its recesses. A counterpoint of difficult intervals, a stretching of harmonic coherence to its limits, a saturation of texture: these are what fugue allows, and it is only in the dramaturgy of classical sonata that fugue takes on this role in the extreme, where the identity of fugue itself signifies an intensification of thematic consciousness: fugue as sign. This E, the defining note of the subject, contains within itself the heavily freighted E-ness that reaches back to measure 15, at a first hint of crisis.

II

The temptation to situate the quintet in a context, to identify its antecedents—its precursors, to think with Harold Bloom in the more aggressive language of influence and its anxieties—is only a response to the call to write it into a history. Rosen (p. 267) hears echoes of Haydn's String Quartet in C Major, op. 33, no. 3: "the same mounting phrase in the cello, the same inner accompanying motion, the same placing of the first violin. . . . Even Haydn's remarkable use of silence . . . is turned to account here." And yet, the two openings are so manifestly different in concept as to suggest some other process of mind. The matter is complicated by the evident, transparent play on Haydn's radical opening bars in the String Quartet in C Major, K. 465, the last of the quartets which Mozart dedicated to this "caro Amico."[3] It is as though the fraught Adagio with which Mozart famously begins is a convoluted response to the problem of beginning itself. For it is clear that Haydn's opening sets loose a theoretical problem of a certain magnitude. The bare sixth is a dissonance, E posing as a root, C as an unprepared neigh-

3. The dedication published with the Artaria print of 1785 is often reprinted and much discussed. Mark Evan Bonds, "The Sincerest Form of Flattery? Mozart's 'Haydn' Quartets and the Question of Influence," *Studi Musicali* 22 (1993): 365–409, reads the rhetorical strategies in the document. Maynard Solomon, *Mozart: A Life* (New York: HarperCollins, 1995), 315, argues that its "imagery seems to resonate with Mozart's very personal yearning for an ideal paternal/filial harmony, for a vigorous, creative, and accepting musical father." I want to suggest that its convoluted conceit may harbor a more complex strain in the relationship, that the identification of Haydn as "father" carries with it that obscure vulnerability that fathers must often endure in the aggression of their sons to supersede them.

Ex. 2.3. Haydn, String Quartet in C Major, op. 33, no. 3, first movement.

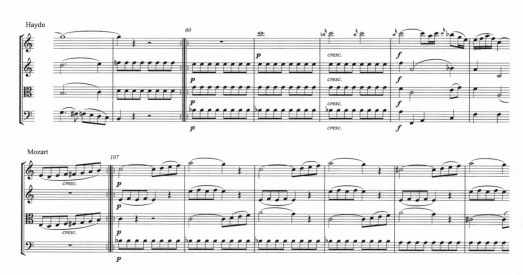

Ex. 2.4. Haydn, op. 33, no. 3, and Mozart, String Quartet in C Major, K. 465:
first movement, beginning of development, compared.

bor to B. And it is precisely this configuration to which the recapitulation addresses itself (see ex. 2.3). The opening of Mozart's Allegro is tame by comparison. But at the outset of the development, those opening bars are recast with a seventh, B♭, squarely in the bass, an echo (if not an allusion more convoluted in how it signifies) of this very moment in the Haydn quartet (see ex. 2.4).

In the quartet, the engagement with Haydn is intense. The quintet, to my ears, spins in some other orbit. If Rosen is right to hear the "same mounting phrase in the cello," it might be worth a moment to ponder the ways in which Mozart's phrase seems determined to obliterate Haydn's, to put it out of mind. The syntax of Mozart's opening paragraph is contingent upon the deep notes with which each arpeggio opens. Those notes themselves become thematic. And yet, a vestige of Haydn's texture is felt here as well. It is as though the quintet, in these opening bars, forces a rehearing—but of what, exactly? Perhaps one might think that Mozart here reenacts the sense of an earlier, and difficult, engagement with Haydn's quartet: the quintet, then, is a response, on the grandest imaginable scale, to that earlier engagement. The symptoms of it can be sniffed out here and there, but in the end, the quintet breaks away.

Its expansive opening was not lost on Beethoven. Rosen (pp. 265–66) notes of the String Quintet, op. 29, composed in 1801, that it possesses "a breadth and a tranquil expansiveness" that stands in contrast to the six quartets of op. 18, evidence that Beethoven understood the "fundamental difference between quartet and quintet" manifest in even the earliest of Mozart's works in the genre. I want, however, to propose that K. 515 seems to have entered into Beethoven's consciousness during the composition of another work noted for its grand expanse: the Quartet in F Major, op. 59, no. 1, composed in 1806.[4] If the famous opening paragraph of its first movement, in increasingly anxious pursuit of a tonic cadence, is nothing like the opening of Mozart's quintet, in other respects, Beethoven's exposition seems to echo Mozart's: in the tonicizing of the dominant of the dominant, and in its brief but consequential closing theme. The timeless expanse of twenty-one bars at the close of Mozart's exposition is compressed here into a two-bar phrase, repeated twice in variant form before the close of the exposition is elided with the opening bars of the development: "*la prima parte solamente una volta*," Beethoven inscribed at the top of the autograph. Even here, one might think that Beethoven means a play upon this moment in K. 515, where the F♮ in the viola at measure 147 leads the music seamlessly back to the tonic. At the repeat of the exposition, this same return to the tonic is interrupted by the deep C♯ in the cello. With Beethoven, it is the G♭ in the cello at measure 108

4. In a conversation recorded in August 1826, Karl Holz turns the talk to string quintets. "Welches von den Mozart'schen halten Sie für das Schönste [Which of those by Mozart do you take to be the most beautiful]?" asks Holz. To Beethoven's (unrecorded) response, Holz writes, "Auch G moll [the G minor too]," from which it might be inferred that Beethoven replied "C dur [the C major]." See *Ludwig van Beethovens Konversationshefte*, vol. 10, ed. Dagmar Beck with the assistance of Günter Brosche (Leipzig: Deutscher Verlag für Musik, 1993), 130.

Ex. 2.5. Beethoven, String Quartet in F Major, op. 59, no. 1, first movement, mm. 80–94.

that interrupts the sense of a return to the tonic, for it is only at that moment that we can know that the exposition will not be repeated.

But it is to Beethoven's fugal moment that I want to turn (see ex. 2.5). It too happens at a moment of crisis in the development, but the crisis differs in every respect from Mozart's. Here, the music settles comfortably — too comfortably, one might think — into Db major. At measure 169, the closing theme is invoked in the three lower strings, and the conversation continues for some fifteen bars, toward a cadence that promises closure on the deepest Db at measure 184. Closure, however, is contravened, the cadence interrupted by a dominant on Bb, setting in motion the first of two voices that together will formulate the double subject of a fugue. The subject in eighth notes is of course an elaboration of the opening motive as it appears at the tail end of the exposition, here in its varied form. The true subject — a counterpoint chiseled in suspended dissonance, expressive intervals, and rhythmic gesture — is yet more abstruse in its relationship to the music of the exposition. That, of course, is much to its point. We are meant to hear it as a kind of abstraction that distills from its running counterpoint a thematic essence, and in so doing, establishes itself as the primary thematic substance of the fugue.

Coming at all this from Mozart's quintet, one might wish to hear in these two fugal moments a kind of colloquy in which the one work engages the other. Both draw on the final measures of the exposition in the formulation

Ex. 2.6. Beethoven, op. 59, no. 1, and Mozart, K. 515: fugue subjects compared.

Ex. 2.7. Beethoven, op. 59, no. 1: earlier version of the principal fugue subject.

of a fugue subject. Then, Beethoven's subject seems to derive its sense of abstraction as much from Mozart's subject as from the thematic surface of its own quartet. (The subjects are shown in ex. 2.6.) Mozart's *Kopfton*, for all that I have suggested of its signifying presence, is missing. But a closer look at Beethoven's autograph score — actually, at a page that was finally stitched into oblivion with the rewriting of the fugue — is revealing in this connection, for it shows Beethoven at work precisely here, as though in search of an opening, if not an actual *Kopfton*: too revelatory, perhaps, in disclosing its source in Mozart's subject, and so the telltale B♭ is expunged.[5] (This earlier layer is shown in ex. 2.7.) Again, fugue subject as intervallic abstraction and as signifier of some deeper inner engagement.

To hear Beethoven's quartet as a text unencumbered by its ritual of creation ought to be enough for any of us. And yet, the convoluted implications in the drafting of these difficult measures leave their mark, suggestive not only of a vigorous process muted in the finality of a final version, but of an engagement with antecedents. The figure of Mozart seems to come alive in

5. The idiosyncrasies of Beethoven's counterpoint are explored in greater depth in my "'*Das Organische der Fuge*': On the Autograph of Beethoven's Quartet in F Major, Opus 59 No. 1," in *The String Quartets of Haydn, Mozart, and Beethoven: Studies of the Autograph Manuscripts*, ed. Christoph Wolff (Cambridge, MA: Harvard University Department of Music, distr. Harvard University Press, 1980), 223–65. An excellent facsimile of Beethoven's autograph manuscript was published as *Beethoven: String Quartet Opus 59 No. 1 (First "Razumovsky" Quartet, in F major)*, with an Introduction by Alan Tyson (London: Scolar Press, 1980).

these draftings, as though enmeshed in the signifying. That Beethoven even in 1806 continued to hear Mozart in his inner ear is plain enough from evidence that is both complex and plenteous.[6] In the end, Beethoven's quartet goes its own way. Its fugal moment, to which there is not the faintest allusion in the heroic celebrations of its coda, simply vanishes. Here, the two works part company.

CODA

"The coda," writes Rosen (p. 273) of the final bars of Mozart's first movement, "is masterly: the closing theme, which in the exposition was a tonic pedal on G, starts once again as a pedal on G, becoming thereby a dominant pedal instead of a tonic." Here I would quibble. The moment is set up by a terrific cadencing that brings the music to a halt on the familiar diminished seventh in anticipation of the big six-four. But the six-four is delayed, and the diminished seventh echoes across a measure of rest. Above the pedal tone on G, the upper voices return to that fugal moment, the whole-note G again placed as the incipit of the subject, now recast in C major. The entries unfold in a kind of unsystematic stretto, the first violin at the fourth entry touching a high E♭, poignant and signifying. Sounding, as all this does, above a *dominant* pedal — more accurately, a protracted six-four before the dominant — the effect is of a cadenza that continues through to the close on the tonic at measure 353, where now the music echoes the closing section of the exposition, the cello finally moving to its deep open-string C for four-and-a-quarter bars toward the very end. But it is the cadenza that lingers in the mind.[7] A prototype for cadenzas of this kind, as though a contrapuntal conversation among the voices, was described eloquently by Emanuel Bach,

6. See, for one, my "Cadenza Contra Text: Mozart in Beethoven's Hands," *19th Century Music* 15(2) (Fall 1991): 116–31, and, slightly revised, in *Unfinished Music*, 211–32. For a remarkable instance from the 1820s, see Bathia Churgin, "Beethoven and Mozart's Requiem: A New Connection," *Journal of Musicology* 5(4) (Fall 1987): 457–77.

7. The defining moment for any cadenza in Mozart is the fermata above the six-four. Here, the fermata is written out in the measure rest, ensuring that the players have no doubt as to where it ends, and the six-four is written into the cadenza itself, a license that only deepens the engagement with the convention. Within the discussion of K. 515, Rosen writes a rich paragraph on the problem of length in sonata movements (269–70), noting the function of the cadenza in the concerto but curiously refusing to note the appropriation of cadenza into such works as K. 515.

in explanation of the extraordinary cadenza in F♯ minor at the end of the Largo in the Fourth Sonata of the *Probestücke* published to accompany the first part of the *Versuch*, in 1753.[8] Bach was writing about performance at a keyboard by a single player who must inhabit the voices embodied in the texture. In chamber music, real bodies inhabit the voices. Mozart had himself composed other cadenzas of this kind, most notably at the close of the finale of the great Quintet for Piano and Winds, K. 452: "I myself consider it to be the best work I have yet composed," Mozart wrote of it.[9]

This astonishing confession tells us much about Mozart in April 1784. But in coming to terms with this music, the critic must do without the help of its author, who of course hears his work with a biased ear. For all that we would give to know what Mozart might have thought of K. 515 after its composition in April 1787, it is to Rosen's "perhaps the most daring of all" that we return. It sets us to imagine how such daring, at its extremity, might be figured, for with Mozart the ritual of creation, rarely exposed, remains inscrutable.

8. The passage is discussed as well in "Cadenza Contra Text," 118–20, and *Unfinished Music*, 214–15.

9. "Ich selbst halte es für das beste was ich noch in meinem leben geschrieben habe." Letter of 10 April 1784; see *Mozart: Briefe und Aufzeichnungen*, ed. Wilhelm A. Bauer, Otto Erich Deutsch, and Joseph Heinz Eibl; Erweiterte Ausgabe, ed. Ulrich Konrad, vol. 3 (Kassel: Bärenreiter, Gemeinsame Ausgabe, 2005), 309; and Emily Anderson, *The Letters of Mozart and His Family* (New York: St Martin's Press, 1966), vol. 2, 873. I have slightly altered Anderson's translation.

3

HEARING THE SILENCE
On a Much-Theorized Moment in a Sonata by Emanuel Bach

In a world circumscribed within Enlightenment aesthetics, there are works now and then that press toward the borders of the cognitive, beyond the conventions that would define their language, and that drive the critical ear to new explanatory models. Such breaches in the wall of convention invigorate the historian's inquiry and cast new light on the paradoxes that encumber the past. I have in mind a deeply enigmatic moment lodged in the midst of the second movement of a sonata by Emanuel Bach. The work in question, uncommonly admired even in its own time for its bold originality, is the Sonata in F Minor, first published in 1781 in the third collection "für Kenner und Liebhaber," but composed (in some form or other) as early as 1763.[1]

I

The entire sonata generated much critical acclaim in the 1770s and 1780s, but it was the second movement, an Andante, that caused considerable head-scratching during the efforts to reclaim Bach's music toward the end

---

1. *Clavier-Sonaten nebst einigen Rondos fürs Forte-Piano für Kenner und Liebhaber*, Dritte Sammlung (Leipzig, im Verlage des Autors, 1781). For a facsimile of the print, see Darrell Berg, ed., *The Collected Works for Solo Keyboard by Carl Philipp Emanuel Bach*, vol. 2, Published Collections in Oblong Format (New York and London: Garland Publishing, 1985), 360–68. E. Eugene Helm, *Thematic Catalogue of the Works of Carl Philipp Emanuel Bach* (New Haven, CT, and London: Yale University Press, 1989), item 173; Wq. 57/6. We infer the date of composition from information provided by Bach himself in an inventory published posthumously as *Verzeichniß des musikalischen Nachlasses des verstorbenen Capellmeisters Carl Philipp Emanuel Bach* (Hamburg: Gottlieb Friedrich Schniebes, 1790), p. 17, item 127. The autograph — or rather, an autograph — once in the possession of Johann Friedrich Reichardt, as he claims in the *Briefe eines aufmerksam Reisenden die Musik betreffend*, vol. 2 (Frankfurt and Breslau, 1776), 10–13, describing a visit to Bach in Hamburg in July 1774, has not survived.

of the nineteenth century and the beginning of the twentieth. This was one of the sonatas included in a landmark collection of Bach's music edited by Heinrich Schenker and that provoked Schenker to publish a *Beitrag zur Ornamentik als Einführung zu Ph. Em. Bachs Klavierwerken*, which begins as a companion to the edition but expands quickly to an investigation of the figures of embellishment in the works of Haydn, Mozart, and Beethoven, drawing upon the appropriate chapters from Bach's *Versuch über die wahre Art das Clavier zu spielen*, then moving beyond to a dialectical inquiry into ornament as a component in the formulation of the structural.[2] Coming to the Sonata in F Minor, here is what Schenker has to say about this extreme passage in the Andante (shown in fig. 3.1): "And then we reach bar 27, unequaled in the entire literature as an example of the most inspired romanticism!"[3] Schenker continues: "Bach obviously created the rests expressly so as to stimulate the spontaneous complicity ['Mittätigkeit'] of the listener through the anticipation of what is to follow."[4]

This "eigenen Mittätigkeit" that Schenker invokes, as a way of explaining an otherwise riddling moment of protracted silence, attributes to Bach a strategy that plays upon the instinct of the listener ("auf den Instinkt des Zuhörers"), and posits a hearing of this repressed music, a fixing of its missing and, to Schenker's ear, self-evident notes. "When the F-major triad occurs, it is easy for the listener to realize what is expected of him, namely that his own instincts must supply the necessary chromatic change from C E♭ G to C E♮ G."[5]

Schenker's hearing of the passage, imagining a plot in which Bach slyly

2. *Ein Beitrag zur Ornamentik als Einführung zu Ph. Em. Bachs Klavierwerken* (Vienna: Universal Edition, 1904, rev. 1908). For an English translation with copious commentary, see Heinrich Schenker, "A Contribution to the Study of Ornamentation," tr. Hedi Siegel, in *The Music Forum*, vol. 4, ed. Felix Salzer (New York: Columbia University Press, 1976), 1–139.

3. "Und nun gar erst das Ereignis des Taktes 27, das in dieser Art wohl einzig in der Gesamtliteratur dasteht, ein Beispiel genialster Romantik!" *Beitrag*, 18; translation from "A Contribution," 39.

4. "Hat er doch offenbar für diesen [Zuhörer] noch eigens die Pausen geschaffen, damit er durch die Erwartung des Kommenden zu einer eigenen Mittätigkeit aufgestachelt werde." *Beitrag*, 19. My translation; for another, see "A Contribution," 41.

5. "Kommt nun der f-dur Dreiklang, wie leicht hat es der Zuhörer zu merken, was der Autor von ihm verlangt: daß er nämlich selbst, aus dem eigenen Instinkt heraus, die hier nötige Chromatisierung des *c es g* nach *c e g* vollziehe." *Beitrag*, 19; see "A Contribution," 41, for a different translation.

engages "the listener" — one with the capacity to engage spontaneously in what Schenker constructs as Bach's manipulative game — means to correct earlier readings of the passage, and pointedly to refute Hans von Bülow's understanding of it. Bülow, in the *Vorwort* to his edition of six sonatas, published by Peters in 1862, offers a broad defense of his editorial meddling:

> No less than the need for a selection, the editor became convinced of the necessity of an "arrangement" [Bearbeitung], a word which one conceives neither pretentiously nor modestly but rather in the sense of a translation from the keyboard language of the eighteenth century into that of the

Figure 3.1. C. P. E. Bach, Sonata in F Minor, Wq 57/6 (H 173), in *Clavier-Sonaten nebst einigen Rondos fürs Forte-Piano für Kenner und Liebhaber . . . von Carl Philipp Emanuel Bach.* Dritte Sammlung (Leipzig, 1781). Second movement, Andante, mm. 24–44.

nineteenth, from the clavichord-like to the pianoforte-like, if I may be permitted this barbaric turn of phrase.[6]

Bülow goes to some length to describe how he understands this delicate business of arrangement, which he claims to have undertaken (in an earlier instance) with "wirklicher Pietät, nicht von Buchstabenpietät [with genuine devotion, not out of a piously literal fidelity]" to Bach's text:

> In a filling out of the often too meager accompaniment of the middle voices; a sealing up of some questionable aphoristic gaps of silence; an enlivening illumination of several fleeting, sketch-like outlines; and finally, carefully detailed performance indications — my additions were limited to a retouching always in analogy with those places where the master applied his practice in more fully-voiced passages.[7]

Setting aside the assumptions underlying his explanatory note that would find little purchase today, nothing quite prepares us for the music that Bülow composes in response to the "aphoristische Pausenlücke" at measure 27. Bülow writes of "a rather curious ellipsis — an aposiopese[8] — which seems to me too angular than that which should have been conveyed. After

6. "Nicht minder als von der Notwendigkeit einer Auslese wurde der Herausgeber von der einer 'Bearbeitung' überzeugt, welches Wort man nicht anspruchsvoller noch anspruchsloser aufzufassen hat, als etwa in dem Sinne einer Übersetzung aus der Klaviersprache des 18. in die des 19. Jahrhunderts, aus dem Clavichordischen in das Pianofortische, wenn mir diese barbarische Wendung gestattet werden kann." *Sechs Sonaten für Klavier allein von C. Ph. Em. Bach*[,] bearbeitet u. mit einem Vorwort herausgegeben von Hans von Bülow (Leipzig: C. F. Peters [preface 1862]), 3.

7. "Ausfüllung der häufig gar zu mageren Begleitung durch passende Mittelstimmen, Verkittung mancher bedenklich aphoristischen Pausenlücke, belebende Kolorierung einzelner flüchtig skizzenhafter Umrisse, endlich sorgfältig detaillierte Vortragsbezeichnung—darauf beschränkt sich meine Zutat, in der ich stets nach Analogie derjenigen Stellen, wo der Meister seine Praxis im vollstimmigerin Satze zur Anwendung bringt, zu retouchieren getrachtet habe." *Ibid.*, 3–4.

8. "*Aposiopese* (from the Greek *aposiopao*, 'to break off, to become silent') is a special case of ellipsis, a rhetorical figure through which a sentence is broken off before it has ended, and its last part replaced by a silence. The breach can produce an emotional overpowering or an unspoken or tacit threat to expression. Sometimes one can lose the thread, or can seek a missing word." Borrowed and edited from the German *Wikipedia* (my translation). For the entry *Aposiopesis* (from the Greek, "becoming silent"), Richard A. Lanham gives: "Stopping suddenly in midcourse, leaving a statement unfinished; sometimes from genuine

Figure 3.2. From *Sechs Sonaten für Klavier allein von C. Ph. Em. Bach*, ed. Hans von Bülow
(Leipzig, 1863), from Sonata in F Minor, Andante.

the C-minor chord in first inversion, pianissimo, F major enters forte."[9] The
passage, in Bülow's edition, is shown in fig. 3.2. Schenker, who gives no hint
of the music that Bülow furnishes, dismisses it peremptorily:

---

passion, sometimes for effect." See his *Handlist of Rhetorical Terms* (Berkeley, Los Angeles,
Oxford: University of California Press, 2nd ed., 1991), 20.

9. "[D]er zweite Satz enthielt kurz vor dem Eintritte des dritten Teils [*sic*], der Rück-
kehr des Hauptmotivs in *F dur*, eine ziemlich wundersame Ellipse oder Aposiopese, die mir
zu kantig erschien, als daß sie nicht hätte vermittelt werden sollen. Nach dem Sextakkorde
von *C moll* pp trat *F dur forte* ein." *Ibid.*, 4. For a brief discussion of Bülow's rewriting of
the passage in the context of a more broadly conceived essay on Bach "reception" and the
concept of *Historismus*, see Regula Rapp, "'Soll ich nach dem Manne der Tagesmode forschen...': Die C.-P.-E.-Bach-Herausgeber Hans von Bülow und Johannes Brahms," in *Carl
Philipp Emanuel Bach: Musik für Europa*, ed. Hans-Günter Ottenberg (Frankfurt [Oder]:
Konzerthalle "Carl Philipp Emanuel Bach," 1998), 506–17, esp. 509–12.

Thus we see how one of the freest sons of the nineteenth century is plagued by the mischievous mockery of a naive grammar (though Heaven only knows of which grammar he was thinking) when confronted by a genius of the eighteenth century who speaks with power and authority. It seems almost childish for him to try so hard to connect C minor and F major, in order to justify what is actually one of Bach's most inspired ideas.[10]

For Hugo Riemann, Bach's text is merely corrupt, a misprint in need of correction. In his notoriously over-edited collection of "ausgewählte Klavier-kompositionen," its luxuriant "Phrasierungszeichen" offering its own "system of musical interpunctuation," Riemann merely replaces the Eb with E♮, throwing in a flat seventh for good measure.[11] Citing the first edition of the sonata (shown above in fig. 3.1) as his primary text, Riemann would surely have seen that the flat before the E is explicit, allowing for no ambiguity in its intent. For Schenker, Bach's text is a subtle subterfuge for a compositional act of a very different kind, masking a "chromatic alteration" from C–Eb to C–E♮ whose ineluctable urgency is so great that, in Schenker's understanding, Bach chose to leave it to the imagination of this imaginary listener, at once benighted and omniscient, for whom Schenker acts as interlocutor, dictating in effect how the silence must be heard.[12]

10. "Bülow bespricht diese Stelle ausdrücklich im Vorwort seiner Ausgabe und nennt sie 'eine ziemlich wundersame Ellipse oder Aposiopese, die mir zu kantig erschien, als daß sie nicht hätte vermittelt werden sollen,' und kurz zuvor 'eine grammatikalische kühnheit von großer Seltenheit, der gegenüber ich mich reaktionär verhalten zu müssen geglaubt habe.' So sehen wir also, wie einen der freiesten Söhne des XIX. Jahrhunderts Kobolde einer naiven Grammatik—weiß der liebe Himmel, an welche er dachte—necken, wo ein Genie des XVIII. Jahrhunderts ein Machtwort gesprochen. Fast kindisch mutet einem die heiße Bemühung an, hier zwischen c-moll und f-dur zu vermitteln, um so, mit gutem Erfolge, den Meister—um eine seiner genialsten Ideen zu bringen." *Beitrag*, 18; "A Contribution," 41. For a thoughtful study of Schenker's argument with Bülow's editorial practice, see Nicholas Cook, "The Editor and the Virtuoso, or Schenker versus Bülow," in Cook, *Music, Performance, Meaning: Selected Essays* (Aldershot, Hampshire, UK; Burlington, VT: Ashgate, 2007), 83–99. The sonata under scrutiny here does not enter into Cook's discussion.

11. C. Ph. Em. Bach, *Ausgewählte Klavierkompositionen*. Mit Fingersatz und Phrasierungsbezeichnung von Dr. Hugo Riemann (Leipzig: Steingräber-Verlag, n.d., plate number 501). In a footnote, Riemann writes "Original *es* statt e♮."

12. In his edition, Schenker writes "hier ist offenbar ein p oder pp vergessen," but in point of fact, the original edition gives *pp* unequivocally. Schenker must have been read-

Schenker's elucidation is a challenge on several fronts. As a first order of business, one might interrogate the chromatic model that Schenker puts before us. Does it serve as a plausible representation of the implications of measure 27? Observing, for one, his misrepresentation of the voicing, it is hardly trivial to note that the E♭ in question is located in the lowest voice, a condition which only strengthens its claim to contrapuntal legitimacy. Consider again how the music goes here. Putting out of mind the unexpected response to it in measure 28 — denying ourselves the privilege of some synoptic view of what lies ahead — there would be no questioning of the compelling logic of the syntax which governs this music precisely as Bach has it. The leading of the bass through the seventh (above a root G) to E♭ is indisputably what we have been led to expect. The declamatory figure in which this resolution is cast, as a response to the intensity of the arpeggiated harmonies that precede it, is utterly new to the piece, the fragility of its voicing, pianissimo, in ironic contrast to the harmonic weight that it bears.

And this brings us to the three beats of rest into which this figure will now resonate. It is worth spending a moment on the phenomenon itself: a silence that functions not within the conventional grammar of phrase articulation, but that interrupts the phrase at a critical moment in the unraveling of its harmony, just as the music has been gearing up for the inexorable moment of return. What, then, *are* we meant to hear in this discomfiting silence at measure 27?

To pose the question is to suggest that there might be some music lurking beneath the silence — unsounded, and yet heard in the mind. In the aesthetics of Enlightenment thought, a tension is cultivated between the conventions of good grammar, of an idealized and self-evident syntax, on the one hand, and, on the other, the intrusion into this perfect world of an element of the unexpected, of the irrational, of some inscrutable originality that means to undo the decorum of the moment. There is, however, an edginess to the question. On the one hand, the speculative mind will wonder if we can be meant to hear in this silence some self-evident, if suppressed, music; and further, whether there is an intention inscribed in its invisible, inaudible subtext that would encourage such a hearing. On the other, the positivist will read Bach's text literally, insisting upon the specificity of the silence for

---

ing from the "Urtextausgabe" edited by Carl Krebs, published in 1895. This was the edition that served as the text for Lothar Hoffmann-Erbrecht's somewhat improved edition of 1953. And it was the Krebs edition that was reprinted by Edwin F. Kalmus in the 1960s.

Ex. 3.1. C. P. E. Bach, Sonata in F Minor, Wq 57/6, Andante:
two hypothetical continuations from m. 27.

what it is, as a thing in itself. But it seems to me that the Enlightenment
mind would recognize the irreconcilability of these two extreme positions
as a condition to be savored, taking pleasure in the dissonance of the moment: a dissonance perceived not as an assertion of some cosmic world force
(Hegelian, one might call it) to be vanquished through acts of heroic tran-
scendence, but as an irresoluble contradiction, an emblem of human nature
in a world apprehended in irony.[13]

In any case, we are put before a challenge to imagine a reasonable continuation to the music that breaks off at measure 27: once more, the confrontation between reason and passion. It is in this spirit that the following
attempts are offered (shown in ex. 3.1).

It is not merely voice-leading that is at issue, nor proper harmonic conduct, but a coherent rhythmic diction. In offering such a reading, I want to
suggest that Bülow's grasp of the passage, for all its anachronistic violation
of Bach's style and diction, yet makes a certain sense when it is heard in re-

13. "Kant apprehended the historical process less as a development from one stage to
another in the life of humanity than as merely a conflict, an *unresolvable* conflict, between
eternally opposed principles of human nature: rational on the one hand, irrational on the
other." So writes Hayden White (emphasis his), one of many remarkable insights into the
Enlightenment mind, in *Metahistory: The Historical Imagination in Nineteenth-Century
Europe* (Baltimore and London: Johns Hopkins University Press, 1973), 58.

sponse to this challenge. I hasten to say that what I am proposing is meant neither as a correction of a flawed passage nor as an alternative to Bach's text — and decidedly not as a *Bearbeitung* (as Bülow has it) — but rather as a hypothetical extension meant to sound somewhere in the mind, insinuated in Bach's script even as it is frustrated in its text.

To hear in this music an instance of *aposiopesis* is to probe into the deeper implications of a syntax otherwise unexplained. Rhetoric has as much to do with the performative aspect of language — whether theatrical, literary, or musical — as with its construction. The rhetorical device imputes agency, a veiled subjectivity of voice. The breaking off in mid-sentence takes on a meaning that moves beyond the grammatical to the affective, our response to it in sympathy with the action, the implicit drama, to which we are witness. We are not asked to complete a fragmentary work, as though its meaning depended on our competency to complete it. Rather, the rupture and the silence at measure 27 is a theatrical moment. We listen for a completion that does not come, for words that are not spoken. The *Affekt* of the passage resides in this sudden and unexpected lapse, as though the train of thought had been interrupted, overwhelmed by the pathos of the moment.

But there is more to this story. The Andante is one of those middle movements that comes to rest on a half cadence before the finale. The relationship of this finale — Andantino grazioso in F minor — to its antecedent — Andante in F major — is of a special kind, about which there will be more to say further on. But the immediate concern is the music at this half cadence.

Rejecting the possibility of a full close at the downbeat of measure 42, this closing music revisits the scene that unfolds from the cadence in D minor, at measure 22, and the moment of rupture — of *aposiopesis* — at measure 27. And it is at just this point that something quite extraordinary happens. It is as though the intense arpeggiation of the four-two chord at measure 26 and its answering figure continue to vibrate in memory, seeming to set off a reply at measure 42. The music is now led through the subdominant minor, a powerful fulcrum for the half cadence on the dominant. The imaginary music conjured in the silence of measure 27 is now reheard, filtered through memory, captured in register, newly inflected toward a cadence whose rhetorical accents must now serve a grander plot in the narrative of the sonata. (The proposed liaison between the two passages is illustrated in ex. 3.2.)

In proposing such a hearing, I emphatically do not mean to argue for a "solution" to an analytical problem, as though Bach had intentionally challenged his player to unmask some inscrutable riddle. Rather, it is in its narra-

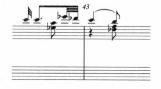

Ex. 3.2. C. P. E. Bach, Sonata in F Minor, Wq 57/6, Andante,
showing putative continuity between m. 27 and m. 42.

tive aspect, in the declamatory accents of its discourse, that this music stakes its claim to meaning. Its fictive voice breaks off at measure 27, the story is interrupted. When it resumes at measure 28, it is as though nothing had happened. But something *has* happened, and when the narrative comes around again to the memory of an event that earlier drove the teller of this tale into silence, it now provokes a return to that moment, as though in contemplation of some lost experience.

II

Students of Emanuel Bach's music will have recognized this very sonata as the topic of an ambitious and influential essay by Johann Nikolaus Forkel. Titled "Ueber eine Sonate aus Carl Phil. Emanuel Bachs dritter Sonatensammlung für Kenner und Liebhaber, in F moll . . . : Ein Sendschreiben an Hrn von ***," Forkel's project is driven by two urgent concerns: the first, to come to terms with a work at once conceptually challenging and exacting in performance, an extreme instance within this multivalent repertory widely admired for its unorthodoxy; the second, to extrapolate from this encounter a broader understanding of sonata: a "theory," Forkel calls it, but the theorizing has little to do with the material content of music itself.[14] Rather, Forkel

14. "On a sonata in F minor from Carl Philipp Emanuel Bach's third sonata collection 'für Kenner und Liebhaber': an open letter to Mr. ***." "Ein vornehmer Mann ersuchte mich, ihm die Schönheiten der erwähnten Sonate zu erklären, die er von einigen Kennern sehr hatte rühmen hören. Hieraus ist dieses Sendschreiben entstanden. Da es nun nicht bloß die Theorie der Sonate überhaupt enthält, sondern auch zugleich eine Recension dieser Sonate ist, so steht es hier hoffentlich nicht am unrechten Orte." [An excellent man begged me to explain to him the beauties in the sonata, about which he had heard much praise from several connoisseurs. Hence this communication. Since it contains not merely a theory of the sonata in general but is at once a review of this sonata, perhaps it is

enters into the discursive, rhetorical, imaginative theater of sonata, a theater occupied preeminently by Emanuel Bach, whose extreme, often obscure language provokes Forkel to these ends. If there were any doubt as to Bach's preeminence, a passage in the article "Sonate" in Sulzer's *Allgemeine Theorie der schönen Künste* (an article very likely written by Johann Abraham Peter Schulz) sets the matter clearly: "A good many keyboard sonatas, some easy, some more difficult, by our Hamburg Bach demonstrate the possibility of achieving character and expression in the sonata. Most of his are so articulate that one believes oneself to be hearing not tones, but a comprehensible language that sets in motion and sustains our imagination and feelings."[15] These words that are at the core of Schulz's appraisal — "sprechend"; "verständliche Sprache" (speech-like; comprehensible language) — locate the distinguishing characteristic of a Bach sonata in something deeply linguistic. It is precisely this aspect that is at the core of Forkel's theorizing as well, wondering aloud whether his reader hasn't noticed "a certain similarity between the sonata in music and the ode in poetry[:] A sequence of highly spirited thoughts [*Begriffe*] that follow upon one another according to the rule of an inspired imagination is an ode; precisely such a sequence of spirited and expressive musical ideas [*Sätze*], when they follow upon one another according to the precepts of a musically inspired imagination is, in music, the Sonata."[16] For

---

not out of place here.] *Musikalischer Almanach für Deutschland auf das Jahr 1784* (Leipzig: im Schwickertschen Verlag, [n.d.]; repr. Hildesheim and New York: Georg Olms, 1974), 22–23.

15. "Die Möglichkeit, Charakter und Ausdruk in Sonaten zu bringen, beweisen eine Menge leichter und schwerer Claviersonaten unsers Hamburger Bachs. Die mehresten derselben sind so sprechend, dass man nicht Töne, sondern eine verständliche Sprache zu vernehmen glaubt, die unsere Einbildung und Empfindungen in Bewegung setzt, und unterhält." From the article "Sonate" in Johann Georg Sulzer, *Allgemeine Theorie der schönen Künste*, vol. 4 (Leipzig: Weidmann, 1792–94; repr. Hildesheim: Georg Olms, 1970), 425. For a slightly different translation, see *Aesthetics and the Art of Musical Composition in the German Enlightenment: Selected Writings of Johann Georg Sulzer and Heinrich Christoph Koch*, ed. Nancy Kovaleff Baker and Thomas Christensen (Cambridge: Cambridge University Press, 1995), 104.

16. "Eine Reihe höchst lebhafter Begriffe, wie sie nach den Gesetzen einer begeisterten Einbildungskraft auf einander folgen, ist eine **Ode**. Eben eine solche Reihe lebhafter, ausdrucksvoller musikalischer Ideen, (Sätze) wenn sie nach der Vorschrift einer musikalisch begeisterten Einbildungskraft auf einander folgen, ist in der Musik die **Sonate**." Forkel, "Sendschreiben," 27. For more on this notion of the "rhetoric of sonata," and on the sonata in question, see my *Unfinished Music*, 7–13.

Forkel, the discourse of sonata is comprehensible only in linguistic terms. Idea [*Idee*] is made synonymous with *Satz*, a word that conjures grammatical construction and syntax: *Empfindung* is aroused by the structure of discourse in all its anomalies, by the idiosyncrasies of language, by bent syntax. If narrative is to be teased out of sonata, it's not the story itself that matters but the linguistic signs of story-making. To be moved by this music—Schulz writes of *Begeisterung* and *Empfindung*, Forkel of *Ausdruck*—is to register in mind the sequence of musical *Sätze*, the ordering of ideas as events that unfold in unexpected ways, that together constitute its story.

If the language in Forkel's simile sounds familiar, that is because it borrows, quite literally and without attribution, from Moses Mendelssohn's definition of *Ode*, cited above in the Preface. Assuming that Forkel had at hand the Mendelssohn piece, already twenty years old, he will have read a bit further to this extraordinary insight: "Mediating thoughts which connect the principal ideas with one another but which in themselves do not possess the highest degree of vivacity [*Lebhaftigkeit*] will be omitted by the poet, and from this arises the apparent lack of order which is attributed to the ode."[17] It is this *apparent* disorder ["anscheinende Unordnung"], obscuring in parataxis the locus of poetic meaning, that is to our point. Forkel's simile is keenly enriched when the apparent disorder that seems to regulate the music in these difficult passages is apprehended in precisely this way: to grasp the meaning hidden in ellipsis.

That Forkel should have chosen the Sonata in F Minor as the basis for his theorizing, seeking an explanatory model in an effort to grasp the significance of this remarkable sonata, is itself worth pondering. It will come as a surprise, and perhaps a disappointment, to find that Forkel is concerned only fleetingly with the actual notes of the sonata, and not at all with the structure of each of its movements, nor with the commonplace notions of tonal design and thematic discourse. What is of central importance is how the three movements of the sonata together constitute a narrative of some kind. The very notion that these movements have something material to do with one another—that the sonata is more than the sum of its parts—is a concept not often (if ever) encountered in critical discourse before 1784,

17. "Mittelbegriffe, welche die Glieder mit einander verbinden, aber selbst nicht den höchsten Grad der Lebhaftigkeit besitzen, werden von dem Odendichter übersprungen, und daraus entstehet die anscheinende Unordnung, die man der Ode zuschreibt." "Gedanken von dem Wesen der Ode. Zergliederung einiger sogenannten Oden der Fr. Karschin," in *Briefe, die Neueste Litteratur betreffend*, 274. Brief (1764), 150.

nor is it likely that it would have occurred to Forkel in the abstract. Rather, it is plainly the case that the three movements of this sonata are not autonomous pieces that might be replaced without damage to the sense of the whole — though indeed, Bach does not hesitate elsewhere to engage in such an exchange of movements.[18] I do not mean this in sanctimonious reverence to an organicist view of the work — anachronistic in any case — but rather to suggest that here, as in few works contemporary with it, a narrative thread makes itself felt. This is what seems to have inspired Forkel to convey in literary or linguistic terms what transpires within this sonata in its passage from one movement to the next. It is not merely that each movement conveys its own mood, but that these shifts in mood (or mode), related to one another, are expressions of a single dramatic expanse.

We can take this further, and in directions only faintly sensed by Forkel (if I do not underestimate his critical acumen). Those who know the first movement will no doubt think of the nettlesome passage before its moment of recapitulation, a moment made prominent in the final pages in the "Sendschreiben." Indeed, it is this passage (shown in ex. 3.3) that Forkel singles out for detailed discussion:

> That place in the second part of the Allegro, where the modulation goes from Ab minor to Fb major, and returns from there in a somewhat rough manner to F minor: perhaps you found this not beautiful. I must confess that, considered quite apart from its relationship to the whole, I found just as little beauty in it. But who would find beauty in the hard, raw, and violent expressions of a spiteful and angry man. I am quite disposed to believe that Bach, whose sense of feeling is otherwise always so exceptionally correct, has here too been guided by no improper feeling, and that under such circumstances, this rough modulation is nothing other than a true expression of what should and must be expressed.[19]

18. In one well-known instance, a new finale for the Fantasia in F♯ Minor, in its version for keyboard and violin (1787; Helm 536), is a transposition and reworking of the finale of the Sonata in Bb Major (1766; Helm 212), for which a replacement finale was now composed. For more on this, see *Unfinished Music*, 140–44.

19. "Sie haben vielleicht diejenige Stelle im zweyten Theil des ersten *Allegro* nicht schön gefunden, wo die Modulation ins As moll, Fes dur, und von da auf eine etwas harte Art wieder zurück ins F moll geht. Ich muß gestehen, daß ich sie, außer ihrer Verbindung mit dem Ganzen betrachtet, eben so wenig schön gefunden habe. Aber wer findet auch wohl die harten, rauhen und heftigen Aeußerungen eines zornigen und unwilligen Menschen schön? Ich bin sehr geneigt zu glauben, daß Bach, dessen Gefühl sonst überall so außer-

Ex. 3.3. C. P. E. Bach, Sonata in F Minor, Wq 57/6, first movement, mm. 53–66.

The intensity of the passage, its assault on the moment of recapitulation, will evoke music composed years later, inevitably bringing to mind certain works by Beethoven.[20] Further, the roughness of the modulation has been exaggerated in a misreading of its actual notes: a failure to recognize Bach's slightly enlarged accidental flat sign as signifying a double-flat, this in mea-

ordentlich richtig ist, auch hier von keinem unrichtigen Gefühl geleitet sey, und daß unter solchen Umständen die erwähnte harte Modulation nichts anders ist, als ein getreuer Ausdruck dessen, was hier ausgedrückt werden sollte und mußte." Forkel, "Sendschreiben," 38.

20. The very opening of the movement has drawn comparison with the opening of the first movement of Beethoven, op. 2, no. 1. See, for one, Hans-Günter Ottenberg, *C. P. E. Bach*, tr. Philip J. Whitmore (Oxford and New York: Oxford University Press, 1987), 194–95; and, from a perspective closer to Schenker's recourse to voice-leading, Reinhard Oppel, "Ueber Beziehungen Beethovens zu Mozart und zu Ph. Em. Bach," *Zeitschrift für Musikwissenschaft* 5 (1922–23): 30–39, esp. 37–38, where Oppel contends that "Beethoven has leaned precisely on Bach's model for the plan of the development," a thesis that would demand more nuance in its argument than Oppel offers.

sures 53–54 and 57–58.[21] With double-flats in place, the passage is less rough
on its surface, if no less challenging in its syntax. It is the E♭♭ at measures
57–58, together with a willful leading of the upper voice from F♭ to F♮, and
the harmonic motion at just that place, that is likely to provoke some analytical gymnastics. The E♭♭ at measure 57 acts as a seventh beneath the root
F♭, with an inclination to descend to the third of a harmony rooted on B♭♭,
to the equal-tempered ear as A major. That inclination is only reinforced in
measure 58, when the uppermost voice moves up to F♮ above the station-
ary E♭♭, an appoggiatura ninth displacing the root F♭. But the harmonies in
measures 59–60 are to be heard unequivocally as the minor subdominant,
B♭ minor, to the six-four above the dominant in F minor. It is the motion
between measure 58 and measure 59 that will not hold: there seems no rea-
sonably convincing way to hear in this interstice a root motion that is syn-
tactically coherent.

All this labored description, if it has any defense, is merely in an effort
to come to a better understanding of Bach's inner ear, to come closer to
his process of mind at just this place. To explain away the passage as an exi-
gency of parsimonious voice-leading — each of the voices moving minimally
or not at all — is to miss the expressive daring of the moment. Only a year
before the composition of the sonata, Bach addressed this kind of syntactical hitch — an ellipsis, he calls it: "a leap without logical connectives" (in
my *Webster's Collegiate*) — in that analysis of a "freie fantasie" in the final
paragraph of Part 2 of his *Versuch*, to return once more to a text that figures
prominently in our opening chapter (see above, fig. 1.4).[22] The two passages
are very different indeed, and so are their contexts. And yet, they have this
in common: that each sounds an extremity of tonal distance, as if the tension at this moment of formal dissonance forces the music to lose itself. The

21. This is the case with the Krebs edition, even in Hoffmann-Erbrecht's revision
(Leipzig, Breitkopf & Härtel, 1954, and many reprintings); and most recently, in Carl
Philipp Emanuel Bach, *"Kenner und Liebhaber" Collections I*, ed. Christopher Hogwood, in
Carl Philipp Emanuel Bach: The Complete Works, series 1, vol. 4.1 (Los Altos, CA: Packard
Humanities Institute, 2009), 124. Schenker, too, misreads the notation, but offers the true
reading as a correction to what he believed was an error of omission. See Philipp Emanuel
Bach, *Klavierwerke*, vol. 2 (Vienna: Universal-Edition [preface: 1902]), 68.

22. For a profound and detailed study of precisely this "miraculous event," as he calls
it, see Heinrich Schenker, "The Art of Improvisation," in *The Masterwork in Music*,
vol. 1 (1925), ed. William Drabkin (Cambridge and New York: Cambridge University
Press, 1994), 10–11.

brief insight in the *Versuch* does indeed give us a rare entry into that inner ear, into Bach's way of conceptualizing what happens at a critical moment in the piece. That the ellipsis between measures 58 and 59 in the first movement is yet more elusive, less responsive to rational explanation, is only a symptom of the greater stakes in the sonata.

We return to the Andante. Heard now in response to the headlong drive toward recapitulation in the first movement, that elliptical moment of silence at measure 27 before *its* recapitulation seems all the more resonant, as though in mute recognition of the abrasive dissonance of this passage in the first movement, its notes flying off the rails, that inspired Forkel to conjure behind the scrim of those notes the animus of some fictional persona not quite in control.

For Forkel, it is, however, the final movement that holds the key to an understanding of the sonata as a whole. If the finale is not unique in how it is made to follow from that half cadence poised on the dominant in the final bars of the movement that precedes it, it is yet uncommon in how closely this Andantino grazioso in F minor follows the Andante in diction, in tempo, even in its inflection of the major mode to minor. But there is more to Forkel's narrative than what might be attributed to the syntax of sonata. "When I think of sonata," writes Forkel, "I think to myself of the expression of a man placed in *Empfindung* or *Begeisterung*" — that is, in a state of feeling, of mind — "who then strives either to sustain this state of mind at a certain point of liveliness (when, *nota bene*, this *Empfindung* is desirable and agreeable); or, if it belongs to the class of disagreeable *Empfindungen*, to modulate it from its elevated position and to transform a disagreeable feeling into something agreeable."[23] These various scenarios eventually generate three "orders" of sonata, the second of which will be brought into play as a model for the sonata at hand, "where a disagreeable *Hauptempfindung*" — a principal feeling — "is suppressed, assuaged, and gradually transformed into something agreeable." More specifically: "the first *Allegro* conveys the expression of a certain animosity, the *Andante* contemplation and deliberation, and the *Andantino grazioso* that follows from these, a rather melan-

23. "Wenn ich mir eine Sonate denke, so denke ich mir den musikalischen Ausdruck eines in Empfindung oder Begeisterung versetzten Menschen, der sich bestrebt, entweder seine Empfindung auf einem gewissen Punkte von Lebhaftigkeit zu erhalten, (wenn es NB. eine wünschenswürdige angenehme Empfindung ist;) oder sie, wenn sie in die Classe der unangenehmen gehört, von ihrer Höhe herunter zu stimmen, und aus einer unangenehmen in eine angenehmere zu verwandeln." Forkel, "*Sendschreiben*," 25.

choly peace of mind." It is this expression of a "melancholy peace of mind and balsamic consolation," this "highest excellence that could be imagined and desired in this character," that in Forkel's view constitutes "the greatest essential value [hauptsächlichste Werth] of the entire sonata."[24]

Without disputing Forkel's keen sense that the sonata is in some measure defined by the "peace of mind" that brings closure in its Andantino grazioso, I think it would be fair to insist that to identify its "hauptsächlichste Werth," if such a thing could ever be established, is a more complicated affair. For Forkel, it is an ethical dimension that holds privilege, the sonata mapping a condition of mind, a metaphor played out in the language of *Empfindungen*. Bach's music, however, seems no less about other things: about agency and voice, less the expression of some fictional construction of ego and id than of plot, hovering equivocally between drama and narrative. If there is some comfort in the *grazioso* of Bach's finale, this may come in exhausted relief from those extreme moments where the music seems to challenge the limits of convention and language. It was prescient of Forkel to seize this sonata as the one with which to define a genre. Writing in 1784, he cannot have known the ways in which its quiddities would come to stand for sonata in the decades to follow.

III

Schenker's reading of this vexing passage from the Andante as "unequaled in the entire literature as an example of the most inspired romanticism" reveals a good deal more about Schenker than it does about Bach. The Romantic temperament finds its sources in a subjectifying poetics of an imaginative world, of Utopian ideals, of a politics born in response to a turbulent Europe coming to terms with catastrophic revolution. Bach cannot think this way; his music works a different arena. Bülow, hearing the music in purely syntactical terms, comes closer to an understanding of how this music might

---

24. ". . . das erste *Allegro* den Ausdruck eines gewissen Unwillens — das *Andante* Betrachtung und Ueberlegung — und das letzte *Andantino grazioso* daraus entstandene, fast möchte ich sagen, etwas melancholische Beruhigung enthalte. Wenn Sie die Sonate von dieser Seite und auf diese Art betrachten, so wird Ihnen Ihr Gefühl bald sagen, daß das letzte Stück eben des melancholisch — beruhigten und fast balsamisch — tröstenden Ausdrucks wegen das vorzüglichste sey, was man sich in diesem Charakter denken und wünschen kann. Auch liegt meiner Meinung nach, hierinn der hauptsächlichste Werth der ganzen Sonata." Forkel, "*Sendschreiben*," 36–37.

have gone on another, less fractious day. And yet, his ingenious revision, for all its musical good sense, is deaf to a central thesis of Enlightenment aesthetics. Bach's radical ellipsis is precisely the point: we are meant to feel the rhetoric of thought broken off. It will not do to suggest, as Bülow's reading does, that the passage is somehow imperfect, even incoherent in its failure to complete itself—that the task of the editor is to finish Bach's work for him. For surely it must have occurred to Bülow that Bach would have been quite capable of completing the passage in just this way. It is implausible even to imagine that Bach's refusal to do so was a matter of neglect, benign or otherwise. Nor does it make sense to accuse Bach of an intention to mislead his reader, in the spirit of some willful insider joke. Context matters. This is a work of considerable gravity—of *gravitas*, as we like to say. Those three long beats of silence are pregnant with meaning, with inner thought, with feeling, with *Empfindung*.

Whose inner thought, whose feeling? The question of agency, of voice, is never far below the surface in Enlightenment narrativity. Reading Sterne, Diderot, Goethe is to participate in a creative process: to reenact a narrative unfolding in all its improvisatory richness. This is what we feel with Bach (better, with the fictional alter ego who voices his text): the grand silence is unexpected, its consequences unpredictable. So that when, at measure 42, the music retrieves that broken phrase, we feel ourselves caught up in the fractured process of remembering, the trace of memory embedded in narrative. It's not our memory that is at issue here, but a fictive memory conjured in the sonata. Such feigned autobiography in Bach's music is somehow unique to keyboard culture in the German Enlightenment and ingrained in a clavichord mystique. It is the performer, bent over her instrument—and not Schenker's *Zuhörer*—who gets caught up in the distracted process of mind and remembering. It is this performer for whom Bach composes—and for the composer himself.

THE KLOPSTOCK MOMENT

4

ODEN VON KLOPSTOCK IN MUSIK GESETZT . . .

I

"The firstborn child of sensibility, the fountainhead of poetic art, and the germ cell of its life is the *ode*."[1] Collecting his thoughts toward a treatise on the topic, Johann Gottfried Herder, writing in 1765, locates the ode at the core of poetic utterance, setting off torrents of brilliant insight, engaging the poetics of antique Greece in battle with the vigorous efforts of contemporary German poets to find a voice (and indeed an authentic poetic language) distinct from its ancient models and true to its own diction. For Herder, the ode was the locus at which the eternal tension between thought and passion, between order and madness, plays itself out. He speaks for the poet himself: "Do not put yourself into a state of sensibility that borders on affect, for otherwise you will be inarticulate, confused, obscure, and laughable to the passionless reader and daring to the obstinate literary critic. . . . Our odes are thus portraits of emotion drawn in perspective, which indeed — " and then, catching himself in mid-thought: "But a raging natural human being?"[2] To speak of "*our* odes" is to move the conversation from the ancients to Herder's contemporaries, even if, in what follows, the two seem indistinguishable. "In the parenthyrsus of his emotional rapture, the odist voices few words, and these entirely with their natural stresses, which only in the most intense passion approach the inarticulate; he does not perform

---

1. "Die erstgeborne Kind der Empfindung, der Ursprung der Dichtkunst, und der Keim ihres Lebens ist die *Ode*." "Fragmente einer Abhandlung über die Ode," in Johann Gottfried Herder, *Sämtliche Werke*, vol. 32, ed. Bernhard Suphan (Berlin, 1899; repr. Hildesheim: Georg Olms, 1968), 62. Johann Gottfried Herder, *Selected Early Works 1764–1767*, ed. Ernest A. Menze and Karl Menges, tr. Menze with Michael Palma (University Park: Pennsylvania State University Press, 1992), 36.

2. "Setze dich nicht in Empfindung, der dem Affekt gränzt: sonst wirst du wortarm, verworren, dunkel, dem kalten Leser lächerlich, und dem eigensinnigen Kunstrichter abentheuerlich scheinen. . . . Unsere Oden sind also perspektivisch gezeichnete Gemälde des Affekts, die freilich — –Aber ein rasender Mensch der Natur?" Herder, *Sämtliche Werke*, vol. 32, 78. *Selected Early Works*, 48.

a pantomime, but rather speaks through unstudied gestures. Simple musical chord progressions—for those are the melodies of the natural odes—descend to the level of his emotive accents and elevate them." And finally, "This bold passion of the parenthyrsus is the creative genius."[3]

What, precisely, did Herder mean by *parenthyrsus*? The well-rehearsed source for its usage is Longinus, who associates it with an extreme, and indeed misplaced, condition of pathos: "it is a pathos unseasonable and empty, where pathos is not necessary; or immoderate, where it should be moderate."[4] Herder might well have had in mind a passage in Winckelmann's famous description of the Laocoon: "All movements and poses of Greek figures marked not by such traits of wisdom, but instead by passion and violence, were the result of an error of conception which the ancient artists called *parenthyrsos* .... The portrayal of suffering alone in Laocoon would have been *parenthyrsos*; therefore the artist, in order to unite the distinctive and the noble qualities of soul, showed him in an action that was closest to a state of tranquility for one in such pain."[5] Writing against Winckelmann's appropriation of the term in his reading of Greek sculpture, Lessing worries a further distinction: "I doubt, indeed, whether this word can be translated into the language of painting. For in oratory and poetry pathos can be carried to extreme without becoming *parenthyrsus*, which is only the extreme of pathos in the wrong place. But in painting the extreme of pathos would always be *parenthyrsus*, whatever its excuse in the circum-

3. "Der Odendichter im Parenthyrsus seiner Affektbegeisterung tönt wenige Worte, und diese ganz mit ihren Naturaccenten, die sich den unartikulirten blos im stärksten Feuer nähern, er tanzt nicht Pantomimisch sondern spricht durch einfältige Geberden. Einfache musikalische Harmoniengänge; — denn das sind die Melodien der Naturoden, — laßen sich zu seinen Affektaccenten herab und erhöhen sie. ... Dieses freche Feuer des Parenthyrsus ist das schöpferische Genie." Herder, *Sämtliche Werke*, vol. 32, 78–79. *Selected Early Works*, 48–49.

4. I take the translation as it is given in Gotthold Ephraim Lessing, *Laocoon: An Essay upon the Limits of Painting and Poetry*, tr. Ellen Frothingham (Boston: Roberts Brothers, 1874; repr. New York: Noonday Press, 1969), 189. The translation by W. R. Roberts, *Longinus on the Sublime* (Cambridge: Cambridge University Press, 1899), is given complete in *Critical Theory Since Plato*, ed. Hazard Adams (New York: Harcourt Brace Jovanovich, 1971), 76–102, esp. 78, where the Greek "pathos" is given as "passion."

5. Johann Joachim Winckelmann, *Gedancken über die Nachahmung der Griechischen Wercke in Mahlerey und Bildhauer-Kunst* (1755); tr. *as Reflections on the Imitation of Greek Works in Painting and Sculpture*, Elfriede Heyer and Roger C. Norton (La Salle, IL: Open Court, 1987), 34–35. I retain the differences in the spelling of *parenthyrsus*.

stances of the persons concerned."[6] Klopstock, too, had something to say
to Winckelmann's notion: "What matters most in the arts is that the master
find the fine line of beauty. Meanwhile, *parenthyrsos* is for the most part to
be discovered where this 'stille Größe' is a bit too calm."[7]

For Herder, *parenthyrsus* is not the misplaced passion that Longinus (and
Winckelmann) read as a flaw in the work, but a legitimate state of height-
ened emotion. And it is this quality that bears on an understanding of ode,
and its place in Enlightenment aesthetics. A few years later, in the midst of
an extremely long and detailed appreciation of ode in the *Allgemeine Theorie der schönen Künste*, Johann Georg Sulzer penetrates to its essence, proposing that

> in every effective [würkende] ode, whether of Hebrew, Greek, or Celtic
> origin, more music will sound than in any other form of poetry. This lies
> in its nature. If one then wished to fashion a work of art from this ode
> created from nature, one reflected in various ways on the prosody (*Syl-
> benmaaß*), and the fine ear of the Greek poet discovered there a variety
> of species. The grouping of the verses into strophes, which would be re-
> peated following a prototype, appeared to be simply spontaneous while
> today they have become law.[8]

6. "Ja ich zweifle sogar, ob sich überhaupt dieses Wort in die Malerei übertragen läßt.
Denn in der Beredsamkeit und Poesie gibt es ein Pathos, das so hoch getrieben werden
kann als möglich, ohne Parenthyrsus zu werden; und nur das höchste Pathos an der unrechten Stelle, ist Parenthyrsus. In der Malerei aber würde das höchste Pathos allezeit
Parenthyrsus sein, wenn es auch durch die Umstände der Person, die es äußert, noch so
wohl entschuldigt werden könnte." *Laokoon: oder über die Grenzen der Malerei und Poesie*, chapter 29, in, for one, Gotthold Ephraim Lessing, *Werke*, vol. 6, *Kunsttheoretische und
kunsthistorische Schriften* (Munich: Carl Hanser Verlag, 1974), 183. For the English, see
Lessing, *Laocoon*, tr. Frothingham, 189.

7. "Eine Beurteilung der Winckelmannischen Gedanken über die Nachahmung der
griechischen Werke in den schönen Künsten" (1760), as given in Friedrich Gottlieb Klopstock, *Ausgewählte Werke*, ed. Karl August Schleiden, with a "Nachwort" by Friedrich
Georg Jünger (Munich: Carl Hanser Verlag, 1962), 1051.

8. "Daher ist zu vermuthen, daß jede würkende Ode, sie bey hebräischen, griechischen,
oder celtischen Ursprunges, in dem Klange mehr Musik verrathen wird, als jede andere
Dichtungsart. Dieses liegt in der Natur. Als man nachher die von der Natur erzeugten
Oden zum Werk der Kunst machte, dachte man vielfältig über das Sylbenmaaß nach, und
das feine Ohr der griechischen Dichter fand mancherley Gattungen desselben. Die Anord-
nung der Verse in Strophen, die nach einem Muster wiederholt werden, scheinet blos zu-

Writing a history tuned to an aesthetic of the Enlightenment, Sulzer imagines the origin of the genre very much as Herder imagines the beginnings of language. The ode has much to do with music — its Greek root *means* song — less because it is designed to be set to music than because at its origin, at least in the Enlightenment imagination, its language virtually sings the qualities of sound and accent that is music at its core: music before music, so to say. The spontaneity of the thing, even in the origin of those antique meters that would become codified as though frozen in time in the recuperations of the eighteenth century, was an irony that Sulzer could not resist: ode as improvisation, Herder's "firstborn child of sensibility."

If the tension between *Leidenschaft* and *Vernunft*, between passion and reason, fuels the engine of Enlightenment aesthetics, Herder and his contemporaries would locate this tension in the ode, where the concentration is extreme. Again, Herder: "Every ode thus reveals in itself a *thread of passion*. . . . The most fervent passion and the coldest perception of reason, in their truth and in their form, are so far removed from one another as to be beyond measure: reason and feeling remain the two poles of humanity."[9] It is the theater of other tensions as well. Toward the end of Sulzer's essay in the *Allgemeine Theorie*, a few lines from Klopstock are given:

> Schreket noch andrer Gesang dich,
>> O Sohn Teutons,
> Als Griechengesang: —
> — So bist du kein Deutscher! ein
>> Nachahmer
> Belastet vom Joche, verkennst du
>> dich selber!

"If, son of Teuton, you fear the lyric in language other than Greek, then you are no German. An imitator burdened by that yoke, you fail to recognize yourself." This bold exhortation (Sulzer gives no source) is drawn from *Der Nachahmer* (1764) — the imitator — one of a number of odes in which Klopstock wrestles with the recovery of a genuine poetic language from the

---

fällig zu seyn, ob sie gleich itzt beynahe zum Gesetz geworden." Georg Sulzer, *Allgemeine Theorie der Schönen Künste*, vol. 3, 540.

9. "In jeder Ode zeigt sich also ein *Faden der Leidenschaft* . . . . Die heiseste Leidenschaft, und die kälteste Empfindung der Vernunft sind in ihrer Wahrheit und Form so weit verschieden, daß ihr Maas verschwindet: Vernunft und Gefühl bleiben die beiden Ende der Menschheit." Herder, *Sämtliche Werke*, vol. 32, 73. Herder, *Selected Early Works*, 44.

ruins of ancient Greece, from a poetry of a time and a cultural place lost to his own.

This loss of time and place seems apropos an effort to grasp today the extent to which Friedrich Gottlieb Klopstock's poetry, and his theorizing of language—most notably in "Von der Nachahmung des griechischen Silbenmaßes im Deutschen" (1755)[10]—sounded the authoritative voice in German letters in the 1760s and 1770s. Even Sulzer's essay seems to have been conceived as an encomium to the Klopstock ode. The epic *Messias*, written entirely in what Klopstock called "[den] deutschen Hexameter"—all 573 pages, in twenty lengthy cantos, or *Gesänge*[11]—was the magisterial work that established his eminence. But it was the publication of the odes, many written in strophic forms inspired by prototypes of ancient Greece and by the odes of Horace, that drew even wider attention among his contemporary poets, together with those composers who recognized the challenge of setting such things to music.

If the eminence of Klopstock's verse by the middle of the 1770s were ever in question, the invocation of his name, somewhat enigmatically, at a critical turn in Goethe's *Die Leiden des jungen Werthers* [The Sorrows of Young Werther] would have relieved its reader of any doubt as to the power of its language to arouse the deepest feelings. "Klopstock!" This is the single word that passes between Charlotte and Werther, uttered at a moment of quiescent passion in the fraught relationship that is at the core of Goethe's epistolary novel. Gathered for a society ball at some country estate, the two have separated themselves off from the others. A thunderstorm passes through. They observe it, silently. Here is Werther:

> She stood there resting on her elbows, gazing deep into the country about us; she looked to the heavens, and at me, and I saw there were tears in her eyes; and she laid her hand on mine and said: "Klopstock!"—At once, I remembered the glorious ode that she had in mind, and sank in the stream of feelings that flooded over me at this one word. It was more than I could bear; I bowed over her hand and kissed it in a stream of ecstatic tears, and again looked into her eyes. Noble poet! If only you could

10. Reprinted in, for one, Klopstock, *Ausgewählte Werke*, ed. Karl August Schleiden (Munich: Carl Hanser Verlag, 1962), 1038–1048. Dismissing French, Italian, and English, each for its own frailties of diction, no other language, claims Klopstock, can achieve the fullness of Greek prosody as can German. See especially p. 1040.

11. I refer to the accessible *Ausgewählte Werke*, 197–770.

have seen the adoration of you in this gaze — and your name, so often profaned, may I never again hear it uttered.[12]

In this remarkable passage, which locates with uncanny precision the *moment* at which the feelings of Lotte and Werther for each other (at the very
least, in Werther's perception) are elevated to a degree of sensuality bordering on the erotic, it is Klopstock who is the catalytic agent. At the mere
uttering of his name, Werther thinks "sogleich" of the ode which, he claims,
Lotte had in mind. If we, readers of Goethe's text, are not given to know
the identity of the ode that Werther brings to mind, we might recognize
the literary point in concealing its identity, in the face of recent attempts
to solve the mystery.[13] In fact, it was only in the second edition, published
in 1787, that the allusion to a specific (if unnamed) ode found its way into
the text.[14] Was it that Goethe, imagining the scene from a later perspective,

12. "Sie stand auf ihren Ellenbogen gestützt, ihr Blick durchdrang die Gegend; sie sah
gen Himmel und auf mich, ich sah ihr Auge tränenvoll, sie legte ihre Hand auf die mei-
nige und sagte: 'Klopstock!' — Ich erinnerte mich sogleich der herrlichen Ode, die ihr in
Gedanken lag, und versank in dem Strome von Empfindungen, den sie in dieser Losung
über mich ausgoß. Ich ertrug's nicht, neigte mich auf ihre Hand und küßte sie unter den
wonnevollsten Tränen. Und sah nach ihrem Auge wieder — Edler! Hättest du deine Vergötterung in diesem Blicke gesehen, und möcht' ich nun deinen so oft entweihten Namen
nie wieder nennen hören!" I cite from *Johann Wolfgang von Goethe. Werke. Hamburger
Ausgabe*, vol. 6, *Romane und Novellen* I, ed. Erich Trunz (Munich: C. H. Beck, 1981), 27.
The translation is drawn largely from *The Sorrows of Young Werther*, tr. Michael Hulse (Penguin Books, 1989), 43; and in some few instances from the translation by Victor Lange in
Goethe: The Collected Works, vol. 11, ed. David E. Wellbery (Princeton, NJ: Princeton University Press, 1988), 19.

13. "Gemeint ist Klopstocks Ode 'Die Frühlingsfeier'" [Klopstock's ode *The Celebration of Spring* is intended], writes Erich Trunz in a note to the text. Goethe, *Werke*, vol. 6,
ed. Trunz, 574. But the argument, in a long disquisition on the ode, offers only circum-
stantial evidence. For an antidote to this way of thinking, see Arnd Bohm, "'Klopstock!'
Once More: Intertextuality in Werther," in *Seminar: A Journal of Germanic Studies* 38(2)
(2002): 116–33. In his "'Klopstock!'" in *Euphorion* 73 (1979): 357–64, Richard Alewyn reflects more broadly on the place of literature in Goethe's novel.

14. For that earlier text, published in 1774, see, for one, *Der junge Goethe, Neu bearbeitete Ausgabe in fünf Bänden*, ed. Hanna Fischer-Lamberg, vol. 4 (Berlin: Walter de Gruyter
& Co., 1968), 120. Curiously, Fischer-Lamberg (358) writes only the following explanatory note: "gemeinsames Gedenken an Klopstocks Ode Die Frühlingsfeyer (1759) mit der
großartigen Schilderung eines Gewitters" [thoughts held in common on Klopstock's ode,
The Celebration of Spring, with its splendid description of a thunderstorm]. We are not told
how she knows this.

felt the need to actualize this Klopstock moment, to enter more intimately into Werther's sensorium (as Laurence Sterne might have put it), even as he tempts his voyeuristic reader to leaf through those odes which would have been in wide circulation by the spring of 1771, the year in which the events of the novel are set—the year too in which the so-called *Hamburger Ausgabe* of the Klopstock odes was published?

To claim to have identified the ode, emblem of a shared intimacy, would be to dispel the aura of not knowing, defeating the subtlety of two minds reading—or misreading—each other, in the play of those elective affinities that Goethe would later explore in *Die Wahlverwandtschaften*. When, on the final page of the novel, it is noted with journalistic dispassion that a copy of *Emilia Galotti* had been left opened on Werther's nightstand, that is precisely the point: to implicate into Goethe's text the stunning final scene of Lessing's grim tragedy. There will be more to say about this below, in chapter 8.

II

"The Ode and the Lied have so much in common that for certain poems, either name seems applicable," writes Sulzer elsewhere in the *Allgemeine Theorie*—this from the article "Lied (Dichtkunst)"—proceeding then to interrogate their differences. At the core of the inquiry is what might be called the strophic imperative, its conditions set forth with a musician's ear for the tension between meter and prosody:

[O]ne could assume that the lied ought always to be sung, and thus disposed so that the melody to one strophe be appropriate as well to all the others; and that the ode serves either simply for reading, or, if it is sung, that each strophe will require its own music. Every verse of the lied ought to constitute a caesura (*Einschnitt*) in the sense of the poem, and each strophe its own *Periode*. Still better, each strophe ought to divide into two periods, so that each ends with a long syllable, for the cadence of the song demands it. The ode doesn't abide by this rule. Its verse doesn't always articulate the sense of the poem, and its strophes do not accord with periods. Further, in the lied, the first strophe must serve as a model for all the others with respect to *Einschnitten*, *Abschnitten*, and *Schlüssen der Perioden*. In the ode on the other hand, the various strophes need be alike only with respect to mechanical meter, without complete regard for the rhythms that arise from the sense of the words. Finally, the lied does not admit variety in poetic feet, which is permitted in the ode; but rather, in all verses only one poetic foot must be maintained throughout—except perchance the final verse of each strophe might have its own meter, as in the Sapphic ode.[15]

A further distinction gets at matters of substance:

> The inner characteristics of the lied ought to agree completely with the external; and with respect to the ideas and expression of feelings, simplicity and uniformity must also be observed. Everything should be said in a single affective tone, because the same melody is repeated throughout. The ode now and then raises itself at certain places above the tone otherwise established, and permits rather more passionate expression of different types, so that one strophe flows gently where the other rushes impetuously.[16]

The discussion is augmented in a rich essay on "Lied (Musik)," written largely by Johann Abraham Peter Schulz, its text resonating with the famous preface to the second edition of Schulz's *Lieder im Volkston* (1785).[17] It is this pull between the repetitive, strophic simplicity of lied and the more ambitious prosody and loftier tone—passionate, lyrical, ethical—of ode that would provoke some of the more invigorating engagements of music and poetry in the 1770s. At the one extreme, the composer is bound to the tightly wrought strophic rule which governs the poem. "The poetic feet must be observed in the melody as precisely as they are observed by the poet," writes Schulz, "and the various syllables which form an indivisible unit (*unzertrennlichen Zusammenhang*) must not be broken by the setting of a perfect consonance ... in the middle of a poetic foot."[18] At the other, the complex internal structure of the ode and its range of expression from one strophe to the next, in counterpoint with an invariable prosody of meter and accent, conspire against the strophic setting even as its external metrical structure encour-

---

15. Sulzer, *Allgemeine Theorie der Schönen Künste*, vol. 3, 252–53.

16. Ibid., 253.

17. Often reprinted, the Preface can be found in Max Friedlaender, *Das deutsche Lied im 18. Jahrhundert: Quellen und Studien* (Stuttgart and Berlin: Cotta'schen Buchhandlung, 1902; repr. Hildesheim: Georg Olms, 1962), vol. 1, part 1, 256–57. On the authorship of the music articles in the *Allgemeine Theorie*, see *Aesthetics and the Art of Musical Composition in the German Enlightenment*, ed. Baker and Christensen, 14.

18. Sulzer, *Allgemeine Theorie*, vol. 3, 278.

ages, if it does not impose, a substratum with which the music must come to terms.

The problem was of a magnitude to inspire Johann Nikolaus Forkel to a formulation as complex in its structure as those odes by Klopstock that seem, paradoxically, to challenge the prospect that they might be set to music. Unsparing in its rush of incongruous metaphors, Forkel's stern admonition comes in a review of *Oden von Klopstock, mit Melodien von Christian Gottlob Neefe* (Flensburg and Leipzig, 1776). "In the composition of the Klopstock odes," he begins,

> Herr Neefe has undertaken a project that our best composers have avoided and against which they have wisely protected themselves ever since these odes first became known. When one considers that, to the composer who wishes to furnish them with a well-fit garment, the high flights of imagination of these excellent poems impose an obligation to fly alongside them at just that height and not perhaps to creep after them from a great distance, in the dust of the earth, then one need hardly allude to these otherwise nearly insurmountable difficulties — the form, the meter, and often the thoroughly singular and unusual construction produced by this great poet — in order to come to a proper understanding of the immensity of the undertaking.[19]

That Neefe himself was fully aware of the challenge speaks through in a letter to Klopstock, on the eve of the publication of these odes. Confessing to an earlier inadequacy, Neefe presses his case:

> Flattering myself that I now possess greater musical knowledge, I have dared once more to compose several of your odes, after I had read them

19. "Herr Neefe hat an der Composition der Klopstockschen Oden eine Arbeit übernommen, die unsere besten Componisten, schon seitdem sie bekannt sind, gescheuet, und sich deswegen auch weislich dafür gehütet haben. . . . Wenn man auch bedenkt, daß blos schon der hohe Schwung dieser vortreflichen Gedichte, dem Tonkünstler, der ihnen ein musikalisches Gewand anpassen will, die Pflicht auferlegt, ihnen in eben der Höhe nachzufliegen, und nicht etwa in einer himmelweiten Entfernung von ihnen, nur auf der Erde im Staube nachzukriechen, so braucht man der übrigen fast ebenfalls unübersteiglichen Schwierigkeiten, die Form, das Metrum, und öfters die ganz eigene und ungewöhnliche Construction dieses großen Dichters verursacht, kaum zu erwähnen, um sich einen richtigen Begriff von der Größe eines solchen Unternehmens zu machen." Johann Nikolaus Forkel, *Musikalisch-kritische Bibliothek*, vol. 1 (Gotha, 1778; repr. Hildesheim: Olms, 1964), 211.

through repeatedly until I understood them and believed that I had penetrated to the entire plan of each of them. I played and sang them to my friends, Prof. [Carl Friedrich] Cramer and Mr. [Johann Martin] Miller (who had become my friends because we were mutual in our veneration of a Klopstock). They assured me that my melodies are in sympathy with your *Empfindungen*, and at the same time encouraged me to make them known to the public.[20]

And in the closing lines of a preamble to his collection, a dedicatory letter to the Frau von Alvensleben — a favored singer who will play a role in the following chapter — Neefe appropriates Werther's Klopstock-moment:

Often, most often, I've said silently to myself: "Klopstock! Noble poet! If only you could have perceived the adoration of you in this voice, and your name, so often profaned, may I never again hear it uttered."[21]

20. "Jetzt, da ich mir schmeichle, mehr musikalische Kenntnisse zu besitzen, habe ich es aufs neue gewagt, einige Ihrer Oden zu komponiren, nachdem ich sie wieder so oft durchgelesen, bis ich sie verstanden und den ganzen Plan einer jeden eingesehen zu haben glaubte. Ich spielt und sang sie meinen Freunden, (die auch darum meine Freunde wurden, weil wir gemeinschaftliche Verehrer eines Klopstocks waren) dem Hrn. Professor Cramer und Herrn Miller vor. Diese versicherten mich, daß meine Melodien mit ihren Empfindungen sympathisirten, ermunterten mich zugleich, sie öffentlich bekannt zu machen." The letter, dated 21 December 1775, is given in La Mara, *Musikerbriefe aus fünf Jahrhunderten*, vol. 1 (Leipzig: Breitkopf & Härtel, [1886]), 280–82; reprinted in Eberhard Möller, "Christian Gottlob Neefe und seine Klopstock-Oden," in *Christian Gottlob Neefe (1748–1798): Eine eigenständige Künstlerpersönlichkeit. Tagesbericht Chemnitz 1998*, ed. Helmut Loos (Chemnitz: Gudrun Schröder Verlag, 1999), 120–21. Curiously, Möller makes no mention of the Forkel review. When La Mara wrote, the letter had earlier been in the possession of Georg Pölchau. Irmgard Leux, in her important *Christian Gottlob Neefe (1748–1798)* (Leipzig: Fr. Kistner & C. F. W. Siegel, 1925), reports that her efforts to locate the letter in either the library of the Singakademie in Berlin, where Pölchau had served under Zelter between 1814 and 1826, or the Staatsbibliothek zu Berlin, which had acquired a substantial portion of the great Pölchau *Nachlass* in 1841, were fruitless.

21. "Oft, sehr oft, habe ich mir im Stillen gesagt: 'Klopstock! Edler! Hättest du deine Vergötterung in dieser Stimme vernommen, und möcht' ich Deinen so oft entweyhten Namen nun nie wieder nennen hören!'" The dedicatory preface may be found in *Oden von Klopstock, mit Melodien von Christian Gottlob Neefe* (Flensburg and Leipzig: in der Kortenschen Buchhandlung, 1776), 1; facsimile repr. as Christian Gottlob Neefe, *Oden von Klopstock*, in *Dokumentation zur Geschichte des deutschen Liedes*, vol. 9, ed. Siegfried Kross (Hildesheim, Zurich, New York: Georg Olms, 2003). For something more on von Alvensleben, and Carl Friedrich Cramer's intention to dedicate to her a gathering of Emanuel

In the substitution of *Stimme* for Goethe's *Blick*, the sensibility of the musician, the acoustic presence of voice, is given privilege in cunning defense of Neefe's enterprise. In an earlier paragraph, the consequences of failure are vividly drawn: "The merely orthodox musician ruins the song that Klopstock, at the height of his fame, sang in his palm grove; and when the diva begins to sing, the feeling soul runs away."[22]

From the litany of solecisms targeted in Forkel's essay, a passage from Neefe's setting of *An Cidli* illuminates the composer's dilemma, its complex counterpoint of meter and syntax challenging the fluid diction of the music.[23] (Neefe's setting, together with the three remaining strophes of the poem, is shown as fig. 4.1.)

Zeit, Verkündigerin der besten Freuden,
Nahe selige Zeit, dich in der Ferne
Auszuforschen, vergoß ich
Trübender Tränen zuviel!

[Time, harbinger of the best joys, near, blessed time: to search you out in the distance I shed too many troubled tears!]

An apostrophe to Time, these opening lines respond to the isolation, grammatically, of the word itself, setting off epistemological questions: Time in what sense? As the infinite scroll against which experience is measured? *Zeit*, its diphthong hedged between two percussive consonants, argues rather for the articulative moment, for *Augenblick*. And then the word vanishes, displaced by "dich," a pronoun that personifies the object of the poet's search, the inspiration of these troubled tears. It is as though Klopstock envisions

---

Bach's songs in 1774, see Gudrun Busch, *C. Ph. E. Bach und seine Lieder* (Regensburg: Gustav Bosse, 1957), 198; and the Introduction to Carl Philipp Emanuel Bach, *The Polyhymnia Portfolio*, ed. Christoph Wolff, in Carl Philipp Emanuel Bach, *The Complete Works*, series 8, vol. 2 (Los Altos, CA: Packard Humanities Institute, 2014), xi–xii.

22. "Der blos orthodoxe Musiker verdirbt das Lied, das Klopstock auf der Lorbeerhöhe und im Palmenhayne sang; und wenn die Operistinn es anstimmt, läuft der Empfindende davon."

23. Cidli is the term of endearment for Meta Moller, to whom Klopstock was engaged in 1752. They married in 1754; she died in childbirth in 1758. In later editions, the poem is renamed *An Sie*, the title by which the settings of Zumsteeg and Schubert are known. Neefe's collection contains two other "Cidli" poems: "Sie schläft. O gieß ihr, Schlummer" (later titled *Ihr Schlummer*) and "Der Liebe Schmerzen" (later titled *Gegenwart der Abwesenden*).

Figure 4.1. Christian Gottlob Neefe, *An Cidli*, in *Oden von Klopstock, mit Melodien von Christian Gottlob Neefe* (Flensburg and Leipzig, 1776), 9.

the moment at which She appears as inseparable from the experience of her presence. The confusion of tense, that moment of time past at the imminent edge of time future, only underscores a further existential paradox, the close proximity of a *nahe Zeit* to be sought in the remote distance, *in der Ferne auszuforschen*.

The convolutions of its deeply metaphoric language point up the tension between those "volkstümliche" lieder that insist upon a strophic setting and the Klopstock ode which resists, strenuously, the conventions of song. Speak this opening line as an actor would: "Zeit," echoing into the rafters, a stolen breath, and then the choriambics etched in the five syllables of "Verkündigerin." However one might think to declaim it, its analogues in the following strophes will each want its own diction. The music of a strophic setting will need to effect a compromise, forfeiting an articulative isolation of that opening "Zeit" to accommodate its analogues in the three strophes that follow.

Unfazed by the strophic problem, Forkel chooses rather to interrogate the boldly protracted setting of "auszuforschen," finding in its rhythmic deviation "no inspiration" but only a violation of "good, pure declamation and of good taste." But surely there is more here to excite the critic's pen than this exclusive focus on the single tone, the unduly lengthened syllable. About the searching harmonies that move through the dissonant flat ninth above D, deepening the expression even as it complicates the strophic problem: not a word.

While Forkel refuses comment on the unseemly fit of this phrase to the parallel text in the remaining strophes, Neefe himself, in the preface to his collection, focuses on the strophic problem quite to the exclusion of all else. "For I wrote out no melody before I had entirely understood the text and felt it, spoke it to myself two or three times out loud, and tested the melody for all strophes. Nevertheless, here and there small adjustments were necessary, and these I have also indicated."[24] And yet, there will be nuances in the declamation from one strophe to the next that will require the sympathetic reading of the performer, to whom Neefe addresses these overly meticulous instructions:

> The singer shall indeed have had to study each poem carefully before he sings it; the Klopstock odes especially demand this preliminary study. For only then will one be able to perform them correctly, and will know where to place the forte and piano in the following strophes of the ode, for the augmenting and diminishing of tone in the voice and the keyboard will not be located in the same place in each strophe. Now and then, an undotted note in the first strophe will have to be dotted in a following strophe in order that the word in question, having a more logical accent, will be strongly enough accented in the performance. And on the contrary, it is sometimes necessary to shorten a note by half and to think of a rest in its place so that things which do not belong together will not be bound up with one another. A composer doesn't always need to indicate those places where such little rules may be applied for the good of the expression. He must also leave something to the individual feeling of the performer.[25]

24. "Denn keine Melodie ist von mir eher aufgeschrieben worden, als ich den Text ganz verstanden und empfunden, mir ihn zwey bis dreymal laut vordeklamirt, und die Melodie nach allen Strophen untersucht hatte. Freylich waren dennoch hier und da kleine Abänderungen in der Melodie nöthig, die ich auch angegeben habe."

25. "Der Sänger soll zwar überhaupt jedes Gedicht vorher aufmerksam studiren, eh er es singt; die klopstockischen Oden aber erfordern dieses vorhergehende Studium besonders.

Yes, but there are limits to what might be asked of the singer where the poetry resists a strophic setting. It is toward these deeper currents of syntactical relationships that Forkel directs his most severe criticism. Focus is sharpened on a passage in the setting of *Bardale*, an ode of eighteen stanzas, constructed rigorously in the antique meter that we know as the Fourth Asclepiad, its first couplet in the familiar hexameter.[26] (The complete song is shown as fig. 4.2.) Forkel dwells on the coordination between what he calls "logische und musikalische Ruhestellen," between cadences in the music and logical points of articulation in the poem.[27] And here a passage from Neefe's setting is shown (see fig. 4.3). "The progression marked by the (*) is somewhat lacking in the genuine stamp of beauty," writes Forkel. "It could be permitted to pass if only the text would not otherwise suffer so powerfully."[28]

Dann erst wird man sie richtig vortragen können; dann wird man das Forte und Piano in den übrigen Strophen einer Ode gehörig zu versetzen wissen; denn die Verstärkung und Verminderung des Tons der Stimme und des Klaviers kann nicht in allen Strophen einerley Sitz behalten. Bisweilen wird man eine in der ersten Strophe unpunktirte Note in einer folgenden punktiren müssen, um das darunter stehende Wort, das vorzüglich viel logischen Accent hat, auch im Gesange stark genug zu accentuiren. Hingegen wird es manchesmal nöthig seyn, eine Note um die Hälfte zu verkürzen, und statt der andern eine Pause hin zu denken, damit das, was nicht zusammen gehört, auch nicht mit einander verbunden werde. Die Stellen, wo solche kleine Regeln zum Besten des Ausdrucks anzuwenden sind, braucht ein Komponist nicht samt und sonders anzugeben. Er muß auch dem eigenen Gefühle des Ausführers Etwas überlassen."

26. First published in 1748 as *Aedon*, the ode was substantially revised for publication in 1771 and retitled *Bardale*. Structurally the same, it is this earlier version, and not the later, that is given in Klopstock, *Ausgewählte Werke*, ed. Schleiden, 34–36. For what may be the earliest critical appreciation of the poem, see C[arl] F[riedrich] Cramer, *Klopstock. Er; und über ihn. Zweiter Theil. 1748–50* (Dessau: in der Gelehrten Buchhandlung, 1781; Leipzig and Altona, 1790), 300–309, where *Bardale* is printed together with the variants found in the earlier *Aedon*. Hölty's *Die Mainacht* is cast in the same strophic meter, its accents painstakingly observed in Brahms's exquisite setting.

For another strophic setting, see Johann Friedrich Reichardt, *Musikalisches Kunstmagazin* [vol. 1] (Berlin: Im Verlage des Verfassers, 1782; repr. Hildesheim: Georg Olms, 1969), 60–61, which Reichardt defended in these self-serving words (63): "In this Ode, I have employed every possible means to make the melody appropriate to all strophes, and yet it was of the utmost urgency here to display the tone of the whole through melodic charm." Measured against even Neefe's modest engagement with Klopstock's challenging poem, Reichardt's claim is overblown.

27. Forkel, *Bibliothek*, 220.

28. Ibid., 221.

2. Hört der Wald dich allein, deine Gespielinnen,
Flattern horchend nur sie dir um den Schattenast;
Singe dann, o Bardale,
Nachtigallen Gesänge nur.

3. Aber tritt er daher, welcher erhabner ist,
Als die Geiste des Hayns, kommt er, der Erde Gott,
Sing dann, glücklicher Sänger,
Tonevoller und lyrischer.

4. Denn sie hören dich auch, die doch unsterblich sind!
Ihren göttlichen Trieb lockt dein Gesang hervor.
Ach Bardale, du singest
Liebe zu, den Unsterblichen!

5. Ich entflog ihr und sang, und der bewegte Hayn
Und die Hügel umher hörten mein flötend Lied!
Und des Baches Gespräche
Sprachen leiser am Ufer hin.

6. Doch der Hügel, der Bach war nicht, die Eiche selbst
War der Gott nicht, und bald senkte der Ton mein Lied.
Denn ich sang dich, o Liebe,
Nicht Göttinnen und Göttern nicht!

7. Jetzo kam sie herauf, unter des Schattens Nacht
Kam die edle Gestalt, lebender als der Hayn!
Schöner, als die Gespiele!
Eine von den Unsterblichen!

8. Welch ein neues Gefühl glühte mir! Ach der Blick
Ihres Auges, der West hielt mich; ich sank schon hin!
Sprach die Stimme den Blick aus;
O so würde sie süßer seyn.

9. Als mein leisester Laut, als mein gesungenster
Und gefühltester Ton, wenn mich die junge Lust
Von dem Zweige des Strauches,
In die Wipfel des Hayns entzückt!

10. Aug', ach Auge, dein Blick bleibt unvergeßlich mir!
Und wie nennet das Lied? singen die Töne dich?
Nennst dich, singen sie: Seele?
Bist du's, das die Unsterblichen

11. Zu Unsterblichen machte? Auge, wem gleich ich dich?
Bist du Blume der Lust, wenn sie der Abendstern
Sanft mit Golde beschimmert?
Oder gleichst du jenem Bach,

12. Der dem Quell kaum entfloß? Schöner erblickte nie
Seine Rosen der Busch! Heller ich selber nie
Mich in einem der Bäche,
Niederschwankend am Frühlingssproß.

13. O, was sprach ihr Blick? Hörtest du, Göttinn, mich?
Eine Nachtigall du? Sang ich vor Liebe dir?
Und was flüstet gelinder
Dir vom schmachtenden Aug herab?

14. Ist das Liebe, was dir zärtlich vom Auge rinnt?
Deinen göttlichen Trieb, lockt ihn mein Lied hervor?
Welche sanfte Bewegung
Hebt dir deine beseelte Brust?

15. Sag, wie heißet der Trieb, welcher dein Herz bewegt?
Neigt ohn ihn dich Amors goldene Schaale noch?
Ist er himmlische Jugend?
Oder Freud in dem Hayn Walhals?

16. O gefeyert sey mir, blumiger zwölfter May,
Da die Göttinn sich saß, aber gefeyerter
Seyst du unter den Mayen,
Wenn ich in den Umarmungen

17. Eines Jünglings sie seh, der die Beredsamkeit
Dieser Augen und euch fühlet, ihr Frühlinge
Dieser lächelnden Mienen,
Und den Geist der dieß Alles schuf.

18. Wars nicht, Fanny, der Tag, wars nicht der zwölfte May,
Als der Schatten dich rief? Wars nicht der zwölfte May,
Der mir, weil ich allein war,
Öd und traurig vorüberfloß?

Figure 4.2. Neefe, *Bardale*, in *Oden von Klopstock*, 4–5.

Figure 4.3. Johann Nikolaus Forkel, *Musikalisch-kritische Bibliothek*, I (Gotha, 1778), 221.

But it is the full close at the dominant, marked by the dagger, that is the primary target of Forkel's inquiry: the violation of syntax at "lehrete sorgsam mich [full close] meine Mutter," shunting the delayed subject of the sentence off to the beginning of a new phrase. Silent on the passage in the example, Forkel here calls up the analogous lines in strophes 9, 11, 12, 16, and 17, in each case constituting an enjambment broken by "this self-same cadence in the dominant." For Neefe, it is apparently the metric structure of the verse that governs the music, overriding the articulative syntax of poetic language — to put the best face on it.

In *Bardale*, the strophic problem is further complicated by the run-on *between* strophes, and here Neefe troubles to write out the slightest of variants for the performance of those strophes linked in this way, eliminating the keyboard postlude between them and adjusting the cadence in the voice to avoid closure on scale degree 1. But it is for the setting of the plangent final strophe that Neefe conjures his most radical swerve. In the course of its first seventeen strophes, it is the nightingale — *Aedon* of Greek mythology, in 1748; *Bardale*, from Nordic mythology, in the revision of 1771 — from whose perspective we witness the passionate summoning of inspiration to sing of love, recalling, in the early strophes, its mother's exhortation:

[strophe 3] "Sing, dann, glücklicher Sänger,/Tönevoller, und lyrischer";
[4] "Ach, Bardale, du singest/Liebe zu, den Unsterblichen!"

[Sing, then, happy singer, with fuller tone and more lyrically. Ah, Bardale, you will sing to love, to the immortal!]

The allure of its song does its incantatory work. A figure at last materializes, goddess-like:

[7] Jetzo kam sie herauf, unter des Schattens Nacht!
Kam die edle Gestalt, lebender, als der Hayn!
Schöner, als die Gefilde!
Eine von der Unsterblichen!

[Now she appeared, under the night of shadows, the noble shape, more alive than the wooded grove! More beautiful than the fields! One of the immortals!]

The poet's surrogate, the nightingale is gradually moved by its own not-so-innocent singing:

[13] O, was sprach itzt ihr Blick? Hörtest du, Göttinn, mich?
Eine Nachtigall du? Sang ich von Liebe dir?
Und was fließet gelinder
Dir vom schmachtenden Aug' herab?

[Oh, what did your glance now say? Did you hear me, goddess? Did you hear a nightingale? Did I sing to you of love? And what is flowing tenderly down from your languishing eye?]

In the final strophes, things heat up considerably:

[16] O gefeyert sey mir, blumiger zwölfter May,
Da die Göttinn ich sah! aber gefeyerter

Seyst du unter den Mayen,
Wenn ich in den Umarmungen

[17] Eines Jünglings sie seh, der die Beredsamkeit
Dieser Augen, und euch fühlet, ihr Frühlinge .
Dieser lächelnden Mi[e]nen
Und den Geist der dieß Alles schuf!

[Oh, twelfth of May, all abloom, how honored was I when I saw the goddess! But how much greater your honor among the days of May were I to see her in the embraces of a youth, the eloquence of these eyes, and you to feel in their spring these smiling countenances and the spirit that created all this!]

And then, this riddling final strophe:

[18] Wars nicht, Fanny, der Tag? Wars nicht der Zwölfte May,
Als der Schatten dich rief? Wars nicht der Zwölfte May,
Der mir, weil ich allein war,
Oed' und traurig vorüberfloß?

[Wasn't this the day, Fanny? Wasn't it the twelfth of May, when "der Schatten" called you?[29] Wasn't it the twelfth of May, which flowed past me, desolate and wretched, for I was alone?]

"And now that last strophe!" writes Carl Friedrich Cramer, on the way to an explanatory gloss of its doleful lines: "the fine turn in which the poet, who himself now speaks, not directly, but through a hint that enables Fanny to grasp that it was her of whom the nightingale spoke; and, through just such a hint, that he was the young lad who would feel the eloquence of these eyes, and whom, desolate and mournful, the twelfth of May would flow past."[30]

---

29. "Der Schatten." Cramer, *Klopstock*, 305, fn. 9, offers a reading: "Als du in den Schatten, in den Wald gingst, wo dich die Nachtigal nämlich gesehen und besungen hat" [As you went into the shadows, into the wood, where the nightingale saw you and sang to you]. In this reading, *Schatten* is a metonym: shade for wood. But "der Schatten dich rief" is no less powerfully suggestive of agency, of a spirit who calls her from the wood into the aura of the nightingale. "Schatten," of course, allows — and in this case, encourages — these shaded meanings.

30. Cramer, *Klopstock*, 305, fn. 8. "Und nun die lezte Stophe! Die feine Wendung womit der Dichter, der jezt selbst spricht, nicht geradezu, sondern durch einer Wink Fanny zu verstehen giebt, sie sei es, von der das die Nachtigal gesagt habe; und eben so durch einen

How then does Neefe respond to this "fine turn" in the final strophe, to
these melancholy reflections of the lover who has been left to ponder his
loneliness? In the wake of seventeen strophic iterations in B major, the turn
to B minor is catastrophic, the prototype now transfigured into a music that
shadows the poet's enigmatic questions, as though in search of the elusive
Fanny, even as its punctuation contradicts, in the basest prosodic sense, the
question to which it is put.[31] The tonicization of G is only underscored in
the cadence on D that follows, but it is the unexpected inflection in the following phrase that catches the ear: the turn upward from that high F♯ to
the keening phrase at "weil ich allein war," finding a high A for the first and
only moment in the song, above the first and only diminished seventh. Compressed into a single bar, these five syllables yet again point up the dissonance
between an obligatory metrical accent (on the conjunction "weil") and the
dislocation, fighting against its weak position, of a word of some signifi-

---

Wink: Er sei der Jüngling, der die Beredsamkeit dieser Augen fühle, und dem der zwölfte
Mai öd' und traurig vorüber geflossen sei."

Why the twelfth of May? "[D]ieser Tag hatte wohl eine besondere Bedeutung für die
Beziehungen des Dichters zu Fanny. Vielleicht war es der Tag der ersten Begegnung" [This
date may well have had a special significance for the relationship of the poet to Fanny.
Perhaps it was the day of their first encounter]. Klopstock, *Ausgewählte Werke*, 1226. The
deeper question is why the poet thought it justifiable to specify a date whose significance
could not be revealed from the evidence of the poem. Cramer (*Klopstock*, 300, fn. 1) reports
on his conversation with Klopstock: "Die Ode scheint in einer ziemlich heitern Stunde ge-
arbeitet zu sein. Die genaue Veranlassung davon weiss ich nicht; [Klopstock] hat mir aber
gesagt, daß es ein für ihn sehr merkwürdiger Tag gewesen sei." [The ode seems to have been
the work of a rather happy hour. I don't know the precise motivation for it, but (Klopstock) told me that it had been a particularly remarkable day for him.]

31. The Fanny of this and other odes is Maria Sophia Schmidt, the passionate and un-
requited love of his early years. In a letter to Fanny of 11 May 1751, Klopstock sets out his
feelings for her in a poetic dialogue in which she plays the reluctant dove: "Komm her,
kleiner Liebling, und setze dich auf meine Leier, und ich will dir ein Lied von einer Fanny
spielen, die der einzige Gedanke meines Lebens ist . . . Warum senkst du deinen schim-
mernden Fittig herunter? Warum wirst du so traurig?" [Come, little darling, and sit at my
lyre and I will sing you a Lied of a Fanny who is the single thought of my life. . . . Why do
your glimmering wings sink down? Why so sad?] To which the answer comes: "Höre auf,
dies Lied zu singen, oder ich fliege in jene dunkeln Schatten und sehe dich nicht wieder."
[Break off this song, or I'll fly into those dark shadows and see you never more.] The letter
can be found in Klopstock, *Ausgewählte Werke*, 1099–1102. The fear that she would dis-
appear into the wooded shadows is a sentiment very close to those closing lines of *Aedon*,
written three years earlier.

cance: the revelatory "ich" with which the poet insinuates himself, finally, as the human voice behind his elaborately wrought conceit.

In the affecting sentiment of these final bars, Neefe will need the acuity of the performer to reach beyond prosody in sympathy with the poet's truer accents. The descent from that high A, calibrated over these three bars, finds its inconclusive closure at F♯ — not, as one might have expected, as the fifth degree above a tonic, but as the root of a dominant, as though breaking off in fragment. In a text whose printing is replete with advice from the composer, there can be no question that the song means to end here: in B minor, and not in an understood *da capo* of the first strophe that would have implicated a return to B major (presumably as a postlude for keyboard alone). The colophon at the end of the print is unconditional. And so we are left to ponder the implications of this "letzte Strophe" that does not close. It is more than a final interrogation mark that is signified here.

And in fact Neefe did some serious pondering of his own. In the "neue sehr vermehrte und verbeßerte Ausgabe" (new greatly enlarged and improved edition) of 1785, *Bardale* is perhaps the most radically revised in the collection, leaving out of discussion the few settings that were replaced wholesale by new ones; several were reprinted without change, *An Cidli* ("Zeit, Verkündigerin") among them.[32] With Forkel's admonition in view, the breach of syntax at "lehrte sorgsam mich [^] meine Mutter" is masked and softened, the music moving now to the dominant of the dominant and revoiced — though Forkel would very likely have continued to hear a bump in the prosody. The first five strophes are sung to the same music, but then, as Klopstock's nightingale rehearses its repertory of feelings and reflections, Neefe's music follows. The sixth strophe — "ein wenig langsam," Neefe instructs — is in B minor, catching the nuance of "bald senkte den Ton mein Lied." With the sight of Her, emerging from the shadows in the next stro-

---

32. Published by Johann Ludwig Gehra in Neuwied, "In Bosslers Notenoffizin zu Speier gedrukt." On this new edition, see Möller, "Christian Gottlob Neefe und seine Klopstock-Oden," 115; and, in the same collection, Friederike Grigat, "Christian Gottlob Neefe und seine Verleger," esp. 203–5. Gehra announced the new edition in a note dated 26 February 1785, inviting subscriptions to an edition that he described as augmented by such various masterpieces as *Dem Unendlichen, Das grosse Halleluja, Dem Erlöser* "und vielen andern, ganz durchcomponirten." The note appeared in the issue dated 22 June 1785 of Carl Friedrich Cramer's *Magazin der Musik*, Zweyter Jahrgang [vol. 2, no. 1] (Hamburg: "in der Musicalischen Niederlage," 1784; repr. [= vol. 3] Hildesheim and New York: Georg Olms, 1971), 677–78.

Ex. 4.1. Passage from Neefe, *Bardale*, version of 1785.

phe, the music returns to B major, now "Lebhaft," and with a lively new figure in the keyboard. The ninth strophe begins in B major and closes in E major; the tenth, again "langsam," begins in E minor and closes on the dominant of G, its question finished at the opening of the eleventh (ex. 4.1).

"And now that last strophe!" — once more. Here again, the music is in B minor, again "langsam." Considerably revised, Neefe's strophe yet finds that same questioning dominant with which the song refused resolution in 1776. But while Klopstock's unanswerable questions continue to reverberate, the music now finds an answer: the piano is given a postlude in B minor, four bars in the tonic. (This final strophe is shown as fig. 4.4.) The song is reconceived, the radical, irresolute ending of 1776 brought to classical decorum, the strophic rule compromised in deference to the obscurities of Klopstock's conceit.

In the music of *An Cidli* and *Bardale*, we hear the modest, understated work of a composer whose literary sensibility sings through in settings that take up the challenge of Klopstock's difficult poetry. It was the setting of *Bardale*, among several others, that Christian Friedrich Daniel Schubart singled out as music that "for the most part measures up to the grand spirit of Klopstock and quite splendidly expresses his deep, melancholy *Empfindung.*"[33]

33. "Die Melodien sind meist dem großen Geiste Klopstocks angemessen und drücken seine tiefe, schwermütige Empfindung ganz vortrefflich aus." Christian Friedrich Daniel Schubart, *Ideen zu einer Aesthetik der Tonkunst*, ed. Ludwig Schubart (Vienna: J. V. Degan, 1806; repr. Hildesheim: Georg Olms, 1969), 118. It must have been the widely circulated earlier version of *Bardale* that Schubart knew, for the material for the *Ideen* was evidently assembled in 1784 and 1785, if we are to believe the account in the *Vorrede* that Schubart's son provided for its publication in 1806.

Figure 4.4. Neefe, *Bardale*, final strophe. From *Oden von Klopstock* (Neuwied: Gehra, [1785]).

Hearing the *Empfindsamkeit* in Neefe's settings, Schubart sets himself at odds with Forkel's schoolmasterly admonitions. It is perhaps a matter of emphasis, these two critical stances, if not a symptom of some deeper aesthetic breach.

5

COMPOSING KLOPSTOCK
Gluck contra Bach

It was the music of two of his most illustrious contemporaries that Neefe recognized in the opening sentence of his *Vorbericht*: "Der Kapellmeister Bach, und der Ritter Gluck, haben in dem göttingischen Musenalmanach gezeigt, daß sich auch klopstockische Oden komponiren lassen" [In the Göttingen *Musenalmanach*, the Kapellmeister Bach and the Ritter Gluck have shown that even the odes of Klopstock can be set to music]. Having begun publication in 1770, each issue of the Göttingen *Musenalmanach* offered an anthology of poems generally gathered within a separately titled *Poetische Blumenlese* together with engraved music on individual plates folded and tipped into the book — six songs in 1774, seven in 1775 — composed at the initiative of its editors, Heinrich Christian Boie and Johann Heinrich Voss. While Bach and Gluck are represented in both volumes, it is their settings of Klopstock in the *Blumenlese* of 1775, edited by Voss, that invite further inquiry: from Bach, a setting of *Lyda*; from Gluck, settings of *Der Jüngling* and *Die frühen Gräber*.

We get some sense of the enterprise from the lively correspondence between the poets of the so-called *Göttinger Hainbund*, whose core members were, after Voss and Boie, Ludwig Christoph Heinrich Hölty, Johann Martin Miller, and Carl Friedrich Cramer.[1] But it was Klopstock, off in Hamburg, who was clearly its *spiritus rector*. Despite the roughly 165 miles between Göttingen and Hamburg, the intellectual relations between them were close. It was at the University of Göttingen that Forkel was lecturing in the early 1770s, about which Voss reported in a letter to Brückner (26 October 1772): "This winter he is reading lectures on the theory of music and its constitution in antiquity."[2] In a letter of 30 March 1774 to Johann Martin

---

1. For a fine account of the *Hainbund* and its significance for Bach's Hamburg years, see Busch, *C. Ph. E. Bach und seine Lieder*, 98 and 118 ff.
2. "Er [Forkel] liest diesen Winter ein Collegium über die theoretische Musik und ihre Beschaffenheit bei den Alten." Busch, *C. Ph. E. Bach und seine Lieder*, 119–20, fn. 80.

Miller and his colleagues in the *Hainbund,* Voss reports from Hamburg on a visit to Klopstock: "Afterward we spoke about the rhythm and the music of prosody. Gluck's *Willkommen [o silberne Mond]* and the *Schlachtgesang* please him thoroughly. The others — *das deutsche Mädchen,* for example — less so, and yet more than Bach's composition. Bach is otherwise said to speak with esteem of Gluck."[3]

"A POET AMONG COMPOSERS"

Readers who know Gluck's setting of *Der Jüngling* will undoubtedly know the version published by Artaria in *Klopstocks Oden und Lieder beym Clavier zu Singen in Musik gesetzt von Herrn Ritter Gluck* (Vienna, 1785) and often reprinted.[4] The version in the *Musenalmanach* of 1775 — the version that Neefe knew — is very different: a simple strophic setting, its barren texture stripped of anything beyond an elocution of Klopstock's resonant prosody. (The two settings are shown as exx. 5.1 and 5.2.) The resonance is palpable in the weighted adverbial incipit at the head of each strophe — Schweigend; Wütend; Ruhig; Jetzo — its spondaic syllables mapping the stations in this allegory of narcissistic youth. Oblivious of the ominous portents that rage about him, the blossom-drenched figure of May sleeps through the violent storm, eliciting from the poet's seat a final admonition: "Auf, und waffne dich mit der Weisheit!"

Schweigend sahe der Mai die bekränzte	Silently, May saw his wreathed,
Leichtwehende Lock' im Silberbach;	lightly flowing locks in the silver brook;

3. "Nachher sprachen wir von der Rhythmik und der Musik des Sylbenmaßes. Glucks Willkommen u. der Schlachtgesang gefallen ihm ganz. Die übrigen, z. E. das deutsche Mädchen nicht völlig, aber mehr doch, als Bachs Composition. Bach soll sonst mit Hochachtung von Gluck sprechen." Carl Philipp Emanuel Bach, *Briefe und Dokumente: Kritische Gesamtausgabe,* ed. Ernst Suchalla (Göttingen: Vandenhoeck & Ruprecht, 1994), 374; and Busch, *C. Ph. E. Bach und seine Lieder,* 122. Both, citing from Voss's autograph in the Bayerische Staatsbibliothek München, give precisely the same excerpt.

4. In, for one, *Lieder und Arien von Chr. W. Gluck,* ed. Max Friedlaender (Leipzig: Peters, [n.d.]); and finally in the splendid edition in Christoph Willibald Gluck, *Oden und Lieder auf Texte von Friedrich Gottlieb Klopstock und Lorenz Leopold Haschka,* ed. Daniela Philippi and Heinrich W. Schwab, in Gluck, *Sämtliche Werke,* Abt. 6: Vokalmusik, Vol. 2 (Kassel, Basel, etc.: Bärenreiter Verlag, 2011).

Rötlich war sein Kranz, wie des Aufgangs,   His crown was flushed like the dawn.
Er sah sich, und lächelte sanft.   He saw himself, and smiled tenderly.

Wütend kam ein Orkan am Gebirg' her!   Furiously, a hurricane approached the
       mountain!
Die Esche, die Tann', und Eiche brach,   The ash, the fir, the oak cracked,
Und mit Felsen stürtzte der Ahorn   and the maple plunged with rocks
Vom bebenden Haupt des Gebirgs.   From the trembling top of the mountain.

Ruhig schlummert' am Bache der Mai ein,   Peacefully, May fell asleep at the brook,
Liess rasen den lauten Donnersturm!   Letting the loud thunderstorm rage!
Lauscht', und schlief, beweht von der Blüte,   He listened, and slept, touched by the blossoms
Und wachte mit Hesperus auf.   And woke with the evening star [Venus].

Jetzo fühlst du noch nichts von dem Elend,   Now you still sense nothing of misery,
Wie Grazien lacht das Leben dir.   Life, like the graces, laughs to you.
Auf, und waffne dich mit der Weisheit!   Up, and arm yourself with wisdom!
Denn, Jüngling, die Blume verblüht!   For, youth, the blossom will wither!

NB. *Die ganze andere Strophe nebst dem andern Vers in der dritten Strophe werden im Singen und Spielen mit Stärke ausgedrückt.*

Ex. 5.1. Christoph Willibald Gluck, *Der Jüngling*, early version, in [*Musenalmanach*:] *Poetische Blumenlese auf das Jahr 1775* (Göttingen and Gotha, 1775), 160–61.

Ex. 5.2. Gluck, *Der Jüngling*, later version, in *Klopstocks Oden und Lieder beym Clavier zu Singen in Musik gesetzt von Herrn Ritter Gluck* (Vienna: Artaria, 1785).

When, a decade later, Gluck revisited the ode for the Artaria publication, he seized the opportunity to move beyond the chaste parsimony of a strophic setting toward a music that would engage the shifting currents of the poem without obscuring Klopstock's fine prosody. While the precise rhythmic declamation of the earlier setting is strictly preserved in each of the four strophes of the new version, in every other respect the poem now erupts in music. No longer merely a doubling of the voice, the "Klavierbegl[eitung]," as it is labeled in the Artaria print, becomes the orchestra in the pit, depicting the imagery of the poem mimetically and in metaphor. Reaching for the tempestuous sublime of the second strophe, the keyboard unleashes a hail of sixteenths — "presto," they are to be played — impelled by the strident, unprepared E♮ of "Wüthend," a note of fury indeed.

In the third strophe the music moves inward. The placid figure of the opening returns, tinged, for a brief moment, in G minor. A remnant of the storm is heard. In the strophic setting of 1775, Gluck instructs his performers to render this passage, together with the entire second strophe, "im Singen und Spielen mit Stärke" — *con forza*, in other words. But this is not what happens in 1785. The thunder rumbles faintly, a momentary inflection heard as if in a dream, as though Gluck could presciently conjure the distant thunder at the end of the slow movement of the *Symphonie fantastique*[5] — or, closer to home, the Klopstock moment in *Werther*: "We went to the window. It thundered off in the distance, and the delicious rain rustled over the land, and the most refreshing fragrance rose up to us in all its intensity in the warm air." Klopstock's second couplet enacts in its four verbs a wonder of syntactic economy: "Lauscht', und schlief, beweht von der Blüte,/Und wachte mit Hesperus auf." *Lauschen*: to listen, but with furtive ear; to doze off. Its two meanings, nearly contradictory, are subtly at play here in the picturing of youth, disturbed in a momentary, half-conscious flutter, unable (or merely disinclined) to register those distant rumblings and falling more deeply into slumber.

With cunning accuracy, Gluck's music manages the transliteration, tone for word. The G♭ at "lauscht,'" an appoggiatura that irritates the dominant, functions as a kind of stage direction (Gluck ever the man of the theater): a dissonant bending that guides the singer to the slightest inflection of the

---

5. As though in homage to what would become Berlioz's passionate devotion to Gluck. For a description, in the *Memoirs*, of Berlioz and Mendelssohn immersed in an aria from *Iphigénie en Tauride*, see chapter 7 below, fn. 16.

head, listening but not hearing. Even registral discrimination serves the poetic scenario, the surreptitious Gb less pronounced, less audible (even whispered) in its lower octave, distinct from the sweep of the descent in the upper voice: F, Eb, Db, C, Bb, A, to the dominant in preparation for the final strophe and the passage from an epic time past to a timeless present. But this Gb has yet another function, more deeply ingrained in the poem: it was a deeper Gb, the lower member of an augmented sixth, that moved the harmony to a structural dominant at "lauten Donnersturm" only an instant earlier.

If these few paragraphs seem obsessively attentive to the nuances of a single moment in the music, consider this remarkable account of Klopstock's meeting in Karlsruhe in 1774 with Gluck, then traveling with his wife and their adopted daughter (and niece) Nanette, who, though only fourteen years old at the time, possessed by all accounts a lovely voice.[6] Here, in Carl Friedrich Cramer's telling, is Klopstock's report of the encounter: "Gluck, at the keyboard, often interrupted her suddenly in the midst of a most delightful performance and, in the very presence of the court, rather harshly, with: 'Stop! That was wrong! Do it again!' And when someone in the company, even a connoisseur, thought they had noticed not the slightest error in intonation or in expression, and said to Gluck, 'But what was the error?,' such a question put him in a complete 'musical indignation': 'What? You don't hear that? Alas for you if you don't hear it. *There* it is!' And then sometimes in the course of a piece there was a fine detail that surely no one other than Gluck noticed, or could have noticed."[7] Klopstock then wished to hear her

6. Charles Burney, visiting Gluck in Vienna during his tour through Germany in 1772, wrote of her performance for him of several scenes from *Alceste*: "She has a powerful and well-toned voice, and sung with infinite taste, feeling, expression, and even execution." Burney goes on at some length about the quality of her study with the famous castrato Giuseppe Millico. See Charles Burney, *An Eighteenth-Century Musical Tour in Central Europe and the Netherlands*, ed. Percy A. Scholes (London: Oxford University Press, 1959), 90.

7. "Demohngeachtet, sagt Kl., unterbrach Gluck am Claviere sie nicht selten plözlich mitten im reizendsten Vortrage eines Stücks, und das in Gegenwart selbst des Hofs, ziemlich hart, durch ein: 'Halt! Das war falsch! Noch einmal!' — Und wenn denn etwa jemand in der Gesellschaft, auch Kenner, die nicht den geringsten Fehler in der Intonation oder dem Ausdruck zu bemerken glaubten, zu Gluck sagten: Aber worinn liegt denn der Fehler? So konnte so eine Frage ihn ganz in musicalischen Unwillen setzen: 'Was? Das hören Sie nicht? Wehe Ihnen, wenn sie das nicht hören! da liegts!' — Und denn wars manchmal eine Nuance von Feinheit, die im Laufe des Stückes gewiß keiner ausser Gluck

sing his *Die frühen Gräber* ("Willkommen, o silberner Mond"): "'This she cannot yet sing,' [Gluck] said, and then he himself sang it for Klopstock with his own voice, full of expression. The piece, for all that, seems very easy; but the affect! From this, one sees what he exacts [of a performance]."[8]

Those demands were made very clear in the famous dedicatory letter to the Duke Don Giovanni di Braganza, published in the preface to the published score of *Paride ed Elena* in 1770:

> Little or nothing, apart from a slight alteration in the mode of expression, would be needed to turn my aria in Orfeo, "Che farò senza Euridice," into a puppet-dance. One note more or less sustained, failure to increase the tempo or make the voice louder, one appoggiatura out of place, a trill, passage-work, or roulade can ruin a whole scene in such an opera, although it does nothing, or only improves, an opera of the common sort. The presence of the composer is therefore as necessary to the performance of this kind of music as, so to say, the presence of the sun to the works of nature. He is absolutely the soul and the life of it, and without him, all is confusion and darkness.[9]

This picture of the composer clinging to his work, dwelling as soul and life in this music that to Cramer seemed "very easy," had serious consequences for the survival of a project that seems to have been his most ambitious and prolonged engagement with the poetry of Klopstock. In a letter to the poet in May 1780, Gluck explains "why I have hesitated so long over *Hermannsschlacht*: I want to make this the last of my musical compositions . . . But al-

---

bemerkt hatte oder bemerken hatte können." Cramer, *Magazin der Musik*, vol. 1, no. 1, 563. For a slightly different, and not altogether accurate, translation, see Patricia Howard, *Gluck: An Eighteenth-Century Portrait in Letters and Documents* (Oxford: Oxford University Press, 1995), 131.

8. "Klopstock wünschte vergeblich seine Sommernacht (Willkommen, o silberner Mond [etc.]) von ihr zu hören. 'Das kann sie noch nicht singen'! sagte er, und sangs denn selber Klopstocken mit seiner eignen ausdrucksvollen Stimme vor. — Gleichwohl ist das Stück dem Anscheine nach sehr leicht; aber der Affect! Man sieht daraus, was er fodert." Cramer, *Magazin der Musik*, vol. 1, no. 1, 564. The correct title of "Willkommen, o silberner Mond" is *Die frühen Gräber*.

9. The original text, in Italian, is given in Ludwig Nohl, *Musiker-Briefe* (Leipzig: Duncker und Humblot, [1866]), 8–11. For translations, see *The Collected Correspondence and Papers of Christoph Willibald Gluck*, ed. Hedwig and E. H. Mueller von Asow, tr. Stewart Thomson (New York: St. Martin's Press, 1962), 27–29; and Patricia Howard, *An Eighteenth-Century Portrait*, 97.

though [it] will be my last work, I believe it will not be the least important of my compositions, because I assembled the principal material for it at a time before age had weakened my creative powers."[10] Indeed, in a letter of 1769 to the poet Johann Gleim, Klopstock reports to have heard from a third source that "Gluck . . . uniquely a poet among composers, has set some strophes from the bardic choruses [of *Hermannsschlacht*] with the full ring of truth. I have actually not yet seen his composition, but all those who have heard it are very taken with it."[11] Four years later, Klopstock had still heard nothing. "Father Denis," writes Gluck, "has told me that you desire to have those strophes I have composed from your Hermannsschlacht. I would long ago have done you this service, had I not been categorically assured that many would not find them to their taste, because they must be sung in a certain style which is not yet much in fashion." This, continues Gluck, is "music that calls for a passionate delivery . . . still completely unknown in your country." Proposing a visit to Hamburg in the coming year, Gluck promises "to sing you not only much from Hermannsschlacht, but also from your sublime odes, in order to show you to what extent I have aspired toward your greatness, or how far I have obscured it by my music."[12]

What kind of work was this *Hermannsschlacht*? "Ein Bardiet für die Schaubühne" — a "Bardiet" for the stage — Klopstock titled it, explaining in an addendum: "Barde, Bardiet, like Bardd, Barddas, in that more recent Celtic language . . . At all events, I've been able to find no truer, no more German word that names a kind of poetry whose content is of the time of the bards, and must be reflected in its imagery," to which he adds that "it is unlikely that the bards, who composed many more lyrical poems than other types, and who at the same time were singers, would have made their other poems for declamation alone."[13] This, however, is not how Gluck seems to

---

10. For the original, see *Briefe von und an Klopstock: Ein Beitrag zur Literaturgeschichte seiner Zeit*, ed. Johann Martin Lappenberg (Brunswick: Westermann, 1867), 294. The translation is taken from Howard, *An Eighteenth-Century Portrait*, 214–15.

11. I take this from Howard, *An Eighteenth-Century Portrait*, 100.

12. The letter is dated 14 August 1773. For the original, see *Briefe von und an Klopstock*, 252–53. The translation is taken from Howard, *An Eighteenth-Century Portrait*, 100–101.

13. "Barde[,] Bardiet, wie Bardd, Barddas, in derjenigen neuern celtischen Sprache . . . Wenigstens habe ich kein eigentlicheres und kein deutscheres Wort finden können, eine Art der Gedichte zu benennen, deren Inhalt aus den Zeiten der Barden seyn, und deren Bildung so scheinen muß." I take the text from *Klopstocks sämmtliche Werke*, vol. 8: *Der Tod Adams. Hermanns Schlacht* (Leipzig: Georg Joachim Göschen, 1823), 243.

have read these bardic choruses. Reichardt, visiting Gluck in Vienna in 1783, describes the composer at his keyboard, singing "with weak and raw voice and palsied tongue, accompanying himself with isolated chords."[14] "It is very difficult to give a clear representation of these performances," Reichardt concludes.

> They seemed almost entirely declamatory, only rarely melodic. It is surely an irretrievable loss that the artist didn't commit them to writing; one would surely have been able, with the greatest certainty, to recognize in them the true genius of the man, for he was bound by none of the conventional demands of the modern stage and singer, but rather followed quite freely his lofty genius, most intimately penetrated by the equal spirit of the great poet."[15]

This seems almost an echo of Burney's lavishly detailed description of his visit a decade earlier, writing of the composer as "not only a friend of poetry, but a poet himself; and if he had language sufficient, of any other kind than that of sound, in which to express his ideas, I am certain that he would be a great poet."[16]

We can only hypothesize — and with great difficulty — a process of mind that would have driven Gluck to withhold this bardic music, releasing it periodically at his own keyboard to those who would be sensitive to the deeply felt inflections of his performance. Was this a music fixed literally in his mind? Or do we imagine it to have been created *de novo* at each performance? If any of it had been committed to writing, surely the intrepid Reichardt would have insisted upon making copies. Was Gluck perform-

---

14. Howard, *An Eighteenth-Century Portrait*, 235. For the original, see "Bruchstücke aus Reichardts Autobiographie," *Allgemeine musikalische Zeitung* 15 (October 1813), col. 670.

15. "Es ist sehr schwer, von diesen Gesängen, nach jenem Vortrage, eine deutliche Vorstellung zu geben; sie schienen fast ganz declamatorisch, sehr selten nur melodisch zu seyn. Es ist gewiss ein unersetzlicher Verlust, dass der Künstler sie nicht aufzeichnete; man hatte daran das eigene Genie des grossen Mannes gewiss am sichersten erkennen können, da er sich dabey durchaus an kein conventionelles Bedürfnis der modernen Bühne und Sänger band; sondern ganz frey seinem hohen Genius folgte, innigst durchdrungen von dem gleichen Geiste des grossen Dichters." "Bruchstücke aus Reichardts Autobiographie," *Allg. mus. Ztg*, 15, col. 670. My translation.

16. Burney, *An Eighteenth-Century Musical Tour in Central Europe and the Netherlands*, 91.

ing from a copy of Klopstock's "Bardiet," or were its strophes committed to memory as well? Why, finally, did nothing of this work survive? Was it simply unimaginable to immobilize in written document this music whose bardic accents were so deeply ingrained in the voice of the composer? Or was it rather that the project never quite formulated itself into something adequately coherent, into a music that *could* be written down?

"A KLOPSTOCK WHO WORKED IN TONES"

I

That other grand figure in Neefe's pantheon was of course Carl Philipp Emanuel Bach. For all his proximity in Hamburg to the great poet, Bach composed only two lieder to texts by Klopstock.[17] The lesser of them is the ubiquitous *Vaterlandslied* ("Ich bin ein deutsches Mädchen"), set as well by Gluck (a setting, we learned, that Klopstock himself was said to have preferred to Bach's), and by Reichardt and Neefe, among many others.[18] But it is the unsettling setting of Klopstock's *Lyda* that has drawn the most attention, and justifiably so. (The song is given as ex. 5.3.) The incentive to compose it came from the editors of the *Musenalmanach*. "I don't have a single song of Bach's," wrote Boie to Voss, in a letter of 13 June 1774. "Couldn't you publish a composition of Klopstock's Lyda? Klopstock changed something in it, and so the piece could appear in our Almanach, where it really belongs."[19] Bach sent two songs to Voss, with a letter dated 5 August 1774, provoking this note from Voss to Ernestine Boie, sister of Heinrich Chris-

17. This is to leave out of discussion the remarkable *Klopstocks Morgengesang am Schöpfungsfeste* of 1783, a setting for chorus and soloists, with strings and flutes, of an ode that Klopstock seems to have written a year earlier, and with the intent that Bach compose music for it. One might even imagine a collaboration between poet and composer, "the result of their intellectual discussions on text and music," as is suggested by Bertil van Boer, the editor of the work in Carl Philipp Emanuel Bach, *Arias and Chamber Cantatas* (*The Complete Works*, series 6, vol. 4) (Los Altos, CA: Packard Humanities Institute, 2010), xii.

18. For one listing, see Max Friedlaender, *Das deutsche Lied im 18. Jahrhundert*, vol. 2: Dichtung (Stuttgart and Berlin: J. G. Cotta, 1902; repr. Hildesheim: Georg Olms, 1962), 127–28.

19. "Lieder für Bach hab ich kein einziges. Können Sie nicht eine Komposition von Klopstocks Lyda herausbringen? Klopstock änderte was daran, und so käme das Stück in unsern Alm.: worin es eigentlich gehört. Sie müssen selbst ein Lied singen, das Bach komponiere." Cited from Busch, *C. Ph. E. Bach und seine Lieder*, 124; see also *Carl Philipp Emanuel Bach: Briefe und Dokumente*, 407.

Ex. 5.3. Carl Philipp Emanuel Bach, *Lyda*, from *Poetische Blumenlese auf das Jahr 1775*, 111.

tian and later Voss's wife: "Last Monday I received a letter from Bach with music to Klopstock's Lyda and to my Schlummernden. They are both splendid. I now have two settings of Lyda, and I must print both. Reichardt's setting is also beautiful, and I would offend him were I to leave it out. But Bach's setting is incomparable, so deeply conceived, so touching. You must have someone play it for you."[20]

Klopstock's iambic trimeter, suggestive more of lied than of ode, appeals in its metric simplicity to the imperatives of a strophic setting even as the internal structure of the poem, in its gradual intensification, its enjambments, and in the run-on between strophes 3 and 4, conspires against it.[21] The placement of the strong verb at the incipit of line 13, setting off an exhortatory diction — "Beschwör' ich dich, Erscheinung" — only concentrates the problem.

Dein süßes Bild, o Lyda,	Thy sweet image, oh Lyda,
Schwebt stets vor meinem Blick;	moves ever before my gaze;
Allein ihn trüben Zähren,	but tears only darken it,
Daß du es selbst nicht bist.	that it is not you yourself.
5 Ich seh' es, wenn der Abend	I see it in the twilight

20. "Vorigen Montag bekam ich einen Brief von Bach, mit Melodien zu Klopstocks Lyda, und zu meiner Schlummernden. Sie sind beyde ganz vortreflich. Zu Lyda hab ich nun zwey Compositionen, die ich beyde drucken muß. Die von Reichardt ist auch schön, und ich würde ihn beleidigen, wenn ich sie wegließe. Aber die von Bach ist unvergleichlich, so tief gedacht, so rührend! Du mußt sie dir von jemand vorspielen laßen." Busch, *C. Ph. E. Bach und seine Lieder*, 125, where the date of the letter is given as 14 August; Bach, *Briefe und Dokumente*, 431, where the date is 15 August. In a letter of 21 July, the poet Hahn wrote Klopstock to report that Voss "thanked Reichardt for the excellent composition of Lyda," and wondered if this might not hinder Bach from composing it as he'd promised. See Friedrich Gottlieb Klopstock, *Werke und Briefe. Historisch-kritische Ausgabe: Briefe*, vol. 6, *1773–75*, part 2: Apparat/Kommentar, ed. Annette Lüchow, with Sabine Tauchert (Berlin and New York: de Gruyter, 2001), letter 166.

21. Evidently written in 1767, the poem was published for the first time in the *Hamburgische Neue Zeitung* in 1773, and then in the *Almanach der deutschen Musen auf 1774* (Leipzig: im Schwickertschen Verlage), where it is titled *An Lyda*; and the *Poetische Blumenlese auf das Jahr 1775* (in *Musenalmanach* 1774 [Göttingen: Bey J. C. Diederich, 1775]) as *Lyda*. In later editions, the poem is called *Edone*, and the text consequently altered: "Edone" in place of "o Lyda" in line 1 and "werd' Edone" in place of "werde Lyda" in line 16. In these early publications, the poem is always printed in two eight-line stanzas. See Friedrich Gottlieb Klopstock, *Oden*, ed. Franz Muncker and Jaro Pawel (Stuttgart: G. J. Göshen, 1889), vol. 1, 212.

Mir dämmert, wenn der Mond	of evening[;] when the moon
Mir glänzt, seh ichs, und weine,	shines on me, I see it and weep,
Daß du es selbst nicht bist.	that it is not you yourself.

9	Bei jenes Tales Blumen,	At every flower of the valley
	Die ich ihr lesen will,	that I would gather for her,
	Bei jenen Myrtenzweigen,	at every myrtle branch
	Die ich ihr flechten will,	that I would weave for her,
13	Beschwör ich dich, Erscheinung,	I implore you, apparition,
	Auf, und verwandle dich!	Up, and transfigure yourself!
	Verwandle dich, Erscheinung,	Transfigure yourself, apparition,
	Und werde Lyda selbst!	and become Lyda herself!

In addition to the engraved music published by Voss, we have Bach's autograph (shown as fig. 5.1), which conveys the text precisely as Voss printed it — with a single exception. With publication imminent, Bach wrote to Voss:

> If it's not too late, dear Herr Voss, you may wish to alter the following in my Lyda:

The *f*[orte] and the wedges must go. The expression "o Lyda" is better if it is softer.[22]

It was not too late. Voss made the change. To those who've more recently studied Bach's illuminating text, the logic of the alteration is apparently beyond dispute. "What a difference between the first and the second versions!" writes Otto Vrieslander, toward the conclusion of a passionate explication of the revision. "One sees how, in the exuberance of the conception, Bach sought to shape an appeal of great pathos and vehemence (*forte* with accent

---

22. "Wenn es noch nicht zu spät ist, liebster Herr Voß, so belieben Sie folgendes in meiner Lyda zu ändern, nehml. [ex.] statt [ex.]. Das F[orte] und die Striche müßen weg. Der Ausdruck, o Lyda, ist beßer, wenn er sanfter ist." Often reproduced, the letter can be found in facsimile in Otto Vrieslander, *Carl Philipp Emanuel Bach* (Munich: R. Piper & Co., 1923), between pp. 112 and 113; and Carl Philipp Emanuel Bach, *Miscellaneous Songs*, ed. Christoph Wolff (CW VI/3) (Los Altos, CA: Packard Humanities Institute, 2014), 244 (commentary) and plate 5. See also *The Letters of C. P. E. Bach*, tr. and ed. Stephen L. Clark (Oxford: Clarendon Press, 1997), 62–63; my translation differs slightly.

Figure 5.1. Carl Philipp Emanuel Bach. Autograph score of *Lyda*. Munich: Bayerische Staatsbibliothek, Mus. Ms. 2774, fol. 6. By kind permission.

wedges!!) but that upon closer examination, became aware of the discrepancy between a lyrical tone and a dramatic outcry, so that this stylistically fatal misalliance had to be fixed in an alteration of the musical substance."[23] Revisions, however, have a life of their own, often obscuring the telling trace of an original conception. We shall want to return to this one.[24]

More unsettling is the strophic problem. Those who have written about Bach's setting, quick to admire the music as an expression of the first (eight-line) strophe, have found its application to the second strophe something of an embarrassment. Vrieslander goes so far as to propose that the second strophe be omitted altogether. Even the formidable Gudrun Busch, writing of such discrepancies within Bach's strophic settings, holds this one up as "perhaps the most extreme example," in effect endorsing Vrieslander's proposal.[25] William Youngren, who "cannot recall another example of a song in which Bach has so completely given up on solving the strophic problem," suggests that "it is as though [Bach] had read only the first stanza of Klopstock's poem."[26]

I think it is safe to assume that Bach would have devoured the complete poem, as would any reader with an ounce of wit, and will have recognized the challenge in finding a music to convey the passionate outburst — *parenthyrsus*, Herder might have called it — of its final lines. Closer to the point, it seems to me that it is precisely here, in coming to grips with the charged language of these final lines, that Bach's music reaches for its ex-

23. Vrieslander actually wrote two explications. The earlier, from which I translate, comes in the important Carl Philipp Emanuel Bach, *Lieder und Gesänge*, ed. with an Introduction by Otto Vrieslander (Munich: Drei Masken Verlag, 1922), xix–xx; the passage is reworded in Otto Vrieslander, *Carl Philipp Emanuel Bach*, 123. Vrieslander's explanation is merely paraphrased (without credit) in Hans-Günter Ottenberg, *Carl Philipp Emanuel Bach*, 215; and in the English translation, tr. Philip J. Whitmore, 155–56. See also *Bach, Briefe und Dokumente*, 441–42, which includes the passage from Vrieslander (1923) and other commentary. The letter to Voss is given as well in Busch, 126; in William H. Youngren, *C. P. E. Bach and the Rebirth of the Strophic Song* (Lanham, MD, and Oxford: Scarecrow Press, 2003), 323; and in *The Letters of C. P. E. Bach*, 62–63, together with reference to other publications of the letter.

24. Bach actually made one more emendation, this an autograph alteration of measures 4–5 to a copy, prepared from the Voss print, by Michel for the so-called Polyhymnia Portfolio (about which see below, fn. 46). The alteration is given in Bach, *Miscellaneous Songs*, 125.

25. "... das vielleicht extremste Beispiel," Busch, *C. Ph. E. Bach und seine Lieder*, 356.

26. Youngren, *C. P. E. Bach and the Rebirth of the Strophic Song*, 324.

treme resources. The new rhythm at measure 13, its affirmatory unfolding in arpeggio, perfectly articulates the imperative "Beschwör ich dich" even as it sits uncomfortably beneath "Ich seh es wenn." This misalignment in the first strophe is only aggravated in the diction of the following lines, and pointedly so at the music that would capture the moment of transfiguration. "Verwandle dich!" pleads Klopstock's overwrought lover, and then a second time: "Verwandle dich, Erscheinung." Here is the gist of the poem, the poet willing into palpable being the distant, imaginary Lyda, as though the apparition could itself enact its own transformation. And here Bach's music seizes the rhetorical intensification of the poetic moment, choreographing its script: the singer, at his keyboard, driving the music to its extremity, to the high G sung against the deep octave C♯s, playing out a harmonic transformation that draws the music away from C major (and its dominant) to this climactic moment that breaks off in mid-sentence. It does not take much argument to hear in these powerful keyboard strokes (marked with articulative "Striche"), moving outward in wedge-like contrary motion, the perfect elocution of the poet's command — and to note, conversely, how incongruously they serve its analogue at line 7 — "mir glänzt, seh ichs" — and the enjambments that complicate the syntax of lines 5–8.

Out of the silence that follows, these weeping chromatics inspired by tears shed in the first strophe take on new meaning in the abject evocation of the shadowy *Erscheinung*, seen darkly through this lens of tears. The resonance, even in their internal morphemes, of "weine" and "Erscheinung," signifiers of each other and analogues in the strophic scheme, fuses in the crucible of Bach's languid phrase. And it is precisely here that time is suspended in the breach between the exhortation "verwandle dich" and the muted, resigned invocation of "Erscheinung." Here once more is the Klopstockian moment, the absent beloved conjured. And it is here that the impassioned vocative "o Lyda!" imprinted at the very beginning of the poem continues to sound, each syllable incisively articulate, precisely as Bach *originally* conceived it. It is as though the music enacts the transformative deed itself: "o Lyda! . . . Verwandle dich." Even those silences — the quarter rest after "Lyda"; the eighth rest after "dich" — seem to resonate within one another, tellingly for the singer at his keyboard.

Still, there can be no getting round the uncomfortable fit of the opening phrases of the song when they are sung to the second strophe. In the most blatant instance, there seems no evident modification that would adapt "Bei jenes Tales Blumen" comfortably to the music of the first phrase, even with Bach's late softening of the articulation at measure 3. At the end of the day, we are left with the enigma of a music that refuses the concessions demanded of a strophic setting, Bach apparently unwilling to engage in the fine-tuning of a single strophe of music to the two octaves of the poem. The high-minded views expressed in Neefe's *Vorbericht* have little purchase here.

Some half-dozen years later, in defense of his own settings of a number of Klopstock's odes, Johann Friedrich Reichardt sized up the problem with rhetorical flourish:

> The most difficult thing is this: To find in a single melody a true declamation for all strophes of the complete ode. It must be a **single** melody in odes which have a unity of feeling, if the impression of that single melody is to be deeply penetrating. And that this melody shall now serve for several strophes of such differing caesuras and periods: here one often exhausts every harmonic, melodic and rhythmic artifice in order to establish and yet conceal the double meaning in this cadence, that phrase, that rhythm, at the very least for the comprehensible performance of manifold and diverse meaning.[27]

Wise words, these are. But the music defended in them suffers from a neutered expression, a poverty of idea, in obedience to strict strophic rule. Reichardt's setting of *Der Jüngling*, cold and stiff, compares unfavorably with Gluck's second version. Carl Friedrich Cramer even thought Gluck's earlier version, in spite of its naive simplicity, "not nearly so monotonous as Reichardt's setting."[28] And the setting of *Bardale*, its single strophe unvaried through all eighteen verses, neglecting even those enjambments that join

27. "Das Schwereste: In einer Melodie für alle Strophen die ganze Ode wahr zu deklamiren. **Eine** Melodie muß es seyn bey Oden, die Einheit der Empfindung haben, wenn der Eindruck der Eine treffende tiefeindringende seyn soll. Daß diese nun für mehrere Strophen von so sehr verschiedenen Abschnitten und Einschnitten passen soll — da erschöpft man oft alle harmonische melodische und rythmische Kunstgriffe, um in dieser Kadenz, in jenem Einschnitte, in jenem Rythmus doppelte Bedeutung, wenigstens für den verständigen Vortrag mannichfaltige Bedeutung, hineinzulegen und zu verbergen." In "Ueber Klopstocks komponirte Oden," 62.

28. This, in a review of Reichardt's *Musikalisches Kunstmagazin*, in Carl Friedrich Cramer, *Magazin der Musik*, vol. 1, 38–39. For Cramer, Reichardt's settings "miss entirely the distinctive characteristics of the Klopstockian meter" [das Unterscheidende der klopstockischen Sylbenmaaße]: the prosody (in Der Jüngling, for one) is "violently damaged" [gewaltsam verletzt].

strophes 8/9, 10/11, and 16/17, manifests none of the response to the sense of the poem evident in either of Neefe's settings. Bach's *Lyda*, straining against whatever rules of prosody might seem appropriate to a reading of Klopstock's poem, plays rather to the tensions within poem and music between the expressive and the measured, the deep saturation of meaning in language and harmony in conflict with the linear measure of prosody. If the equilibrium sought in Reichardt's homily is refused, something of value is gained. "Incomparable," Voss thought Bach's song, "so deeply conceived, so touching." Precisely.

II

Not more than a year after the composition of *Lyda*, Bach was induced to set another poem in search of the absent lover, contending once more with the permeable membrane between lied and ode. Untitled, the song is known by its opening line: "Auf den Flügeln des Morgenrots." (It is given as ex. 5.4.) Here is the first of its six strophes:

Auf den Flügeln des Morgenrots	On the wings of dawn
über weinende Fluren hin	over weeping meadows
schwebt der Seufzer meines Herzens	the sigh of my heart
meiner Betty entgegen.[29]	drifts toward my Betty.

The Betty who inspired these lines was the Frau von Alvensleben to whom Neefe was to inscribe the dedicatory preface to his *Oden von Klopstock* (see above, chapter 4). But it was Carl Friedrich Cramer from whose heart issued this winged sigh to the distant beloved (a familiar trope to which we shall return in the next chapter) and who must then have invited Bach to compose it, presumably as an offering in homage to this unhappily married woman with whom Cramer was then carrying on a passionate, and apparently quite indiscreet, affair.[30]

Much of the business of the poem is shrouded in a veil of semiconsciousness. In a dream, the beloved is heard to utter the words he longs to

29. Bach's setting is to be found in the *Miscellaneous Songs*, ed. Christoph Wolff (CW, VI/3), 160, together with the poem complete in its six stanzas.

30. For more on this, see Rüdiger Schütt, "Von Kiel nach Paris: Carl Friedrich Cramer in den Jahren 1775 bis 1805," in *Ein Mann von Feuer und Talenten: Leben und Werk von Carl Friedrich Cramer*, ed. Rüdiger Schütt (Göttingen: Wallstein, 2005), esp. 16–17; and Ludwig Krähe, *Carl Friedrich Cramer bis zu seiner Amtsenthebung* (Berlin: Mayer & Müller, 1907), 96–102, 128–34.

hear: "Mein Liebling, ich liebe dich!" she sings, and then sinks into his arms "an den schwellenden Busen." The fantasy continues to its salacious end:

Und ich wusste nicht, wie mir war!	And I was unaware how I was!
Wonneschauer durchbebten mich;	A shudder of rapture coursed through me.
Tag und Licht ward um mich Dämmerung,	Day and light dimmed about me.
Frühling glänzt auf der Heide.	Spring gleamed on the meadow.

The dream dissolves, and the poet calls out in despair: "Betty, Betty, wo bist du?" The language has a familiar ring. "Auf den Flügeln der Ruh, in Morgenlüften" is the image that opens the third strophe of Klopstock's *An Cidli* ("Zeit, Verkündigerin"). The willing into focus of the astigmatic image of the absent lover is of course the conceit in Klopstock's *Lyda*, just as Cramer's "Betty, wo bist du?" echoes Klopstock's "Verwandle dich . . . und werde Lyda selbst!"

These linguistic traces, slight as they are, might yet be read as symptoms of a more extensive veneration of Klopstock — an obsession, even — that produced work of significance. Cramer's ambitious *Klopstock. Er; und über ihn*, its five volumes published between 1780 and 1792, in many printings, is a remarkable chronological study, textual and critical, drawing unabashedly upon what the author claims to have been intimate conversations with his magisterial subject. An earlier work — *Klopstock (In Fragmenten aus Briefen von Tellow an Elisa)*[31] — fuses fiction and criticism, and includes this intimate account of a performance of Neefe's setting of *Selmar und Selma*:

> We were all gathered together, and Windeme and Gerstenberg, at my clavichord, sang Neefe's intimate music. Fritz Stollberg paced around the room with great steps, the others stood at the keyboard. He [Klopstock] sat in the corner on the little yellow armchair, and I next to him. He listened.[32]

The Neefe setting was among the works published in his *Oden von Klopstock* in 1776. In August of that year, Klopstock wrote from Hamburg: "The day before our departure for Kiel, Carl Cramer came to us. He, Gerstenberg and

31. Hamburg: Schniebes, 1777; a second volume, *Fortsetzung*, followed from Schniebes in 1778.

32. *Klopstock (In Fragmenten)*, vol. 1, 130. "Wir alle waren versammelt, Windeme und Gerstenberg sangen an meinem Claviere nach Neefens inniger Melodie. Fritz Stollberg ging mit großen Schritten im Zimmer umher, die andern standen ums Clavier, er saß im Winkel des Saals in dem kleinen gelben Lehnstuhl, ich by ihm. Er hörte zu."

Noodt traveled with us to Eutin to Fritz Stolberg," bringing together again the cast of characters in Cramer's account.[33] "Windeme" was Klopstock's poetic name for Johanna Elizabeth von Winthem, the niece of Meta Moller, Klopstock's first wife.[34] The sensitivity of her singing inspired Cramer to invoke her name in describing the similar effect made upon him by the singing of Gluck's niece Nanette, who, he wrote, achieves "the perfectly sublime simplicity and genuine expression (missing in most opera singers) of a *Windeme*, and which she can have learned only through the instruction of her uncle."[35]

Cramer was here reporting on the earlier of two meetings between Gluck and Klopstock in Karlsruhe, Gluck and family en route to Paris from Vienna in the autumn of 1774. On the return trip in March of 1775, Klopstock again met Gluck in Karlsruhe, accompanying him then as far as Rastatt.[36] In a delightfully witty, mock-legal memorandum to the venerable poet, and dated "Rastatt am 17. März 1775," the sixteen-year-old Nanette wrote "under each of these arias — the aria in which Orpheus calls after Eurydice, and the aria in which Alceste calls after her children — I shall put a few words, in which shall be contained, so far as words can contain such things, the nature, method, constituents, and essence, and as it were the nuances of my magical musical performance, so that the aforesaid Klopstock can, on his part, send these my words, together with the arias, to his niece in Hamburg...."[37] That the *empfindsame* voices of these young women might have touched in this seductive scenario drawn up in Nanette's imagination must in turn excite ours. Nieces

33. Klopstock, *Ausgewählte Werke*, 1170; Johann Martin Lappenberg, *Briefe von und an Klopstock: Ein Beitrag zur Literaturgeschichte seiner Zeit* (Braunschweig: Westermann, 1867; repr. Bern: Herbert Lang, 1970), 276.

34. For more on her, see, for one, Klopstock, *Werke und Briefe. Historisch-kritische Ausgabe: Briefe*, vol. 6, 1773–75, part 2, 295 and 705; *Briefe*, vol. 7, 1776–82, part 2, Apparat/Kommentar, ed. Helmut Riege (Berlin and New York: de Gruyter, 1982), 328–29.

35. ". . . die ganze hohe Einfalt und Wahrheit des Ausdrucks einer **Windeme**, die den meisten Opernsängerinnen fehlt, und die nur der Unterricht ihres Oheims ihr geben konnte." Carl Friedrich Cramer, *Magazin der Musik*, vol. 1, no. 1, 563.

36. In a letter to Voss dated "Carlsruhe den 24ten März — 75," Klopstock writes: "Gluk u seine Niece haben uns auf ihrer Rükreise nach Wien 4 Tage hintereinander hohe Wollüste der Musik geniessen lassen" [On their return trip to Vienna, Gluk and his niece have afforded us 4 days of the most sublime pleasure of music]. Klopstock, *Werke und Briefe*, vol. 6, part 2, 200–201.

37. The original text can be found in Ludwig Nohl, *Musiker-Briefe* (Leipzig: Duncker und Humblot, [1867]), 29–30; the translation is drawn from Howard, *An Eighteenth-Century Portrait*, 134–35.

of Klopstock and Gluck, each was drawn into a more intimate relationship with their iconic uncles: Nanette as Gluck's adopted daughter, Winthem eventually as Klopstock's wife, as if to legitimize that other intimacy bodied forth in a music of poetic utterance that so deeply moved all who heard them sing.[38] This luminous moment was lamentably brief. Nanette succumbed to smallpox only thirteen months later, at age seventeen. "How desolate and lonely is everything about me now," Gluck wrote to Klopstock. "She was my only hope, my comfort, and the inspiration of my work."[39]

The poetic evidence that Windeme and Bach ever made music together is inscribed in the opening lines of Klopstock's *Klage*:[40]

Klaget alle mit mir, Vertraute	Lament with me, all you
Der Göttin Polyhymnia!	friends of the goddess Polyhymnia!
Windeme sang, es ertönten	Windeme sang, accompanied by the
Bachs und Lolli's Saiten zu dem Gesange:	chords of Bach and Lolli:
Und ich war fern, und hört es nicht ...	Yet I was far off, and heard it not.

This Bach can only have been Carl Philipp Emanuel. Winthem sang in the famous performance of Handel's *Messiah* in Hamburg under Bach's direction on 31 December 1775, its English text replaced with Klopstock's German.[41] Antonio Lolli, the virtuoso violinist employed at Stuttgart since 1758, is known to have toured through Hamburg in January of 1773, a vivid account of his performance captured by Matthias Claudius in the pages of his

---

38. Klopstock, who moved permanently from Denmark to Hamburg in late 1770, gives his address as "bey Hr. Von Winthem" in a letter to Ebert dated 11 June 1771 (see Klopstock, *Werke und Briefe*, vol. 5, part 1, Nr. 188) and seems to have moved in with the family the following year (*Briefe*, vol. 5, part 2, 295). Whatever the nature of his relationship to his niece in the intervening years, the matter was consummated finally in 1791, when the two were married, a few years after the death of Johanna's husband. For an account of this relationship and its perception, see Franz Muncker, *Friedrich Gottlieb Klopstock: Geschichte seines Lebens und seiner Schriften* (Stuttgart: Göschen, "Ausgabe in einem Bande," 1893), 429–30.

39. Howard, *An Eighteenth-Century Portrait*, 160.

40. The poem was first published in the *Poetische Blumenlese für das Jahr 1776*, in *Musenalmanach für das Jahr 1776* von der Verfassern der bish. Götting. Musenalm. herausgegeben von J. H. Voß (Lauenburg gedruckt bey Berenberg), 188.

41. Bach, *Briefe und Dokumente*, 554–55. The event was discussed in Voss's letter of 5 January 1776 to Ernestine Boie.

Wandsbecker Bothe.[42] Bach owned an undated pastel portrait of Lolli by the Hamburg artist Hardrich.[43] But there is otherwise no evidence that the two performed together.

Bach's setting of "Auf den Flügeln des Morgenrots," never published, was very likely meant to appear in a miscellaneous collection of his music that Cramer had been planning to publish, as he reports in a letter of 30 October 1775 to Gerstenberg: "Bach has granted me permission to collect and publish his scattered pieces and for this he will give me some pieces that are still unpublished. I've asked this of him for I want to give this pleasure to my Betty, to whom I intend to dedicate a poem of rather long breath. . . ."[44] The poem "of rather long breath" [etwas longue haleine] may well have been the ten strophes of *An Betty* ("Sie ist, sie ist herabgesunken") whose complete text is printed alongside a setting by Neefe in his *Lieder mit Klaviermelodien* (Glogau: Christian Friedrich Günthen, 1776), attributed to "Cramer." And it is in this volume that we find as well Neefe's impressive setting of "Auf den Flügeln des Morgenrots," under the title *Ein Traum.*[45] That these poems of Cramer's have survived at all owes in good measure to their publication in Neefe's collection, where they are printed complete in all their strophes.

This miscellany of Bach's music that Cramer was intent upon publishing in 1775 evolved over the years into a much larger project, the so-called Poly-

42. *Wandsbecker Bothe.* Anno 1773, Nr. 8, "13ten Januar." The performance is described in an account dated 11 January, in which it is announced that Lolli has agreed to give another concert on the 13th. Might Klopstock have heard him? If Emanuel Bach participated in some way, no evidence of it is recorded in any of the Bach *Dokumente.* The date of Lolli's visit contradicts Albert Mell in the article on Lolli in the *New Grove Dictionary of Music & Musicians* (London and New York: Macmillan, 1980), vol. 11, 137, and reprinted in the second ed. (UK: Macmillan; US: Grove's Dictionaries, 2001), vol. 15, 82, where we read that Lolli "toured northern Germany with concerts at Hamburg, Lübeck and Stettin . . . at the end of 1773." Mell's article was revised by Norbert Dubowy for the "zweite, neubearbeitete Ausgabe" of *Musik in Geschichte und Gegenwart,* ed. Ludwig Finscher, Personenteil 11 (Bärenreiter, 2004), cols. 423–27, but the date of the Hamburg visit is retained.

43. See *Carl Philipp Emanuel Bach. Portrait Collection I: Catalogue,* ed. Annette Richards (CW VIII/4.1) (Los Altos, CA: Packard Humanities Institute, 2012), 121, and 48 for something on Hardrich.

44. For the German text, see *Bach, Briefe und Dokumente,* 523–24, which takes its text from Busch, *Lieder,* 198. For another translation, see Bach, *Polyhymnia Portfolio,* xi.

45. The setting was published by Friedlaender, *Das deutsche Lied im 18. Jahrhundert,* vol. 1, part 2: 144, though with the text of only the first strophe.

hymnia Portfolio that remained essentially unrealized until the publication, in facsimile, of its reconstruction in 2014.[46] Cramer's waning interest in the project led Bach, only months before his death in 1788, to pursue the publication of a volume titled *Neue Lieder-Melodien* (Lübeck: Donatius, 1789), which was to include only those songs previously unpublished.[47] Tellingly, "Auf den Flügeln des Morgenrots" was excluded. In the copious repertory of Bach's lieder, it is one of only nine that remained in manuscript and was never published. It has survived not, alas, in Bach's autograph, but in a copy prepared by Johann Heinrich Michel, Bach's favored Hamburg copyist, in a manuscript of fifty-two pages that would have constituted a chunk of the greater Polyhymnia Portfolio.[48]

Ignorant of the circumstances under which Bach agreed to compose something to these intimate lines, we are left only with eight bars of a music that seems uncomfortable in its fit with Cramer's verse, playing willfully with its diction, indifferent to its prosody. (The song is shown as ex. 5.4.) The syllables of its opening phrase do not roll off the tongue. Difficult to sing, the constricted glottal stops at "[Flü−] geln des" conspire against the expanse sketched in these cosmic wings that carry the dawn. But then the music gathers itself beneath the "weeping meadows" of its second line, the bass finding an octave C♮ while the voice arches its expressive sixth up to E. Through the characteristic convolutions of poetic syntax, a subject finally emerges: it is this *Seufzer*, a cry from the heart that must in turn find its mark. And it is here that Bach's music finds *its* mark. At "meiner Betty" — at the utterance of the name — the bass reaches down to a solitary B♯, a diminished ninth below that earlier C♮, its enharmonic inverse. In its isolation deep in the register of Bach's clavichord (and the lower extremity in many contemporary instruments), in the timbral buzz of that low string, in its striking dissonance against the B♮ in the voice, this B♯ astonishes at the

---

46. Bach, *Polyhymnia Portfolio*, its genesis and reconstruction explained in the introductory material, pp. xi–xvii.

47. As was reported by Bach to Breitkopf in a letter of 6 August 1788. See *The Letters of C. P. E. Bach*, 284; *Bach, Briefe und Dokumente*, 1281–82; and *Polyhymnia Portfolio*, xiii.

48. The Michel copy is shown in *Polyhymnia Portfolio*, 82, where it is untitled, its poet unidentified, and its other strophes not given. Michel prepared another copy that was given by Bach's widow in 1791 to J. J. H. Westphal (1756–1825), whose massive collection of manuscripts and prints are today at the Royal Conservatory of Music in Brussels. See Ulrich Leisinger and Peter Wollny, *Die Bach Quellen der Bibliotheken in Brüssel. Katalog* (Hildesheim, Zürich, New York: Georg Olms, 1997), 54 (fn. 95), 266.

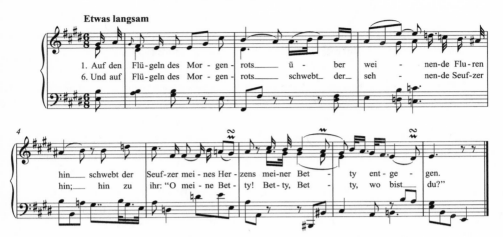

Ex. 5.4. Carl Philipp Emanuel Bach, *"Auf den Flügeln des Morgenrots."*

incision with which it marks the moment of revelation, the privacy of this intimate name made public, marking as well the moment at which the music reveals itself in relation to the poem.

But what, precisely, is revealed? Is it the twinge of the poet's longing made palpable? Or is there some subtle interplay here, Bach insinuating himself— or his surrogate instrument—into the poet's scenario, disturbing ever so slightly the innocent surface of the poem, hinting at the imbroglio implicit between and beneath its lines? The music is of course powerless to confirm anything of the sort. And yet that B♯ will be felt, acutely by singer and player, as an irritant, shrewdly placed as if to probe the source of such questioning. We are left only to wonder how Cramer would have heard the song, and whether his Betty ever did hear it.

III

"With a total of more than 250 individual pieces, Carl Philipp Emanuel Bach ranks among the most prolific composers of lieder in eighteenth-century Germany." So it reads in the Preface to the Lieder volumes in the *Complete Works*; in the pages of its three volumes dedicated to the songs, we are able finally to gain some perspective in this vast expanse that occupied Bach for some forty-seven years.[49] To reduce all this to a focus on these few songs,

49. This only sets in bolder relief the extraordinary achievement of Gudrun Busch, who was able to make her way through this repertory—by her count, comprising some

as though oblivious of the rich contexts from which they are drawn, may seem an extravagant abuse of an author's privilege. Yet, the fixing of these intense, singular moments captures something of the complex process in which a poem that probes the interiors of language draws forth a music engaged in a probe of its own, poem and music in search of one another. Busch puts it well, identifying a turn in the development of the secular song that "takes shape from that moment in 1773 when Bach is brought into association with the poets of the *Hainbund*: subjective experience, simple form and folk-like diction in their work guide Bach's song to a true apex in two distinct ways: on the one hand, as simple folk-like, often accented declamatory song with an emphatic simplification of all means; on the other, as an exaggeration of sensibility, as in 'Lyda,'" from which she concludes that the years 1773–77 "may be regarded as a peak in Bach's song production."[50]

Lyda is a remarkable song, capturing within its few phrases the vivid expression of a profound musical mind coming to terms — its own terms — with this poignant and subtle ode by a poet whose name was often coupled with Bach's. As early as 1774, Reichardt heard the uncommon difficulty of Bach's music as comparable to reading Klopstock: "Bach wishes to please everyone as little as does Klopstock," he writes, and continues: "Do you not then realize that an original idea often demands an expression that is unusual to us? And what indeed is the difficult other than something unusual, that which does not appear to us every day?"[51] In a provocative essay of 1800,

---

291 numbers — when virtually none of it was readily available, and during those years immediately after the war when the impediments to access of library archives were extreme. Her doctoral dissertation of 1956 (reprinted by Bosse in 1957) stands even now as an indispensable resource.

50. "Um so erfreulicher gestaltet sich die Entwicklung des weltlichen Liedes von dem Augenblick an, der Bach 1773 die Verbindung mit den Dichtern des Hainbundes bringt: Erlebnisgehalt, einfach Form und volkstümliche Diktion ihrer Werke führen Bachs Lied zu einem wirklichen Höhepunkt in zwei Ausprägungen: einmal als schlicht volkstümliches, oft akzentuierend deklamiertes Lied bei betonter Vereinfachung aller Mittel . . . ; zum andern als empfindsame Übersteigerung wie in der 'Lyda.' . . . Wir dürfen die Jahre 1773–1777 als Höhepunkt in Bachs Liedschaffen betrachten." Busch, *C. Ph. E. Bach und seine Lieder*, 383.

51. "Bach will eben so wenig Allen gefallen, als es Klopstock. Sehen sie denn das nicht ein, daß ein Originalgedanke oft auch einen solchen Ausdruck erfordert, der uns ungewöhnlich ist? Und was ist das Schwere wohl anders, als etwas Ungewöhnliches, was uns nicht täglich vorkommt?" Reichardt, *Briefe eines aufmerksamen Reisenden die Musik betreffend*, vol. 1, 113, 120. The passage is cited in Ernst Fritz Schmid, *Carl Philipp Emanuel Bach*

Johann Karl Friedrich Triest depicted Bach as "ein Klopstock, der Töne statt Worte gebrachte" — a Klopstock who worked in tones instead of words.[52] And it was Klopstock himself who, in his inscription written in 1791 for a monument to Bach designed by the architect Johann August Arens, wrote of this "profound harmonist" who "united novelty with beauty; was great in music accompanied by words, greater in bold, wordless music."[53]

Favoring the boldness in Bach's "wordless" music, Klopstock's distinction captures something of the inner tension that seems to play itself out in the setting of *Lyda*, a struggle to reconcile the prosody of Klopstock's complex syntax, as it might be conveyed in a compliant diction, with the urge that one senses often in Bach's keyboard music toward "Originalgedanke" (in Reichardt's word), toward an expression, at and in the keyboard, of a music that would, in Forkel's conceit, find the altitude of Klopstock's "high flights of imagination." Retrieving once more Forkel's simile of ode and sonata, we might imagine that embedded within the syntactical dissonances of the Klopstock ode is a sonata waiting to be sprung; that within the striking turns of phrase of the Bach sonata, its syntactical dissonances, its obscurities, its speech-like inflections, are the symptoms of poetic utterance. Ode and sonata, word and tone, Klopstock and Bach: to the theorist, these are familiar binaries, each pair setting loose, equation-like, its complex array of differences, oppositions, commonalities. But for the musician and the poet alive in their work, it is the immediacy of process that matters: the touching of minds and sensibilities across the thresholds of poetry and music, for this brief incandescent moment.

---

und seine Kammermusik (Kassel: Bärenreiter, 1931), 84. Extended to the music of Beethoven, the idea of the difficult as a condition to be sought is the topic of an essay by Klaus Kropfinger, " 'Denn was schwer ist, ist auch schön, gut, gross,' " *Bonner Beethoven-Studien* 3 (2003): 81–100.

52. J. K. F. Triest, "Bemerkungen über die Ausbildung der Tonkunst in Deutschland im achtzehnten Jahrhundert," *Allgemeine musikalische Zeitung*, vol. 3 (1800–1801), col. 300 ff. Cited in Ottenberg, *Carl Philipp Emanuel Bach*, 270; and *Carl Philipp Emanuel Bach*, tr. Whitmore, 200, where the translation differs from mine.

53. The full inscription, often reproduced, can be found together with a translation in Annette Richards, "An Enduring Monument: C. P. E. Bach and the Musical Sublime," in *C. P. E. Bach Studies*, ed. Annette Richards (Cambridge: Cambridge University Press, 2006), 149: "Karl Philipp Emanuel Bach, der tiefsinnige Harmonist, vereinte die Neuheit mit der Schönheit; war groß in der vom Worte geleiteten Musik, größer in der kühnen, wortlosen."

6

BEETHOVEN
In Search of Klopstock

"But I don't much like to write songs," he is alleged to have said. Put into Beethoven's mouth by the ever-inventive Friedrich Rochlitz, these words served Hans Boettcher as the opening salvo of his pioneering *Beethoven als Liederkomponist* (1928) not because he believed that Beethoven had actually spoken them but because they had been taken to signify the inferior place of the Beethoven lied in the culture of both the performance of Beethoven's music and the literature about him in the 101 years since his death.[1]

If we've moved well beyond the need for a revisionist assessment of Beethoven's lieder, it is yet good to remind ourselves of the earnestness with which Beethoven engaged the challenge that poetry always puts before its reader. That this was recognized by his contemporaries is affectingly captured on a page in a conversation book of January 1824: "If only you knew how often I sing your lieder," wrote the visitor, the distinguished singer Caroline Unger, and then in answer to what must have been Beethoven's mischievous reply: "That's difficult to decide, for I love them all."[2] To put the matter in rough quantitative terms, the 102 items in Helga Lühning's fastidious edition of the lieder for the Beethoven-Haus *Werke* offers a fresh perspective on the extent of the enterprise.[3] This is to leave out of the conversation the 179 settings, mainly for piano trio, of those "folk" songs, mainly from the

1. "Ich schreibe nur nicht gern Lieder." Hans Boettcher, *Beethoven als Liederkomponist* (Augsburg: Dr. Benno Filser Verlag, 1928), 1.

2. *Ludwig van Beethovens Konversationshefte*, vol. 5, ed. Karl-Heinz Köhler and Grita Herre, with the assistance of Peter Pötschner (Leipzig: VEB Deutscher Verlag für Musik, 1970), 79. And in August 1823, Carl Czerny was moved to write "I know nothing more beautiful for song than your cycle *An die ferne Geliebte*." *Konversationshefte*, vol. 4 (1968), 58. On Unger, see Theodor Frimmel, *Beethoven Handbuch*, vol. 2 (Leipzig: Breitkopf & Härtel, 1926), 345.

3. Beethoven, *Werke: Gesamtausgabe*, Abteilung 12, vol. 1: *Lieder und Gesänge mit Klavierbegleitung*, ed. Helga Lühning (Munich: G. Henle Verlag, 1990).

British Isles, that George Thomson sent Beethoven between 1809 and 1820, a richly diverse repertory that has only recently begun to move out of the shadows and into the canon.[4] Quite distinct from these repertories of finished works are those occasional engagements with poems (and poets) obscured among the pages of Beethoven's sketches and drafts.

Taking the measure of Beethoven's achievement here means setting its considerable repertory in a larger context. There is the evolution of the genre itself, its radical reformulation from Johann Abraham Peter Schulz's *Lieder im Volkston* of 1782, which will stand here for the hundreds of publications inventoried in Max Friedlaender's *Das deutsche Lied im 18. Jahrhundert*, to Schubert's Heine-Lieder of 1828, whose neo-*Volkston* is now tinged in the sardonic ironies of Romantic discontent.[5] Never a willing co-conspirator in matters of genre, Beethoven plants himself against its shifting currents. Further, Beethoven's engagement with the poem is often an encounter with the poet, enmeshed in those webs of culture and psyche that we are continually disentangling in his other music.

I

By the later 1780s, the august figure of Klopstock and the formidable complexities of his poetry must have given pause to a young composer in search of texts to sing. During these years of his apprenticeship, Beethoven seems to have kept his distance from Klopstock, perhaps in sober recognition of the daunting challenges that Forkel, in his excoriating review of Neefe's *Oden von Klopstock*, identified in the setting of these exemplary odes to music; or perhaps gleaned from Neefe himself, guiding his young student to the advice offered in the *Vorbericht* to his own ambitious enterprise.[6] Did this refined poetry, in its complex syntax, its often arcane evocation of antiquity, hold less appeal for the adolescent Beethoven, caught up in the new sensibilities,

4. For a comprehensive study, see Barry Cooper, *Beethoven's Folksong Settings: Chronology, Sources, Style* (Oxford: Clarendon Press, 1994). One volume has now appeared in Beethoven, *Werke*: Abteilung 11, no. 1: *Schottische und walisische Lieder*, ed. Petra Weber-Bockholdt (Munich: G. Henle Verlag, 1999).

5. Max Friedlaender, *Das deutsche Lied im 18. Jahrhundert: Quellen und Studien*, 2 vols. in 3 (Stuttgart and Berlin: Cotta'schen Buchhandlung, 1902; repr. Hildesheim: Goerg Olms, 1962). On the *Lieder im Volkston*, see vol. 1, part 1, 254–61.

6. Neefe's publication and Forkel's review are examined above in chapter 4.

literary and political, of the *Illuminaten* in Bonn?[7] The late coming to terms with a Klopstock problem (or however we think to construct Beethoven's resistance in the Bonn years to an encounter with Klopstock) seems evident in a letter of January 1824 to Georg Kiesewetter. Complaining about Josef Karl Bernard's text for "Der Sieg des Kreuzes" (which, in the end, Beethoven did not set), Beethoven adds: "But so far as I am concerned, I prefer to set to music the works of poets like Homer, Klopstock and Schiller. For at any rate, even though in their works there are difficulties to overcome [*Schwierigkeiten zu besiegen*], these immortal poets are worth the trouble."[8] Indeed, one might imagine Beethoven having thought "precisely *because* there are difficulties to overcome, these immortal poets are worth the trouble." In a note to the publisher S. A. Steiner in the winter of 1822–23, Beethoven writes: "If only you could procure for me for a few days the works of the poets Klopstock and Gleim, but in good copies of most recent editions."[9] And in the "Appraisal of the Books belonging to the Estate of Herr Ludwig van Beethoven," prepared for the auction of the *Nachlaß*, we find as item 28: "Klopstock. Werke, Troppau, 1785"; and in item 39, another volume listed as "Klopstock, Werke," without date.[10]

While there is no Klopstock to be found in any edition of the lieder, the

---

7. For a rich study of intellectual life in Bonn during those years, in such institutions as the *Lesegesellschaft* (a reading society) and the *Illuminaten*, see Sieghard Brandenburg, "Beethovens politische Erfahrungen in Bonn," in *Beethoven: Zwischen Revolution und Restauration*, ed. Helga Lühning and Sieghard Brandenburg (Bonn: Beethoven-Haus, 1989), esp. 34–41.

8. "[. . .] was mich aber angeht, so will ich lieber selbst *Homer*, Klopstok Schiller in Musik sezen, wenigstens wenn man auch Schwierigkeiten zu besiegen hat, so verdienen dieses diese unsterblichen Dichter –" *Ludwig van Beethoven. Briefwechsel Gesamtausgabe*, vol. 5 (1823–24), ed. Sieghard Brandenburg (Munich: G. Henle, 1996), 260; Emily Anderson, ed. and tr., *The Letters of Beethoven*, vol. 3 (London: Macmillan & Co.; New York: St. Martin's Press, 1961), 1105.

9. "wenn ihr mir doch auf einige [Tage] die Dichter Klopstock Gleim jedoch nach guten neuesten Original Ausgaben verschaffen könntet?!!" *Briefwechsel Gesamtausgabe*, vol. 4 (1817–22), 560; Anderson, *Letters*, vol. 2, 635, puts the letter in the year 1816.

10. See Hanns Jäger-Sunstenau, "Beethoven-Akten im Wiener Landesarchiv," in *Beethoven-Studien: Festgabe der Österreichischen Akademie der Wissenschaften zum 200. Geburtstag von Ludwig van Beethoven*, ed. Erich Schenk (Vienna: Hermann Böhlaus, 1970), 11–36. A more detailed annotation is given in Albert Leitzmann, *Ludwig van Beethoven: Berichte der Zeitgenossen, Briefe und persönliche Aufzeichnungen*, vol. 2 (Briefe und persönliche Aufzeichnungen) (Leipzig: Insel-Verlag, 1921), 379–83. See also Theodore Albrecht,

Ex. 6.1. Beethoven, *Das Rosenband* (Klopstock). Sketch. Kraków: Biblioteka Jagiellonska [formerly Berlin: Staatsbibliothek] Mus. ms. autogr. Beethoven Landsberg 6, 145.

sketch papers tell a different story. The earliest entry is lodged among intensive work on massive projects in the sketchbook Landsberg 6 (the so-called "Eroica" sketchbook), dateable to the winter of 1803–04. The text is Klopstock's *Das Rosenband*, and we have only a single line of music (shown as ex. 6.1).[11] Here is the poem:

Im Frühlingsschatten fand ich sie,	In spring's shade I found her
Da band ich sie mit Rosenbändern:	and with rosy ribbons bound her:
Sie fühlt es nicht und schlummerte.	She felt it not and slumbered.
Ich sah sie an; mein Leben hing	At her I gazed; my life hung,
Mit diesem Blick an ihrem Leben:	in that gaze, on hers:
Ich fühlt' es wohl und wußt' es nicht.	That I sensed and did not know.
Doch lispelt ich ihr sprachlos zu	But to her wordlessly I murmured
Und rauschte mit den Rosenbändern:	and stirred the rosy ribbons:
Da wachte sie vom Schlummer auf.	Then from her slumber she awoke.
Sie sah mich an; ihr Leben hing	She gazed at me; her life hung,
Mit diesem Blick an meinem Leben:	in that gaze, on mine:
Und um uns ward's Elysium.	And about us it was Elysium.

Nothing could be simpler. In the midst of nearly 200 pages of drafts for the immense expanses of the first movement of the *Eroica* Symphony, for the *Waldstein* Sonata, and among extensive plottings for the opening scene of *Vestas Feuer* (a first encounter with the challenges of opera after Mozart), works each meant to establish a bold public presence, here is a modest turn

---

tr. and ed., *Letters to Beethoven and Other Correspondence*, vol. 3 (Lincoln and London: University of Nebraska Press, 1996), 231–38.

11. The transcription is taken from *Beethoven's "Eroica" Sketchbook: A Critical Edition*, tr., ed., and with a commentary by Lewis Lockwood and Alan Gosman, 2 vols. (Urbana, Chicago, and Springfield: University of Illinois Press, 2013), 145 in the pagination of the sketchbook proper.

inward, to Klopstock's intimate poem, its syntactical inflections and enjambments appropriate more to ode than to lied. What was it, we may ask,
that drew Beethoven to these subtleties — to lovers whose existence hangs on
the fleeting glance, on impalpable feeling, on the "sprachlos" whisper, where
the only action is of the sleeping lover at that erotic moment of awakening?
Consumed in the challenges of these imposing projects, here is Beethoven
distracting himself, finding a volume of Klopstock's odes, leafing through,
reading for the music in the poem. The opening syncope is already a kind
of reading, a searching, in its implied inner voices, of the lover hidden "im
Frühlingsschatten." Of those "Schwierigkeiten zu besiegen" (as he wrote to
Kiesewetter), there are plenty in this little poem, different in kind from the
epic challenges to which most of the sketchbook is devoted.

Klopstock's modest poem remained with Beethoven, for he returned to
it again three years later, in the midst of another major instrumental project. On a leaf of sketches now sewn in with the miscellaneous papers known
by the signature Grasnick 20b at the Berlin Staatsbibliothek, amid entries
for the Quartet in E Minor, op. 59, no. 2, is a more ambitious draft that envisions the entire poem in a single sweep.[12] (It is shown in transcription as
ex. 6.2 and in facsimile as fig. 6.1.) There's not much detail. Beethoven both-
ered to write only the initial word of each strophe. The harmonic track has
to be imagined. The third strophe is tinged in minor: "moll," Beethoven reminds himself. But it is in the fourth strophe, the source of the gaze shifted,
that Beethoven's music moves beyond the purely lyrical. At that moment of
awakening, it is she who now sees him: "with this glance, her life hung on
my life," writes the poet, and the moment of ecstasy is bathed in the aura of
Elysium, a word that seems always to arouse Beethoven. If my proposed text
underlay is right, then Beethoven's *fortissimo* is placed on "meinem Leben,"
the climactic half note and the protracted dominant only reinforcing the
breach of strophic diction. The moment seems to touch a nerve, or perhaps
some deeper well of feeling, provoking a music more about triumph than
Eros. But the project is dropped — or rather, postponed. Returning to the
draft evidently years later, Beethoven scrawled "Klopstock" in broad pen-

---

12. Alan Tyson dates "the substance of Beethoven's work on the Quartets in the time
from April to November 1806"; see his "The 'Razumovsky' Quartets: Some Aspects of the
Sources," in *Beethoven Studies*, vol. 3, ed. Alan Tyson (Cambridge: Cambridge University
Press, 1982), 109, and 114 for the Klopstock entry in Grasnick 20b. These latter sketches are
entered in Bartlitz, *Die Beethoven-Sammlung in der Musikabteilung der Deutschen Staatsbibliothek*, 109.

Ex. 6.2. Beethoven, *Das Rosenband*. Draft. Berlin: Staatsbibliothek,
Mus. ms. autogr. Beethoven Grasnick 20b, fol. 18r. By kind permission.

ciled script at the top of the page, then adding "Rosenband, glaube ich"
[Rosenband, I believe] at the bottom.[13]

The encounter with Klopstock continued. On a loose leaf currently
housed with a sketchbook (Landsberg 5) used during the year 1809, Beethoven grappled with another of the less metrically complex, more lyrical odes
in the Klopstock repertory.[14] "Dein süßes Bild, Edone,/Schwebt stets vor
meinem Blick" [thy sweet image, Edone, moves ever before my gaze]: these
opening lines will of course bring to mind Emanuel Bach's setting of *Lyda*,

13. I'm much indebted to Clemens Brenneis, of the Staatsbibliothek zu Berlin, for gra-
ciously helping decipher those last words.

14. Inventoried with the sketchbook in most accounts, the leaf has no evident claim
to a place in the now-reconstructed book. The peregrinations of the leaf in the course of
the nineteenth century are difficult to establish. Gustav Nottebohm's study of the sketchbook omits any mention of the leaf; see his *Zweite Beethoveniana: Nachgelassene Aufsätze* (Leipzig: C. F. Peters, 1887), 255–75. Alfred Christlieb Kalischer, "Die Beethoven-
Autographe der Königl. Bibliothek zu Berlin," in *Monatshefte für Musikgeschichte*, vol.
28, no. 2 (1896), 10, identifies "Liederskizze 'Dein süsses Bild'" on p. 3a. The leaf is not
included in Clemens Brenneis's fine edition of the sketchbook: *Ludwig van Beethoven:
Ein Skizzenbuch aus dem Jahre 1809 (Landsberg 5)*, 2 vols., ed. Clemens Brenneis (Bonn:
Beethoven-Haus, 1993), where it is nonetheless numbered 111/112 in the representation of
its current structure.

Figure 6.1. *Das Rosenband*. Facsimile of draft. Berlin: Staatsbibliothek,
Mus. ms. autogr. Beethoven Grasnick 20b, fol. 18r. By kind permission.

of which much was made in the previous chapter.[15] There is no evidence that
Beethoven knew Bach's setting, though Neefe must surely have known it
well. The few decipherable phrases on the sketch leaf, written in ink against
a backdrop of smudged penciled notations, do little more than establish Beethoven once again reading Klopstock, reading less for those grand antique
themes, ethical and heroic, to which Klopstock is often drawn — no less than
Beethoven would be drawn in his instrumental projects from these years —

15. On the complicated publication history of the ode, see Klopstock, *Oden*, ed.
Muncker and Pawel, vol. 1, 212. In its earliest publications, in the *Hamburgische Neue Zeitung* (1773), the *Leipziger Almanach der deutschen Musen* (1774), and the *Göttinger Musenalmanach* (1775), the ode is entitled *An Lyda*, or (in 1775) simply *Lyda*. Only in later publications is the title given as *Edone*. Hans Boettcher claims that Beethoven found *Edone*
in vol. 6 of the *Göttinger Musen-Almanach*, but this is implausible; see his *Beethoven als
Liederkomponist*, 39.

Figure 6.2. Facsimile of sketch leaf now housed with the sketchbook Berlin:
Staatsbibliothek, Mus. ms. autogr. Beethoven Landsberg 5. By kind permission.

than for the sensibilities of the inner, love-obsessed poet. (A facsimile of the
sketch is shown in fig. 6.2.)

Finally, the opening line of another Klopstock poem was written into a
bifolium (now at the Royal Library in The Hague) that otherwise contains
sketches for the Cello Sonata in D, op. 102, no. 2, very likely from the summer of 1815. "Willkommen, o silberner Mond," Beethoven scribbles, barely
legibly. These are the familiar opening words of Klopstock's *Die frühen
Gräber*, an ode that inspired the famous setting by Gluck.[16] They are juxta-
posed on the sketch leaf, these few words, with some music set in quartet

16. Late in the summer of 1815, Schubert too was thinking of Klopstock. On 14 September, he composed settings of *Die frühen Gräber*, *Die Sommernacht*, *An Sie* ("Zeit, Verkündigerin"), *Vaterlandslied*, and *Selma und Selmar*, to be followed the next day by *Dem
Unendlichen*. The irony is poignant: Schubert and Beethoven in 1815 — the whiz kid Schubert, racing through what would be his most prolific year; the iconic Beethoven, struggling

score, Klopstock's prosody evident in none of its phrases. Jos van der Zanden has recently gone to some length to establish a relationship between poetic text and music, but in the end the argument ventures beyond what the scant evidence will allow. The document remains inscrutable.[17]

II

Another item in Beethoven's library was a collection of Ludwig Hölty's *Gedichte*, in an edition of 1815. The date is suggestive, and it must remain so, for we cannot know precisely when Beethoven acquired the Hölty volume. Still, Klopstock's address to this "silberner Mond" resonates sympathetically with a poem by Hölty, another apostrophe to the moon:

Dein Silber schien	Through the green oak
Durch Eichengrün,	that brought cooling,
Das Kühlung gab,	your silver shone down
Auf mich herab,	on me, O Moon, and
O Mond, und lachte Ruh	smiled gently at this
Mir frohen Knaben zu.	happy lad.
Wann itzt dein Licht	When now your light
Durchs Fenster bricht,	breaks through the window,
Lachts keine Ruh	no smile brings peace to
Mir Jüngling zu,	the young man,
Siehts meine Wange blaß,	sees only my pale cheek,
Mein Aug von Thränen naß.	my eye wet with tears.
Wann, lieber Freund,	When, dear friend,
Ach, wann bescheint	O when will your
Dein Silberschein[,]	silver light illuminate
Den Leichenstein,	the tombstone that
Der meine Asche birgt,	conceals my ashes,
Wenn Minneharm mich würgt?	should the sorrow of love strangle me?

through a midlife reckoning—each probing the poetry of Klopstock (among others) in search of solutions.

17. See Jos van der Zanden, "A Beethoven Sketchleaf in the Hague," in *Bonner Beethoven-Studien* 3 (2003): 153–67, esp. 155–57, and 161 for a facsimile of the page in question.

This was a poem that absorbed Beethoven in Bonn, for we have his music written out twice in manuscripts that must date from 1790. (The later version is shown as ex. 6.3.) The poem that Beethoven knew was published posthumously by Voss in his *Musenalmanach* for 1779, in a version that expurgates Hölty's final couplet, transforming the morbid death wish of the lovesick poet — "Der meine Asche birgt,/Wenn Minneharm mich würgt" — into the sentimental complaint of a young man on his deathbed.[18] Here is how that third strophe goes in Voss's revision:

Bald, lieber Freund,	Soon, dear friend
Ach bald bescheint	ah, soon will your
Dein Silberschein	silver gleam illuminate
Den Leichenstein,	the tombstone
Der meine Asche birgt,	that will contain my ashes,
Des Jünglings Asche birgt!	contain the ashes of youth!

As everyone knew by 1779, this exceptionally gifted poet had succumbed to tuberculosis three years earlier, at age twenty-seven, and so Hölty's original lines (which Beethoven could not have known) might be read to conflate the agony of the love-death with the affliction of the bedridden consumptive.

For Hölty, in the intensity of those too few years with poetry, Klopstock was the master poet haunting the correspondence with his compatriots in the Göttingen *Hainbund*. Among them, it was Hölty who came closest to Klopstock in his embrace of the strophic forms of antiquity, even as he sings with a lyrical voice distinctly his own. "I've written various poems during your absence," he writes to Heinrich Christian Boie in a letter of 3 January 1774, "but they are not yet sufficiently ripe to be put before Klopstock, and further, I must not press my work on him."[19] In an intimate letter to Charlotte von Einem, the much-courted muse to the poets of the *Hainbund*,

18. The extent and substance of Voss's rewritings of Hölty's poems, and the relationship between the two men, is well documented. For a foundational study, see Wilhelm Michael, *Überlieferung und Reihenfolge der Gedichte Höltys* (Halle: Max Niemeyer, 1909), esp. 29–49.

19. "Ich habe verschiedne Gedichte während Ihrer Abwesenheit gemacht, sie sind aber noch nicht reif genug, um Klopstock vorgelegt zu werden, und überdies mag ich ihm meine Sachen nicht aufdringen." See, for one, Ludwig Christoph Heinrich Hölty, *Werke und Briefe*, with a "*Vorwort*" by Uwe Berger (Berlin and Weimar: Aufbau-Verlag, 1966), 227.

Ex. 6.3. Beethoven, *Klage* (Hölty), WoO 113.

kei - ne Ruh' mir Jüng - ling zu, sieht's mei - ne Wan - ge

blaß, _____ mein Au - ge trä - nen naß. Bald, lie - ber Freund, ach

bald be - scheint dein Sil - ber - schein den Lei - chen stein, der mei - ne A - sche

birgt, des Jüng - lings A - sche birgt.

Hölty advises her to protect her health: "Remain cozy indoors and sit by a warm oven and read Klopstock's Odes. Then the veil will at once fall from your eyes and, like Lotte's flowers, you'll be able to appear at the dance."[20] The reference is quite possibly to Goethe's *Die Leiden des jungen Werthers* (1774), about which Hölty wrote Johann Martin Miller a few weeks earlier: "Goethe's *Leiden* is meeting with exceptional approval here. It's already sold out."[21] This Charlotte also took the role of Goethe's Charlotte in a house performance at which Hölty and Miller seem to have participated.[22] Between the lines in these letters, one might sense a subliminal tension, if not quite a tectonic shift, between the legacy of the magisterial Klopstock and the fresh voice of a new generation, the *empfindsame* intensity of Goethe's early writing tendering a new poetics of experience.

In his penetrating study of Beethoven's Bonn years, Ludwig Schiedermair thinks the closing bars of Beethoven's setting, with its octaves in the keyboard sounding a death knell, "point to a deeper psychic resonance in the young musician who takes the poetic text not merely as a model to be illustrated in music but as something that he experiences and shapes."[23] And still one must wonder how Hölty's original line — "Wenn Minneharm mich würgt" — in the bitter and unexpected twist of its irony, might have found expression in Beethoven's final bars. No less touching is the music of the first strophe, in its response to Hölty's convoluted syntax. Insinuating a past tense, the music remembers a friendlier moon whose light will too soon find the pallid cheek, the eye wet with tears. Beethoven sings it twice, this apostrophic "O Mond," first, in fluent response to the poetic enjambment, and then again: harmonically, a simple variant, yet in its diction a disconsolate cry from the heart, reinforced in those deep octaves in the bass. *An den*

20. "Hüten Sie fein das Zimmer und setzen sich hinter den warmen Ofen und lesen Klopstocks Oden. Dann werden Sie die Verhüllung bald wieder vom Gesicht nehmen und, als die Blume der Lotten, auf dem Ball erscheinen können." Hölty, *Werke und Briefe*, 237.

21. "Goethens 'Leiden' finden hier außerordentlichen Beifall, alle Exemplare sind schon vergriffen." Hölty, *Werke und Briefe*, 236.

22. The performance is described by Charlotte von Einem, as reported in Ernst Buchholz, *Der Konrektor von Einem und seine Tochter Charlotte* (Münden: W. Klugkist, 1899), 17–18.

23. ". . . deutet auf ein tieferes seelisches Mitschwingen des jungen Musikers, der hier den Vorgang des Textes nicht nur musikalisch zu illustrieren sucht, sondern ihn selbst miterlebt und gestaltet." Schiedermair, *Der junge Beethoven*, 349.

Mond, Hölty called his poem, a title that reveals more than Voss's generic *Klage*. And then the poem and the music move into a painful present. We are in E minor now. At "mein Auge tränennaß," the music reaches for the difficult interval, the dissonant inflection, the bass plotting its chromatic descent to the dominant, and then postponing resolution until the final word.

Hölty's "eye wet with tears" brings to mind another lament on the topic, another instance of Beethoven's extreme response. "Trocknet nicht," wrote Goethe — indeed, wrote four times, its eight words comprising nearly a third of a poem that manages to see the world through the tear-stained, astigmatic eye of this unhappy lover. Beethoven, composing in 1810 — his Goethe year, by most accounts — knew the poem (*Wonne der Wehmut*) as it was revised for publication in 1789.[24] (Beethoven's setting is shown as ex. 6.4.)

Trocknet nicht, trocknet nicht,	Do not dry, do not dry,
Tränen der ewigen Liebe!	Tears of eternal love!
Ach, nur dem halbgetrockneten Auge	Ah, to the merely half-dry eye
Wie öde, wie tot die Welt ihm erscheint!	How bleak, how dead the world appears!
Trocknet nicht, trocknet nicht,	Do not dry, do not dry,
Tränen unglücklicher Liebe!	Tears of unhappy love!

Tear: No other word is quite so intimately endowed, so heavily freighted with the signifiers of love and loss. For Lessing, writing in the 1750s, "all sorrow accompanied by tears is a sorrow over something good that has been lost."[25] The involuntary flow of tears serves the poet too readily as metonymy for the consummate *Augenblick* of the love-act, the thing itself, in its saline residue, a vanishing trace of what is no longer. It's the half-dried eye that the poet fears, clinging to the tear that has been shed, the remnant of a passion that will not come again. Twenty years after the setting of Hölty's *Klage*, here is another song in E major, another swerve to E minor. Goethe's "Tränen unglücklicher Liebe," a condition that Beethoven, in 1810, would have

24. For the original text, see, for one, Johann Wolfgang von Goethe, *Werke. Hamburger Ausgabe in 14 Bänden*, vol. 1, 104; and the note on 528.

25. "[A]lle Betrübnis, welche von Tränen begleitet wird, ist eine Betrübnis über ein verlornes Gut; kein anderer Schmerz, keine andre unangenehme Empfindung wird von Tränen begleitet." From a letter to Moses Mendelssohn, 13 November 1756, published in *Briefwechsel über das Trauerspiel*, in Gotthold Ephraim Lessing, *Werke*, vol. 4: *Dramaturgische Schriften* (Munich: Carl Hanser Verlag, 1973), 166. Lessing's thought is put into a larger context in our final chapter.

Ex. 6.4. Beethoven, *Wonne der Wehmut* (Goethe), op. 83, no. 1.

understood all too well, provokes a pair of extraordinary phrases. The first of them is very nearly a rehearing of Hölty's "mein Auge tränennaß," as though the earlier song continued to sound, etched in memory. But it's the second phrase, in its rewriting of the opening of the song, that signifies something more, in its preemptive capturing, a quarter note too soon, of "Tränen," its high G♮ sounding as a dissonant ninth above the implicit root F♯, the first *forte* in the song, sustained through a diminuendo, as though to accompany the tear as it evaporates. Beethoven's autograph, now in the Goethe-Schiller Archiv in Weimar, is a composing score, and a page from it (see fig. 6.3) records something of the angst of this rewriting, measure 17 originally to have recapitulated measure 2. It catches Beethoven in the act, rereading, finding that strident G♮ through a performance of the poem.

One more song suggests itself here, again in E major, and returning us to 1815. The poet is now Christian Ludwig Reissig: from the magisterial figures of Klopstock and Goethe, and the much-admired Hölty, to this dilettante, as Beethoven described him (and worse) in his correspondence with Breitkopf & Härtel.[26] Beethoven's setting of Reissig's *Sehnsucht* is yet another landmark, its muted lyricism often heard as a premonition of the third movement, "Gesangvoll, mit innigster Empfindung," of the Piano Sonata in E Major, op. 109. (The first strophe is shown as ex. 6.5.) Some forty years ago, Lewis Lockwood taught us to understand the "thirty-one entries for the song spread over five pages" in the so-called Scheide Sketchbook *not*, as Nottebohm had earlier suggested, as a "melody gathered together from portions of the whole, built up in a steady metamorphosis," but as a process of a different kind, manifoldly more complex than the reasoned product of, in Nottebohm's words, "assiduous, continuous labor."[27] And Georg Kinsky,

26. See the letters of 4 February 1810 and 15 October 1810, *Briefwechsel Gesamtausgabe*, vol. 2, 106 and 163; Anderson, *Letters*, 262–63 and 298.

27. "Beethoven's Sketches for *Sehnsucht* (WoO 146)," in *Beethoven Studies* [vol. 1], ed.

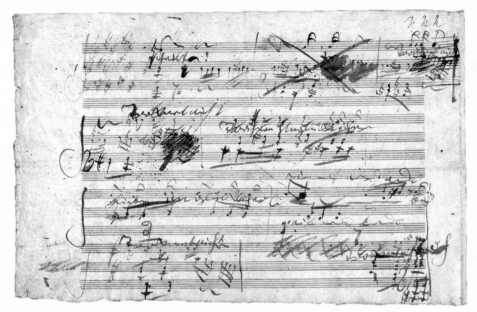

Figure 6.3. Beethoven, *Wonne der Wehmut*. Facsimile from composing score of a preliminary version, Hess 142. Klassik Stiftung Weimar: Goethe-Schiller Archiv. By kind permission.

echoing Nottebohm, was struck by the "16 (!) different versions of the opening measures — a proof of the fact that even short lied melodies owe not to the inspiration of the moment but to the improvements of restless work and polishing."[28]

I would propose to worry that complexity a bit further. This dizzying

---

Alan Tyson (New York: W. W. Norton, 1973), 97–122, esp. 103 and 121. The passage from Nottebohm will be found in his *Zweite Beethoveniana*, 332. The sketchbook belongs today to the Scheide Library in the Department of Rare Books and Special Collections at the Princeton University Library.

28. "16 (!) verschiedenen Fassungen der Anfangstakte — ein Beleg für die Tatsache, daß Beethoven auch kurze Liedmelodien nicht einer Augenblickseingebung verdankt, sondern in rastlosem Arbeiten und Feilen verbessert" [16 different versions of the opening measures — proof of the fact that Beethoven owed not even brief song melodies to the inspiration of the moment, but rather improved them through restless work and polish]. Georg Kinsky, *Manuskripte, Briefe, Dokumente von Scarlatti bis Stravinsky. Katalog der Musikautographen-Sammlung Louis Koch* (Stuttgart: Hoffmannsche Buchdruckerei Felix Krais, 1953), 70.

Ex. 6.5. Beethoven, *Sehnsucht* (Reissig), WoO 146, mm. 1–15.

array of sketches is in the service of a song that never moves beyond the simple declamation of its iambic trimeter, coming as close as Beethoven ever came — even more so than in those settings for Thomson — to the precepts taught in Schulz's *Lieder im Volkston*, whose lengthy, manifesto-like preface in the second edition (Berlin: Decker, 1785) seems nearly a script for Beethoven's project in 1815:

> For only through a striking similarity of the musical accent with the poetic accent of the song; through a melody in which the progression never raises itself above the movement of the text, nor sinks below it, which adapts to the declamation and meter of the words like a garment to the body, and which moreover flows on in very singable intervals, in a range adapted to all voices, and in the easiest modulations (*Modulationen*), and finally through the utmost perfection of all the parts to one another, by means of which the melody is given that rounded arch which, in the province of the small, is so indispensable to every work of art, does the Lied obtain that illusion that is the topic of discussion here: the illusion of the unsought, the artless, the familiar (den Schein des Ungesuchten, des Kunstlosen, des Bekannten): in a word, the *Volkston*, by which means it impresses itself so immediately and continuously upon the ear.[29]

Tellingly, Beethoven refuses even the slightest harmonic inflection beyond a single A♯ in the bass (and its repetition two bars later). The voice is purer still, circling around itself almost exclusively within the intervallic confines of a fifth, purged of even a single chromatic tone. The boldest, most expressive moment, harmonically, might be the low G♯ in the piano in the very first measure: an expansive deep breath before the constraints to follow. A late revision in the autograph score, canceling a lovely (and perfectly logical) tertiary dominant, only underscores the point (see ex. 6.6).

There is a poignance in this picture of Beethoven, in 1815, laboring so obsessively to find Schulz's "Schein des Ungesuchten, des Kunstlosen" — "ohne Kunstgepräng erklungen," as Alois Jeitteles would have Beethoven sing in the final song of *An die ferne Geliebte*, the cycle that followed directly in this very sketchbook. The sentiment echoes a few lines in Schulz's article "Lied (Musik)" in Sulzer's *Allegemeine Theorie*: "The Lied, according to its nature, must be set very simply," he writes, now quoting Klopstock:

---

29. Often reprinted, the preface, which Schulz dated "Berlin im November 1784," can be found in Friedlaender, *Das deutsche Lied im 18. Jahrhundert*, vol. 1, part 1, 256–57.

Ex. 6.6. Beethoven, *Sehnsucht*, WoO 146, mm. 5–6, early version, from Beethoven's autograph (Berlin: Staatsbibliothek, Mus. ms. autogr. Beethoven Grasnick 18).

—als ob kunstlos aus der Seele
Schnell es strömte. —[30]

To hear this turn in his later years to the directness of song penetrating into the fabric of the late quartets and sonatas is now a commonplace in Beethoven criticism. Joseph Kerman even wrote of being "ravished by the sheer songfulness of the last quartets."[31] To complicate the picture a bit, I'd like to suggest that the grain of voice manifest in the late works has its roots in Beethoven's earliest endeavors to create song, to find music in the poem. Within the severe, self-imposed restraint of the Reissig setting—repression seems hardly too strong a word for it—traces of that Hölty lied of 1790 sound through. Even its opening bars seem echoed in the little refrain that mediates between Reissig's strophes. So, too, the slippage in the bass—A♯, A♮, G♯—at "auf mich herab, O Mond" has its moment at "geheimnisvolles Schweigen" toward the cadence of the Reissig strophe, putting us in mind of the great phrase at bars 17 and 18 of *Wonne der Wehmut*.

The retrieval of a *Volkston* in 1815, recalibrated in the accents of a sensibility caught between the poetics of Enlightenment and the aftermath of Revolution, is yet another instance of revisionist memory. To read a poem, to conjure it in music, whatever else might be subsumed in the act, is an expedition into the interiors of mind. In the play of memory, the return home, imaginary and poetic, is a powerful agent in this reconfiguring. Revisiting Klopstock in 1804 and again in 1807, 1810, and 1815, Beethoven struggles

30. "—as though it flowed from the soul, spontaneously and without artifice" (Klopstock, from the ode *Die Chöre*). Sulzer, *Allgemeine Theorie der schönen Künste*, vol. 3, 278.
31. Joseph Kerman, *The Beethoven Quartets* (New York: Alfred A. Knopf, 1967), 195.

to come to terms with the poet whom he could not find in Bonn. The failure, each time, to engage the poem with the intensity that he brought to Reissig's *Sehnsucht* reminds us of those "Schwierigkeiten zu besiegen," that phrase with which, in 1824, he captured the challenge that such poetry must always put to the reader intent upon drawing from it a music commensurate with its linguistic idiosyncrasies, a challenge no less evident to a Neefe writing in 1776. For reasons that escape interrogation, these few exquisite poems that drew Beethoven to Klopstock, in their complex subtlety, proved incommensurate with the urgency to establish a fresh voice. The world of 1815 — Beethoven's world, in any case — was no longer Klopstock's. At the end of the day, these intensely private moments reading Klopstock remained precisely that: private moments, and no more.

DRAMMA PER MUSICA

7

ANAGNORISIS
Gluck and the Theater of Recognition

Students of the *Poetics* will recall Aristotle's investment in Recognition (*Anagnorisis*) — a "change from ignorance to knowledge," as he puts it — as an indispensable engine of dramatic plot. Here is the familiar passage:

> The kind of recognition most integral to the plot and action is a joint recognition and reversal that will yield either pity or fear, just the type of actions of which tragedy is taken to be a mimesis. Because recognition is recognition between people, some cases involve only the relation of one party to the other, while in others there is need for double recognition: thus Iphigeneia was recognized by Orestes through the sending of the letter, but for Iphigeneia to recognize his relation to herself required a further recognition.[1]

It is of course the *Iphigenia in Tauris* of Euripides to which Aristotle refers, to the process of recollection in which Iphigenia, the daughter of Agamemnon, and Orestes, his son, long ago separated, will finally recognize each other. Marked for sacrifice by her father's oath, covertly rescued at the last possible moment by the goddess Artemis, Iphigenia is delivered to Tauris, there to serve King Thoas in the ritual sacrifice to the goddess of those who come as foreigners to this place: "an ancient and cruel custom," Iphigenia complains in her opening soliloquy. "Can She hear me?" she cries out in anguished appeal to the goddess.[2] Orestes, together with Pylades, his brother-in-law by marriage to Electra, that other suffering daughter of Agamemnon, arrives at Tauris in quest of a wooden likeness of Artemis that Orestes has

---

1. I draw this from Stephen Halliwell's edition and translation of Aristotle's *Poetics* in the Loeb Classical Library series (Cambridge, MA: Harvard University Press, 2nd ed., 1995, repr. with corrections, 1999), 67.

2. My text is the translation by Witter Bynner, in *Greek Tragedies*, vol. 2, ed. David Grene and Richmond Lattimore (Chicago and London: University of Chicago Press, 1960), 116.

been charged to bring home to Greece, in part as atonement for the murder of Clytemnestra, his mother.

The scene of recognition unfolds methodically, Iphigenia questioning the two captives, probing for what she can learn of her family: of Agamemnon first of all, but then, poignantly, of Orestes. It's like the peeling of an onion, layer upon layer. For Euripides, it is not so much the dramatic moment of recognition that is the point, but rather the searching process through which recognition comes: a narrative pieced together from the shards of memory, even while Orestes must conceal his identity, for the unnamed Iphigenia stands before him as the enemy.

I

In a scene that was originally to have come at the close of act 2 of Gluck's *Iphigénie en Tauride* (1779), the image of Clytemnestra appears to the increasingly unstable Oreste in his uneasy sleep, tormented for his matricide by the Furies (les Euménides), who enact a "Ballet-Pantomime de terreur." At the very end of the scene, at the stage instruction "apercevant Iphigénie," Oreste cries out: "Ma mère! Ciel!" In a revelatory letter of 17 June 1778 to his librettist, Nicolas François Guillard, Gluck argues that the act must not end here: "The Eumenides appear to Oreste only in a dream and in his imagination," he writes. "[Ending the act here] would destroy the idea that in seeing Iphigénie he sees his mother. He must be still immersed in his dream when he says the words 'Ma mère! Ciel!' otherwise they will be of no effect."[3] What is gained in Gluck's scenario is the staging of a legitimate confusion in the mind of the not-quite-conscious Oreste between the oneiric figure of Clytemnestra and the actual presence, on stage in full view, of Iphigénie, the horror of the matricide, and all that it conceals of deeper maternal intimacies, transferred subliminally to the image, faintly remembered, of a sister whom he cannot recognize.

The liaison between the end of this scene and the opening of the next, in

3. For two translations of the complete letter in English, see *The Collected Correspondence and Papers of Christoph Willibald Gluck*, ed. Hedwig and E. H. Mueller von Asow, tr. Stewart Thomson, 130–32; and Howard, *An Eighteenth-Century Portrait*, 187–90. The original text is given in Gluck, *Sämtliche Werke*, Serie I, vol. 9, *Iphigénie en Tauride*, ed. Gerhard Croll (Kassel: Bärenreiter Verlag, 1973), vi–vii. A facsimile of the letter is to be found as a frontispiece of the edition of the opera, ed. F. Pelletan and B. Damcke (Paris: Simon Richault, [1874]).

which Iphigénie appears with her entourage, is one of the signal moments in the opera, Iphigénie coming into view just as Oreste utters those horrific words that awaken him from his dream.[4] The awakening is captured in an extreme diminished seventh, echoed in Iphigénie's chilling response to what she has witnessed: "I see all the horror that my presence inspires in you," she sings. These are her first words to him. In the imagined conflation of mother and sister, more is at stake than the irony of a doubly mistaken identity. The music captures that disquieting moment at which one awakens from a dream, that instant in which the dream image is at once transfigured into the waking present. It is at this cathartic moment that Iphigénie and Oreste set eyes on each other for the first time in the opera. The process of recognition begins here, intuitively and through the recesses of the subconscious. "Quels traits! Quel étonnant rapport!"—What features! What striking similarity!—sings Oreste in stage whisper, upon hearing her voice for the first time. (See ex. 7.1.)

And now the intense questioning begins. "The word 'Agamemnon' which Oreste repeats three times is significant," writes Gluck to Guillard, and continues: "Iphigénie rips his words from him, almost by force." "Agamemnon" is the word that Iphigénie does indeed rip from him, driven, as she is, to learn something of the fate of her father. Oreste can do no more than cry out the name. The orchestra amplifies the cry in another diminished seventh, and the repetition intensifies the dissonance. "This suffering that grips you: where does it come from?" she asks. "D'ou naît la douleur qui vous presse?" And when she learns of Agamemnon's death through what Oreste calls *parricide*, she in turn cries out: "Je me meurs," and it is this impassioned reaction that leads Oreste to ask himself "Quelle est donc cette femme?"—Who is this woman? (See ex. 7.2.)

In stunned response to the litany of these unspeakable acts, Iphigénie orders a funereal ceremony to honor the memory of this "héros qui n'est plus"—this hero who is no more—unaware still that it is her brother to whom she has been listening. In the measured rhythms of a regal menuetto, the orchestra intones a strophe of twenty-six measures before the chorus of priestesses takes up the lament: "Contemplez ces tristes apprêts." *Lente-*

---

4. In fact, the scene change is marked precisely at the moment of Iphigénie's appearance, coordinate with the moment of Oreste's three bars before the end of the Choeur des Euménides, though some later scores mark the change at the beginning of Iphigénie's recitative.

Ex. 7.1. Gluck, *Iphigénie en Tauride*, act 2, scene 5.

IPHIGÉNIE

Je vois tou - te l'hor - reur que ma pré - sen - ce vous ins - pi - re; mais au fond de mon

coeur, é - tran ger mal - heu - reux, si vos yeux pou - vaient li - re, au - tant que je vous plains, vous

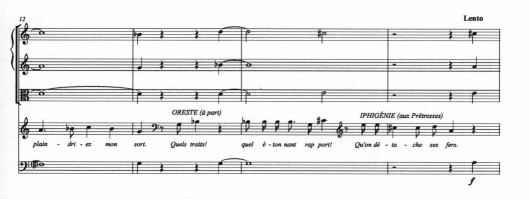

ORESTE (à part)

IPHIGÉNIE (aux Prêtresses)

plain - dri - ez mon sort. Quels traits! quel é - ton nant rap port! Qu'on dé - ta - che ses fers.

Ex. 7.2. Gluck, *Iphigénie en Tauride*, act 2, scene 5.

ment, it is marked, but the meter (3/8) and the diction urge a tempo that will move the procession along without loss of the grand sweep of its larger rhythms.[5] In its somber strophic simplicity, the music traces an expansive tonal arch, from C major to C minor, from E♭ major to E♭ minor, retracing itself through E♭ major and C minor to a final, symmetry-inducing C major. The sheer repetition, the subtle permutation of its few phrases against this shifting harmonic backdrop, is overwhelming in its effect. In the midst of the formal threnody, in its alternation of orchestra and chorus, nothing quite prepares us for Iphigénie's outburst, "Ô mon frère, daignez entendre les accents de ma douleur," the cumulative effect of the larger design establishing a context for Iphigénie's profoundly felt apostrophe. It is in her second quatrain — "que les regrets de ta soeur jusqu'a toi puissent descendre!" — and only here, that the music modulates within its sung phrases (shown in ex. 7.3). The inflection from E♭ major to C minor, a commonplace in normal tonal discourse, here assumes catastrophic significance. Dwelling for two full bars on a Neapolitan sixth, with its fraught D♭, the phrase breaches the formal patterning and opens a wound in the austere surface of the music, disturbing its chaste decorum. Against the disciplined phrases of the chorus, the voice of a distraught Iphigénie, marked in its nuance and timbre, draws its phrases from a deep well of suffering.

It is well known that a portion of the music for this extraordinary scene originated decades earlier, composed for *La clemenza di Tito*, first performed in Naples in 1752. But the matter is complicated. Readers of that letter to Guillard during preliminary work on *Iphigénie en Tauride* in 1778 will have puzzled over this passage:

> We come to the air which ends the [second] act during the funeral sacrifices. I would like an air in which the words express both the situation and the music. The meaning should always be completed at the end of the line, not at the beginning, nor half-way through the following line. This is as essential a quality in an air as it is bad in recitative; it constitutes the difference between them; the airs are then better adapted to a flowing melody. We come to the meter of the air I am interested in.[6]

<hr/>

5. A fine performance by the Boston Baroque ensemble, conducted by Martin Pearlman with Christine Goerke singing Iphigénie, captures this perfectly. The tempo is roughly the eighth-note at 106. Telarc CD 80546, recorded in 1999.

6. Howard, *An Eighteenth-Century Portrait*, 188.

Ex. 7.3. Gluck, *Iphigénie en Tauride*, act 2, scene 6: from the chorus
"Contemplez ces tristes apprêts," mm. 210–30, piano reduction.

And here Gluck writes out the full quatrain of "Se mai senti spirarti sul volto," marking those syllables "that must be long and sonorous":

> After these four lines—or eight if you wish, provided that they all have the same metre—will come the chorus, "Contemplez ces tristes apprêts," which seems to me very apt for the situation. I would like the [solo] air here to have roughly the same meaning. After the chorus, either the air will return da capo, or else just the first four lines that you will have written will be sung. I explain myself a little confusedly because my head is excited by the music.

Sesto's aria "Se mai senti spirarti" is in fact the prototype for the aria "Ô malheureuse Iphigénie" that precedes the funeral procession. In both, the key is G major; in both, the solo oboe is given the capacious opening theme. Alterations are largely inconsequential, with the single and telling formal exception that the middle section of Sesto's aria, in 3/8 meter and marked *grazioso*, would be removed from Iphigénie's aria and remade as the closing chorus, preceded by its own *accompagnato*. But it is clear enough from the letter to Guillard that Gluck's original intention had been to preserve the formal da capo of the original aria, even if its middle section would be sung by the chorus. The libretto, printed before the first performance and dated 11 May 1779—the first performance took place on 18 May—betrays some ambiguity as to the original state of things. Here is how the text looked at that stage:

Iphigénie
    O mon frere daigne entendre
    Les accens de ma douleur:
    Que les regrets de ta soeur,
    Jusqu'à-toi puissent descendres!

Les Prêtresses
    Contemplés ces tristes apprêts [etc.]

(L'Air et le choeur se chantent sur un air Pantomime qui regle la marche des cérémonies. Iphigénie et les Prêtresses reprennent le choeur, et sortent du Théâtre en continuant les chants funèbres.) [The aria and the chorus are sung to a music of pantomime which regulates the ceremonial march. Iphigénie and the priestesses take up the chorus and leave the stage while continuing the funereal song.]

From this one might infer that Iphigénie was to have sung her lines before the chorus sings: that the two were imagined as a pair: aria, then chorus.

Much has been made of Gluck's habitual self-borrowings. In his path-breaking study, Klaus Hortschansky reads the letter to Guillard as an argument in support of the view that Gluck began the borrowing with the middle section—with the chorus "Contemplez ces tristes apprêts"—and only then asked Guillard to provide a text for Iphigénie that would accord with the music for the main section of Sesto's aria.[7] In another reading of this letter, Michel Noiray comes to a similar conclusion: "Once Gluck had decided to use the middle section of Sesto's aria . . . for the mourning procession of the priestesses, the idea came to him, quite obviously, to take up the principal part of the aria, and to repeat it, da capo, after the chorus."[8] If there is sense in these readings, surely the greater issue must engage the transformation of what was essentially a trio-like middle section of thirty-seven bars in the original aria—thirty-four bars, really, with a three-bar close in E minor to negotiate the return to the G major of the aria—into a formidable work of 137 bars, and of a very different kind. Alterations to its surface, its spiky dotted rhythms replaced with phrases of even sixteenths, its texture enriched with suspensions, recast the tone of the piece, suggesting something closer to the "*stille Grösse*," in Winckelmann's famous phrase, that, to the Enlightenment sensibility of 1779, would have conjured the solemnity of some antique past.[9] The orchestration, too, is noteworthy. The oboes and

---

7. Klaus Hortschansky, *Parodie und Entlehnung im Schaffen Christoph Willibald Glucks* (*Analecta Musicologica*, 13) (Cologne: Arno Volk Verlag Hans Gerig KG, 1973), 218.

8. "Nachdem Gluck beschlossen hatte, für die Trauerprozession der Priesterinnen die Musik von 'Al mio spirto dal seno disciolto,' d. h. den Mittelteil von Sestos Arie . . . zu verwenden, kam ihm selbstverständlich der Gedanke, auch den Hauptteil der Arie zu übernehmen und nach dem Chor *da capo* zu wiederholen." Michel Noiray, "Der Brief Glucks an Guillard: Zum Parodieverfahren in zwei Arien der 'Iphigénie en Tauride,'" in *Christoph Willibald Gluck und die Opernreform*, ed. Klaus Hortschansky (Wege der Forschung, 613) (Darmstadt: Wissenschaftliche Buchgesellschaft, 1989), 373–89; here, 376.

9. Winckelmann, *Gedancken über die Nachahmung der Griechischen Wercke in der Mahlerey und Bildhauer-Kunst*. For a reprint with facing English translation, see Winckelmann, *Reflections on the Imitation of Greek Works in Painting and Sculpture*, 32–33. In a study that will have some resonance to the readers of these pages, Simon Richter argues that in *Iphigénie en Tauride*, Gluck "is enacting a musical version of Winckelmann's classical aesthetics," and, "more tentatively, that knowledge of Winckelmann's aesthetics may have consequences for the way in which *Iphigénie* is performed, staged, and interpreted."

flutes are silent for forty-two bars, and one must wonder whether this is a remnant of the original trio, where the oboes (having had much to do in the aria) are excused. In their place, Gluck presses into service a pair of clarinets, and the effect is very beautiful. When the music reaches E♭ major, the clarinets (in C) are relieved by the flutes and oboes, who play until measure 68: here, Iphigénie begins her lament, and the clarinets join her.

To those who have been moved by the solemnity of this music, it will come as something of a shock to learn that in its early history it was suppressed, together with the recitative that precedes it. Indeed, it was removed as early as 1781 for the recasting of the work in German for performances at the Burgtheater in Vienna (about which, more below).[10] But there is evidence that the chorus was removed earlier still, during its first run in Paris.[11] In both Paris and Vienna, the chorus was replaced with a brief instrumental piece in C minor: an Air-Pantomime in Paris, a Sinfonia in Vienna. And in a score that Berlioz copied at the Conservatoire in Paris in 1824, he enters a note after the aria "O malheureuse Iphigénie": "A l'opera le second acte finit ici. Le recit: et le choeur suivant sont supprimés."[12] If we cannot know the motives behind the decision to remove the chorus, the effect is clear. In the pacing of the opera, the chorus, for all its beauties, slows the action. Time itself seems to stop. But the Enlightenment mind had little patience for timeless ceremony when it was perceived to impede dramatic action. It would take nearly a hundred years, in the restoration of Pelletan and Damcke in 1874, to recognize what had been lost.[13]

See his "Sculpture, Music, Text: Winckelmann, Herder and Gluck's *Iphigénie en Tauride*," *Goethe Yearbook*, vol. 8 (1996), 165–66.

10. See Gluck, *Sämtliche Werke*, Serie I, vol. 11: *Iphigenie auf Tauris*, ed. Gerhard Croll (1965), viii–ix.

11. Gluck, *Sämtliche Werke*, Serie I, vol. 9, 364. In their edition of 1874, Pelletan and Damcke (xx–xxi) too surmised that the suppression was enacted during the first run of the opera in Paris.

12. "At the Opera, the second act ends here. The recitative and the following chorus are suppressed." For something on the Berlioz score, see below, fn. 16.

13. Indeed, the suppression has survived into the twenty-first century at the Metropolitan Opera in New York in 2007 and in a revival of 2011, perhaps to reinforce a reading of the opera that emphasized its brutalities over against the ritual equipoise of classical tragedy.

II

In a probing study of the opera, Carl Dahlhaus is at pains to demonstrate the ethical dimension in Iphigénie's bearing, in opposition to the pathetic in Oreste, identifying passages in her music that are regulated by a "Pathos der Einfachheit," and what he calls "ein Stil der 'noblesse,'" invoking as well Winckelmann's famous "edel Einfalt."[14] Unquestionably, Gluck's music points up these overarching differences in character. And yet, there is a complexity to Iphigénie that is missed in the reductiveness of such a reading. This troubled woman, so deeply enmeshed in the machinations of the gods, is altogether human, and it is the *empfindsame* core of her being that finds expression in the poignance of her music. Guided, as she is, by an ethos of sterner fiber, moments such as these are all the more revealing of a woman who feels.

Tellingly, it is precisely this ethical dimension that hangs heavy over the portrayal of her character in Goethe's *Iphigenie auf Tauris*. In the justifying of her difficult decisions, Iphigenie is impelled, time and again, to defend heart over mind. In act 1, Thoas (for Goethe, more *Mensch* than tyrant) tries in vain to persuade Iphigenie, who yearns for a return to her home and family, to remain in Tauris as his partner. Thoas: "Es spricht kein Gott, es spricht dein eignes Herz." Iphigenie: "Sie reden nur durch unser Herz zu uns"—the gods speak to us only through our hearts. In act 4, urging her to flee with them while they can, Pylades appeals to reason. "Ich untersuche nicht, ich fühle nur," responds Iphigenie: "I do not analyze, I only feel." There is of course much more to her story than that, and one might suppose that in the appeal to the heart, Goethe is only questioning the assumed impregnability of cold reason, playing out (as he did, a few years earlier, in *Werther*) the deeper wiring in this dialectical interrogation.

Gluck's Iphigénie knows nothing of Goethe's Iphigenie. The two were conceived in ignorance of one another, both in 1779. And yet, this same conflict between the implacable rule of law—the ethical dimension, in Dahlhaus's reading—and the inner, feeling self drives much of her behavior. Perhaps her most moving music comes in the touching *accompagnato* at

---

14. Carl Dahlhaus, "Ethos und Pathos in Glucks Iphigenie auf Tauris," in *Die Musikforschung* 27 (1974): 289–300. Reprint in Dahlhaus, *Gesammelte Schriften*, vol. 5 (Laaber Verlag, 2003), 441–53, esp. 451.

the opening of act 3. Deciding now to send one of her prisoners to inform Électre of her fate, Iphigénie admits to herself "la pitié la plus tendre" that she feels for the one whom, only moments later, she will select for freedom:

Mon coeur s'unit à lui par des rapports secrets . . .	My heart is drawn to him by some secret bond.
Oreste serait de son âge;	Oreste would be his age;
Ce captif malheureux m'en rappelle l'image,	This poor captive reminds me of him,
Et sa noble fierté m'en retrace les traits!	In his noble pride I see his features!

Just as Oreste confuses the dreamed image of Clytemnestra with an intuited sense that the woman before him is his sister, so Iphigénie intuits the trace of Oreste (whom she has not seen for fifteen years) in the bearing of this anonymous prisoner who is in fact her brother. The confusion of identities now overwhelms her: "D'une image, hélas! trop chérie, j'aime encore à m'entretenir" [I wish still to keep before me an image alas too cherished!]. These are the disconsolate words with which Iphigénie begins her affecting soliloquy, an aria in G minor that takes up the thread, both in its music and language, of her lines in the chorus at the end of act 3. Cavatina, it might better be called, its thirty-nine bars a distillation of thought and feeling, its phrases edging only slightly above the fluid line between speech and song.[15] (The closing bars are shown as ex. 7.4.) In its second quatrain, Iphigénie is overcome with the sense that her longing for Oreste is in vain—cherished images, but hopeless: "Inutiles et chers transports! Chassons une vaine chimère!" It is only the simplest gesture in the strings that manages to draw some music from the muted Iphigénie, a subtle rapport between strings and voice, here and in the keening line that follows: "Ah! ce n'est plus qu'aux sombres bords que je puis retrouver mon frère" [Ah, it is only at the dark

15. "Gegenüber die Seria-Aria . . . nimmt die Cavatina durch ihre drei wichtigsten Kennzeichen (Stellung am Szenenanfang; Kürze; musikalische, formale und dramatische Offenheit) eine Gegenposition ein" [Through its three most important characteristics–in its placement at the beginning of a scene, its brevity, its musical, formal and dramatic ingenuousness—the cavatina takes a position in opposition to the seria aria], writes Helga Lühning in "Die Cavatina in der italienischen Oper um 1800," in *Analecta Musicologica* 21 (1982): 333–34. Iphigénie's "D'une image, hélas" meets these criteria, to which might be added the marking "à demi" in the strings, suggesting that the whole piece is to be performed *sotto voce*. On the meaning of "demi-jeu" and "à demi," see Jean-Jacques Rousseau, *Dictionnaire de Musique* (Paris, 1768; facsimile repr. Geneva: Editions Minkoff, 1998), 141.

Ex. 7.4. Gluck, *Iphigénie en Tauride*, act 3, scene 1:
from the aria "D'une image, hélas!" mm. 27–39.

shores that I will be able to find my brother again].[16] Finally, the concise epilogue in the strings, its serpentine phrases over-articulated as though in stammered speech, exposes a music internalized: Iphigénie singing within herself, unable to put words to all that she feels. As it turns out, these unusual phrase articulations in the first violins are a matter of some dispute. They are to be found, entered in red crayon, in a score prepared by the scribe Lefebvre, copyist and librarian at the Académie Royale de Musique;[17] but in the first edition (Paris: au Bureau du Journal de Musique) and a first issue (or "Titelauflage") (Paris: chez Deslauriers), the phrasing is normalized.[18]

The distinction is not trivial, and it is tempting to hear a significant, if distant, echo of Iphigénie's music in another cavatina-like aria in G minor. When, in the second act of Mozart's *Die Zauberflöte*, Pamina sings "Ach, ich fühl's," her plangent accents seem almost a rehearing, intensified, of the music of Gluck's troubled heroine.[19] In its rhythmic displacements, in the staggered entries of the winds against the strings in those octave doublings

16. Readers of Berlioz's *Memoirs* will think here of his account, while visiting Mendelssohn in Leipzig in 1843, of their time together in Rome in 1831: "How many times, stretched morosely on his sofa, did I sing the aria from *Iphigénie en Tauride*, 'D'un image, hélas! trop chérie,' while he accompanied, soberly seated at the piano. And he would exclaim, 'It's beautiful, so beautiful! I could go on hearing that all day, always, and never grow tired of it.' And we would begin all over again." See *The Memoirs of Hector Berlioz*, tr. and ed. David Cairns (New York and London: Alfred A. Knopf, 2002[1969]), 296. Indeed, a younger Berlioz sat at the library of the Conservatoire in 1824 and copied, meticulously, the score of the complete opera. At the bottom of the second page of this aria, he wrote of the E natural in the basses at measures 21 and 34: "Quiconque, etant dans les dispositions nécessaires, n'a pas tremblé de tous ses membres en entendant ce mi ♮ des Basses est evidemment privé de toute sensibilité pour la musique dramatique" [Whoever, upon hearing this E♮ in the bass, and being of the necessary frame of mind, has not trembled in all his limbs obviously lacks all feeling for dramatic music]. The Berlioz score is today at the Morgan Library in New York, and is accessible through its digital "Music Manuscripts Online."

17. The manuscript is at Paris, Bibliothèque de l'Opéra, A. 267 a². For a description, see Gluck, *Sämtliche Werke*, Serie I, vol. 9, 338. These unorthodox phrasings are retained in the score edited by Pelletan and Damcke (Richault, [1874]), and in the miniature score "edited from the available editions" by Hermann Abert for the Edition Eulenburg [n.d.].

18. And it is this normalized phrasing that is given in the edition for the *Sämtliche Werke*.

19. Similarities between Iphigenie's aria, in its German version, and Pamina's were noted by Gernot Gruber, "Gluck und Mozart," *Hamburger Jahrbuch für Musikwissenschaft* 5 (1981): 169–86, esp. 178–82, where even more space is given to Tamino's "Bildnis" aria for its inner resonance with Iphigenie's sentiments.

so characteristic of Mozart's wind writing, in its expanding counterpoint, the four increasingly complex bars of this epilogue infiltrate the psyche of a Pamina close to the edge. And yet, the simple, direct speech of Gluck's epilogue does its work no less poignantly, however we think to articulate its phrases. There will be more to say about the touching of these two moments, Mozart's and Gluck's, in our final chapter.

III

In Euripides, the unraveling of plot hinges upon the letter that Iphigenia entrusts to Pylades, who is charged to deliver it to her brother, whom she believes still to be in Greece. "Say this to him," she begins. "Say to Orestes, son of Agamemnon, 'A greeting comes from one you think is dead.' Tell him, 'Your sister is not dead at Aulis but is alive.'" Upon hearing this, Orestes must now find ways to convince Iphigenia that her brother stands before her. Recognition comes early in the play, and the denouement is in the subterfuge by which Iphigenia plots the escape from the grip of King Thoas. The goddess Athena intercedes, assuring calm seas and safe escape. "The man who thinks he ever stood a chance against the Gods was born a fool," concludes the chastened Thoas.

With Gluck the unraveling is more devious, less driven by the implacable gods. If, from their first encounter in act 2, Iphigénie and Oreste have aroused vaguely sympathetic feelings in each other, their identities remain occluded. True recognition comes late, at the extreme moment of sacrifice. Iphigénie, knife in hand, is the reluctant agent of the deed: "Tout mon sang se glace dans mon Coeur" — The blood freezes in my heart. "Frappez," urges an impatient chorus. Under the knife, Oreste construes his fate as the just sequel to his sister's sacrifice: "Ainsi tu péris en Aulide, Iphigénie, ô ma soeur" — Thus did you perish in Aulis, Iphigénie, o my sister. Unfolding slowly, the revelatory words seem to penetrate almost before they are uttered. Iphigénie sings "Mon frère!" even as Oreste sings "Ma soeur!" to a sister whom he continues to think is no longer among the living. In response to this sudden reversal of fortune, he manages only to stammer: "Où suis-je! Se peut-il? . . ." — Where am I? Can it be? (See ex. 7.5.)

"It is sometimes necessary to ignore the old rules and to make new ones for oneself in order to create grand effects," wrote Gluck, in 1775, to his librettist le Baillit du Roullet during the composition of *Alceste*. "You are writing for the lyric theatre and not a tragedy for actors, and that totally

Ex. 7.5. Gluck, *Iphigénie en Tauride*, act 4, scene 2; at the moment of recognition.

changes the way you have to set about it. . . . These old Greeks were men with one nose and a pair of eyes, just like us. We do not have to submit to their rules like servile peasants. On the contrary, we must throw off their clothes, break free of the chains they would bind us with, and seek to become original."[20]

If this sage advice to du Roullet suggests a distinction of and about genre — the constraints of classical tragedy over against the new rhythms of "reform" opera — a deeper current seems to run through Gluck's words: a theater of human interactions driven by a newly conceived musical pacing

20. Letter of 2 December 1775. For the full text in English, see Asow, *Collected Correspondence*, 75; Howard, *An Eighteenth-Century Portrait*, 153.

toward the moment of revelation, of catastrophe averted. For Gluck, for the man of Enlightenment theater, it is less about the substance of what is revealed than the tension and expectation before the moment of *anagnorisis*: of recognition. It's not that Euripides and Aristotle are refused, only that the emphasis is placed elsewhere, removed from the thing recognized to the experience of recognition: How does it feel, this shuddering moment of awareness? What happens in the mind — and, for that matter, in the body?

IV

This concentration of the senses, in reading the art of Greek antiquity, was much on Lessing's mind in his essay on the Laocoon. Winckelmann's apprehending of the sculpture group as an exemplification of "noble simplicity and quiet grandeur" provoked Lessing, in 1766, to his exploration of the boundaries between painting and "Poesie," as he puts it in the subtitle of the essay.[21] (An illustration of the sculpture group is shown as fig. 7.1.) For Lessing, it is not merely that the visual arts labor in the province of timeless space while the poetic and dramatic arts traffic in the temporal. Rather, it is a paradox that drives much of the argument: of painting that must insinuate the before and after, of poetry that must situate its subject spatially. The focus is then narrowed to this "single moment of time to which art must confine itself. In the whole course of an action," writes Lessing, "no moment is so disadvantageous as the moment of its culmination."[22] When Laocoon sighs, imagination can hear him scream; but if he screams, the mind is limited to imagining him in some less interesting condition. Timomachus, he continues, "did not paint Medea at that moment [*Augenblicke*] in which she actually murdered her children, but several moments before, when motherly love is still struggling with jealousy. We anticipate the result and tremble at the idea of soon seeing Medea in her unmitigated ferocity, our imagination far outstripping anything the painter could have shown us of that terrible moment."[23]

21. Lessing, *Laokoon, oder über die Grenzen der Mahlerey und Poesie*. My source is Lessing: *Werke*, vol. 6: Kunsttheoretische und kunsthistorische Schriften. Translations are my own, indebted in part to *Laocoon*, tr. Frothingham; and *Laocoön: An Essay on the Limits of Painting and Poetry*, tr. Edward Allen McCormick (Indianapolis and New York: Bobbs-Merrill, 1962).

22. *Laokoon*, 25–26; *Laocoon*, tr. Frothingham, 16–17.

23. *Laokoon*, 27; *Laocoon*, tr. Frothingham, 18, but translation here modified.

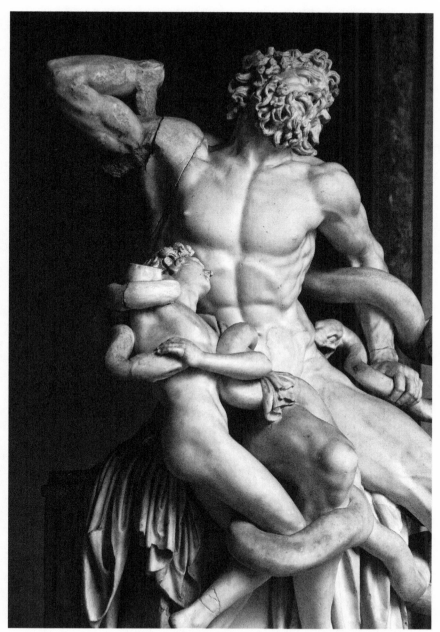

Figure 7.1. Laocoön and His Sons. Museo Pio-Clementino, Vatican. By kind permission.

It was very likely this concentration on the moment, and a formulation some lines earlier to the effect that this single moment must express nothing that can be apprehended as exclusively transitory (". . . was sich nicht anders als transitorisch denken"), that inspired Goethe, in an essay on the Laocoon published in 1798, to an intense interrogation of what might be called the phenomenon of the moment, and of its apperception.[24] "Äußerst wichtig ist dieses Kunstwerk durch die Darstellung des Moments," he writes — the utmost significance of this work of art lies in its representation of the Moment.[25] But it must be a moment in transition — "ein vorübergehender Moment" — that is captured if the work is to convey a real sense of motion. To experience the sense of movement in the Laocoon group, Goethe proposes that we "face the sculpture from a proper distance, eyes closed. If you open and then immediately close your eyes, you can see the whole marble in motion, and you will even expect the whole group to have changed its position before you glance at it a second time. I would describe the sculpture as a frozen lightning bolt, a wave petrified at the very instant it is about to break upon the shore."[26]

Determined to come to an understanding of the precise arrangement of the figures in the group, and in particular of the posture of the father in all the parts of his body, Goethe imagines the "instantaneous moment at feel-

24. "Über Laokoon," in *Propyläen. Eine periodische Schrift, herausgegeben von Goethe*, vol. 1, no. 1 (J. G. Cotta, 1798). I take the text from Johann Wolfgang von Goethe, *Werke. Hamburger Ausgabe in 14 Bänden*, vol. 12: *Schriften zur Kunst*, ed. Erich Trunz, commentary Herbert von Einem (Munich: C. H. Beck, 1981), 56–66. For an English version, see Johann Wolfgang von Goethe, *Essays on Art and Literature*, ed. John Gearey, tr. Ellen von Nardroff and Ernest H. von Nardroff (Princeton, NJ: Princeton University Press, 1994), 15–23. Goethe's essay is thoughtfully studied in its historical contexts in Simon Richter, *Laocoon's Body and the Aesthetics of Pain: Winckelmann, Lessing, Herder, Moritz, Goethe* (Detroit: Wayne State University Press, 1992), esp. 164–79, which constitutes one stop in an impressive critical survey of the formidable literature around the sculpture group. Lynn Catterson, "Michelangelo's *Laocoön?*" in *Artibus et Historiae* 26(52) (2005): 29–56, takes the ambivalent stylistic issues that have plagued the dating of the work in antiquity and the coincidences of its discovery outside Rome in 1506, in which Michelangelo played a part, to be grounds for proposing the work as a "forgery" from the workshop of Michelangelo. Whatever the merits of her thesis, it provokes us to ponder the fragility of those grand pronouncements from which theories of the art of antiquity are drawn.

25. "Über Laokoon," 59. The translation here is my own.

26. "Über Laokoon," 60; *Essays on Art and Literature*, 18.

ing the wound" as "the principal cause of the motion in its entirety."[27] "Die Schlange hat nicht gebissen, sondern sie beißt," writes Goethe, in a powerful economy of expression that translates weakly as "the snake has not bitten, but rather bites." It is this critical distinction that Goethe wants, between the deed accomplished and the anticipation of it, capturing the snake at the very moment of the puncture — even if the sculpture itself allows no such definitive distinction. A theorem is derived from all this close analysis: "The most sublime expression of pathos which art can portray is captured in the suspended transition from one condition to the other."[28] For Lessing, the freezing of an action in extreme transition is a degradation of the work of art, an aesthetic deformation, a wasting of the imagination. For Goethe, writing thirty-two years later, it is precisely the tension of the moment that is of its essence. If Lessing and Goethe might disagree as to the precise moment wherein this tension is most aptly captured, they do not disagree as to the efficacy of the affect.

This sensitivity to a moment held in suspended transition comes through in a remarkable entry dated Naples, 13 March 1787, in the *Italienische Reise*. On 6 September 1786, only days before his departure for the great journey through Italy, Goethe wrote to Charlotte von Stein that, acting on Herder's counsel, he'd decided to take *Iphigenie* along. The task ahead was to transform its original prose into a uniformity of metric verse that would approach a prosody of antiquity.[29] The work remained much on his mind in the months that followed, and was the topic of frequent readings among friends, one of whom was the artist Angelika Kauffmann, in close contact with Goethe during much of his Italian travels. This entry of 13 March describes her project:

Angelika has undertaken to paint a scene from my Iphigenie. The idea is a very happy one, and she will realize it admirably. It is the moment when

27. "Um die Stellung des Vaters sowohl im ganzen als nach allen Teilen des Körpers zu erklären, scheint es mir am vorteilhaftesten, das augenblickliche Gefühl der Wunde als die Hauptursache der ganzen Bewegung anzugeben." "Über Laokoon," 60.

28. "Der höchste pathetische Ausdruck, den sie darstellen kann, schwebt auf dem Uebergange eines Zustandes in den andern." "Über Laokoon," 62; *Essays on Art and Literature*, 20.

29. The relevant passages from these months are given in the section "Goethe und seine Zeitgenossen über 'Iphigenie auf Tauris,'" in Johann Wolfgang von Goethe, *Werke: Hamburger Ausgabe in 14 Bänden*, vol. 5, Dramatische Dichtungen III, 406–8, and, for a discussion of the process by Dieter Lohmeier, 421.

Orest, recovering from his swoon, finds himself in the company of his sister and his friend [Pylades]. She has conveyed in the simultaneity of the group that which these three characters speak one after another, and transformed their words into gesture. One sees in this how delicately she feels and how she knows to arrogate to herself that which is innate in her art. And this is indeed the turning point of the play.[30]

What has survived of Kauffmann's work is not the painting but a drawing, something of a preparatory sketch, that captures those qualities that so struck Goethe.[31] (It is shown as fig. 7.2.) Did Goethe know it? He writes as though he had some actual image in sight. But it is that last line that wants unpacking: ". . . es ist wirklich die Achse des Stücks." This moment in act 3, scene 3, is a protracted one. It is not that instantaneous flash of recognition that is the revelatory moment withheld until the closing scenes of Gluck's opera, but rather a gradual coming to terms with the troubled implications of what these characters now know about one another, and how they will cast their future. And yet it is the collapsing of this scene into what Goethe here calls "den Moment" — its portrayal in the Kauffmann drawing as a moment, and Goethe's apperception of it as such — that is much to our point.[32]

30. "Angelika hat aus meiner 'Iphigenie' ein Bild zu malen unternommen; der Gedanke ist sehr glücklich, und sie wird ihn trefflich ausführen. Den Moment, da sich Orest in der Nähe der Schwester und des Freundes wiederfindet. Das, was die drei Personen hintereinander sprechen, hat sie in eine gleichzeitige Gruppe gebracht und jene Worte in Gebärden verwandelt. Man sieht auch hieran, wie zart sie fühlt und wie sie sich zuzueignen weiß, was in ihr Fach gehört. Und es ist wirklich die Achse des Stücks." Goethe, *Werke: Hamburger Ausgabe*, vol. 11, Autobiographische Schriften III, *Italienische Reise*, 205. My translation differs in certain respects from the rather freer one in Goethe, *Italian Journey (1786–1788)*, tr. W. H. Auden and Elizabeth Mayer (New York: Schocken Books, 1968), 196.

31. Two drawings, actually, one an enhanced variant of the other. Presumably the earlier of the two, now at the Goethe-Museum Düsseldorf, Anton- und Katharina-Kippenberg Stiftung, is in fragile condition, with one edge torn away; the three figures regard one another with mouths closed. In the second drawing (shown in fig. 7.2), now at the Goethe Museum, Klassik Stiftung Weimar, the three are in quite the same configuration, but with mouths slightly open, as though in simultaneous conversation, Pylades grasping Orest's arm with both his hands. There is an urgency to the moment, in this second drawing, that is missing in the first.

32. For more on the confluence of these ideas around Goethe's notion of the "prägnanter Augenblick" in Kauffmann's *Iphigenie* drawings, see Waltraud Maierhofer, "Angelika

Figure 7.2. Angelika Kauffmann. Depiction of Goethe, *Iphigenie auf Tauris*, act 3, scene 3.
Klassik Stiftung Weimar, Herzogin Anna Amalia Bibliothek. By kind permission.

V

Something very close to this image of action frozen in indeterminate time—
kairos, as the ancient Greeks named it—is effectively captured at that extreme moment in Gluck's opera, the knife suspended as though between
ignorance and recognition. It is somehow reassuring to discover that the
capturing of the moment did not come easily to Gluck. An early state—
evidently the original one, to judge from the surviving autograph documents[33]—shows the passage shaded quite differently. The violins, marked
"très doux," intone an expansive melody above a Neapolitan sixth, joined at
mid-phrase by Oreste, who, in this singing, will reveal his identity at once,

Kauffmann Reads Goethe: Illustration and Symbolic Representation in the Göschen Edition," *Sophie Journal* (online) 2(1) (2012), esp. 12–13.

33. In a full score in the hand of a copyist and containing numerous additions and
emendations in Gluck's hand.

and without suspense. (This is shown in ex. 7.6.) One can hear Gluck worrying: How is Iphigénie to act while this ravishing phrase unfolds? How can she restrain herself, how repress her response? What happens to the knife? The man of the theater worries about such things.[34] And so the passage is rewritten.

One other document is of great interest here. In preparation for the German translation of the opera for performance in Vienna in October 1781 — "ein tragisches Singspiel," the printed libretto calls it — Gluck wrote out the voice parts only, on leaves the greater number of which are now at the Morgan Library.[35] The full passage is shown as ex. 7.7, from which it might seem that in finding a new diction for the German, Gluck failed to adjust the motion of the voice against the B♮ in the second violins, the string parts having been retained from the Paris version. But if the oversight can be defended as an offspring of contrapuntal voicing, it is the momentary dissonance at "warst," coming precisely at the change of harmony, that brings a new poignancy to a phrase that Orest had every reason to think his last. Evidently, this final authorized text reinstates the prose syntax of the original version (as shown in ex. 7.6) and yet retains the music of the revision (as in ex. 7.5) as it is preserved in the publication of the score in 1779. One must wonder whether Gluck's translator, the poet Johann Baptist von Alxinger (much admired by Mozart), wasn't working from the libretto published for the Paris production, which confirms that even Gluck's earliest setting of the passage constitutes a rewriting of the Guillard text.

In their too-brief moment of recognition, Iphigénie and Oreste seem on the printed page barely able to hear each other. Onstage they sing, and the studied accents of Gluck's finely calibrated phrase intensify the moment of recognition in a suspended tension that, recalling Goethe's lapidary depiction of the Laocoon moment, captures "the most sublime expression of pathos."

34. As Julie Cumming reminds us, this original version was in fact lifted quite literally from Gluck's pantomime ballet *Sémiramis*. See her "Gluck's Iphigenia Operas: Sources and Strategies," in *Opera and the Enlightenment*, ed. Thomas Bauman and Marita Petzoldt Mc-Clymonds (Cambridge: Cambridge University Press, 1995), 217–40, esp. 227–36.

35. The manuscript belongs to the Mary Flagler Cary collection at the Morgan Library, and can be viewed in its entirety at its digital website. For a facsimile of its first page and a description of the manuscript and its history, see J. Rigbie Turner, *Four Centuries of Opera: Manuscripts and Printed Editions in the Pierpont Morgan Library* (New York: Pierpont Morgan Library in association with Dover Publications, 1983), 32–33.

Ex. 7.6. Gluck, *Iphigénie en Tauride*, act 4, scene 2: earlier version of the recognition scene.

Ex. 7.7. Gluck, *Iphigenie auf Tauris* (1781), act 4, scene 2: at the moment of recognition.

EPILOGUE

At the end of 1780, six months before Gluck was preparing for the Viennese production of *Iphigenia auf Tauris*,[36] Mozart was in Munich composing *Idomeneo*, and contending with his father, home in Salzburg, who was serving as the interlocutor for the librettist Varesco. Impatient with the drawn-out exchange in act 1 between Idomeneo and Idamante, whose identities are unknown to one another, Mozart pleads for drastic cuts. Leopold argues for the defense: "If you consult the draft [of the libretto]," he writes, "you will see that it was suggested that this recitative should be lengthened a bit, so that father and son should not recognize one another too quickly. And now you want to make it ridiculous by having them recognize one another after

36. The actual title in Alxinger's printed libretto (Vienna: Beym Logenmeister, 1781) is *Iphigenia in Tauris*, but the editors of the Gluck *Sämtliche Werke* have chosen to adopt the wording that, following Goethe's title, has become common practice. See Serie I, vol. 11, *Vorwort*, xii.

they have exchanged only a few words."[37] The case is built at great length, even as Leopold accedes finally to a less drastic cut (to which the paste-overs and cross-hatchings in Mozart's autograph score vividly attest[38]), and concludes finally: "In this way the recitative will be shortened by a minute, yes, in puncto, by a whole minute. Great gain, indeed! Or do you want to make father and son run up and recognize one another just as Arlequin and Brigella, who are disguised as servants in a foreign country, meet, recognize and embrace each other immediately? Remember that this is one of *the finest scenes in the whole opera*, nay, the principal scene, on which the entire sequel of events [ganze Folge der Geschichte] depends."

The thirty-six letters between Salzburg and Munich from 8 November 1780 through 22 January 1781 record a dramatic narrative of their own, in its episodic arguments toward the mounting of a *dramma per musica* and in the playing out of a psychological agon between this real father and son: the brilliance of a young composer intuiting the swift stage business of Enlightenment opera in conflict with a father who, in league with Varesco, continues to defend the proprieties of an older theater. It is tempting to read this conversation against the backdrop of Gluck's exchange, two years earlier, with Guillard. For all their other differences, not least the forty-two years in age, Mozart shares with Gluck an intuitive feel for the operatic stage, the pacing of dramatic action driven by a new sense of musical time. Only months later, now in Vienna, Gluck's *Iphigenie auf Tauris* held the stage while an anxious Mozart waited, preparing to mount his new *Singspiel*. If Mozart's *Entführung* works a very different genre, its captive woman sings with a pathos worthy of Gluck's mythic heroine. Konstanze's *Traurigkeit* is the consuming topic of our final chapter.

---

37. Letter of 22 December 1780. For the original, see *Mozart: Briefe und Aufzeichnungen. Gesamtausgabe*, vol. 3, 68; and Anderson, *The Letters of Mozart and His Family*, 695.

38. See Wolfgang Amadeus Mozart, *Idomeneo, K. 366, with Ballet K. 367. Facsimile of the Autograph Score*, Introductory Essay by Hans Joachim Kreutzer, Musicological Introduction by Bruce Alan Brown (Los Altos, CA: Packard Humanities Institute, 2006), vol. 1, esp. 137–40.

8

CHERUBINO'S LEAP

I

Who *is* Cherubino? A participant in what might be called a contrapuntal subplot, at once extraneous and yet essential to the ligaments of the drama, the ubiquitous Cherubino implicates himself in the action at every turn. The Count seems destined to discover him in unsuspected places at unsuspected times. His flirtations with the Countess, with Susanna, with Barbarina—he would even consider Marcellina (though perhaps only in Beaumarchais)—all have repercussions in the opera. He is the butt of the finale to act 1, Figaro's spirited farewell to the newly commissioned officer in the Count's regiment ("Non piu andrai, farfallone amoroso"—amorous butterfly!). At the outset of the terzetto earlier in act 1 ("Cosa sento"), Cherubino, concealed onstage, is the topic of heated dispute. At once *Schwerpunkt* and perfect turn at the center of this elaborate ensemble, the moment of his discovery is precisely calibrated: "Cherubino Uncovered," as Carolyn Abbate puts it in the title of a chapter in *Unsung Voices*.[1]

There is something elusive, if not inscrutable, about this Cherubino. His sexuality, which seems the essence of his character, is veiled in ambivalence. Omniscient witnesses to the opera, *we* know that there's a woman in those clothes, but by the conventions of theater, in the enclosed world of the stage, the players (and Cherubino himself) do not—though it would be the rare performer who didn't act out this secret knowledge in some way.[2] Beaumarchais, in his preliminary notes on the characters, spends more time on Chérubin than on any other:

1. Carolyn Abbate, *Unsung Voices: Opera and Musical Narrative in the Nineteenth Century* (Princeton, NJ: Princeton University Press, 1991); the chapter is titled "Cherubino Uncovered: Reflexivity in Operatic Narration," on the terzetto in act 1.

2. For an interesting commentary on the place of Cherubino in the operatic convention of cross-dressing, see Heather Hadlock, "The Career of Cherubino, or the Trouser Role Grows Up," in *Siren Songs: Representations of Gender and Sexuality in Opera*, ed. Mary Ann Smart (Princeton, NJ, and Oxford: Princeton University Press, 2000), esp. 67–72.

This role can be played as it should only by a young and very lovely woman. In our theaters we have no very young men sufficiently developed to feel the subtleties in it. Timid to excess in front of the countess, elsewhere charming and naughty, an anxious desire is at the bottom of his character. He rushes at puberty, but without plan, without knowledge, and given entirely to each event. Finally, he is what every mother would perhaps wish at the bottom of her heart that her son would become, whatever she might suffer for it.[3]

For all the wit in Beaumarchais's note, one must wonder if there isn't some less pragmatic explanation, a trace of androgyny in the character itself. Cherubino is in any case ever in disguise, or in costume, or in hiding. In act 1, he hides behind a chair and then slips into it, hidden under one of Susanna's dresses. At the end of the act, he acquires the trappings of the military man. In act 2, Susanna and the Countess fit him out in one of Susanna's dresses, to plant him among the women.

An unwitting catalyst in his social interactions, there is in Cherubino a touch of the divine, suggesting rather a timeless, mythic Eros, a Cupid (even a Peter Pan), than a partner in some reasoned conversation. He is a poet, a singer. His "Voi che sapete" is a canzonetta that he himself has composed — about, of course, love. Kierkegaard even conjures him as a pubescent Don Giovanni, "though without this being understood in a ridiculous way, as if the Page by becoming older became Don Juan" — a complex and yet troubling speculation, because it's the innocence of Cherubino that we cherish.[4]

---

3. "Ce rôle ne peut être joué, comme il l'a été, que par une jeune et très jolie femme; nous n'avons point à nos théâtres de très jeune homme assez formé pour en bien sentir les finesses. Timide a l'excès devant la Comtesse, ailleurs un charmant polisson, un désir inquiet et vague est le fond de son caractère. Il s'élance à la puberté, mais sans projet, sans connaissance, et tout entier a chaque événement; enfin il est ce que toute mère, au fond du coeur, voudrait peut-être que fût son fils, quoiqu'elle dût beaucoup en souffrir." Translation my own. For a translation of the play, see Beaumarchais, *The Figaro Plays*, tr. John Wells, ed. John Leigh (London: J. M. Dent, 1997), where the "Author's Notes on the Characters" is much truncated, and the note on Chérubin omitted altogether.

4. See "The Immediate Stages of the Erotic, or the Musical Erotic," in Søren Kierkegaard, *Either/Or*, tr. David F. Swenson and Lillian Marvin Swenson, rev. and Foreword by Howard A. Johnson (Princeton, NJ: Princeton University Press, rev. 1959), vol. 1, 99. Wye Allanbrook worries the commonalities and differences keenly in her *Rhythmic Gesture in Mozart: Le Nozze di Figaro and Don Giovanni* (Chicago and London: University of Chicago Press, 1983), 263 and 376 (fn. 18).

To imagine Don Giovanni in adolescence is to picture the hip teenager busy plotting a licentious future, the idea of innocence itself questioned and refused.

At the very end of her brilliant study of the opera, Wye Allanbrook returns finally to Cherubino: "a touchstone," she calls him,

> without whose charismatic presence the transformations wrought during the mad day would never have taken place. Under his aegis Susanna and the Countess have drawn closer together, Figaro has learned to listen as well as to act, and the Countess has faced out the Count to bring him back to her, for at least a moment reconciled. Cherubino is emblematic of the fragile traits possessed by some humans which enable them to discover a special place, a "room of their own," a tranquil refuge to which they may also draw fellow seekers less well endowed than they.[5]

For Allanbrook, Cherubino is at the core of the opera, its "presiding genius," figuratively and literally.

II

But in his music — a music that he inhabits like a skin — he is touchingly human: the extreme adolescent in search of identity, discovering a libido which he doesn't yet know how to control. "Non so più cosa son, cosa faccio" gives the impression of an improvisation. The spontaneity of the thing is contagious. The phrases roll off without effort. The form seems very much of the moment. We are made to witness the intimacy of this search for self, a self-awareness made even erotic in the final couplet: "E se non v'è chi m'oda,/ Parlo d'amor con me" [and if there is no one who will hear me, I will speak with myself of love]. The music choreographs Cherubino's pensive, erogenous groping, the starting and stopping, the reflective Adagio that gives on to a "primo tempo" at "parlo d'amor con me" that is never quite at tempo, for the slightly chromatic ascent, *crescendo*, is composed to linger at this wistful moment. The sudden *piano* at "me" — the twinge at the appoggiatura, a tonic in first inversion, the fermata — arrests the moment: Cherubino, taken by surprise at his own conclusion. (See ex. 8.1.)

Earlier in this existential self-interrogation, Cherubino seeks to understand the root and the nature of his desire. The telling lines come at the end

5. Allanbrook, *Rhythmic Gesture in Mozart*, 193–94.

Ex. 8.1. Mozart, *Le nozze di Figaro*, act 1, scene 5: Cherubino,
from the aria "Non so più cosa son," mm. 88–100.

of the second quatrain: "E a parlare mi sforza d'amore/Un desio ch'io non posso spiegar" [and a desire that I can't explain forces me to speak of love]. In its convolutions and inversions, the syntax seems designed to put great stress on the subject, this "desire" that Cherubino can't explain but that he recognizes as the force beneath his irrepressible talk of love. Mozart seizes the moment. (See ex. 8.2.) "Un desio" is sung twice within the phrase, the phrase itself sung a second time, its shifting harmonies finding the ineffable source of Cherubino's introspection. The poignance of the harmony at measure 32 captures this elusive desire that can't be understood. The harmony can be parsed simply enough: Cherubino's appoggiatura D♭ resolves to the "added sixth" of a minor subdominant, a harmony reserved always for such moments, its effect enhanced as an alteration of the analogous moment at measure 27, where the D♭ is a ninth above the root of a dominant of the dominant.

There is of course more to all this than the naming of chords. The G♭ in the minor subdominant is a tone of affect, subtle in its implication of a flatted ninth above the root F in the four-two chord to which it will resolve. Gone before we've had a chance to register its effect, this ephemeral G♭ yet lives on in memory.

There are of course other G♭s in the opera, but only one other that speaks out with similar effect. When the Countess Almaviva takes the stage at the beginning of act 2, the ritornello with which her cavatina opens seeks to define her in every sense as inhabiting a world unavailable to a Cherubino. In its aristocratic demeanor, its measured diction, the music masks the woman who grieves beneath these artful formalities.[6] It may be worth a moment to consider the formal plotting of the cavatina. The ritornello is uncommonly long: seventeen full bars, *larghetto*, before the Countess utters a word.[7] Da Ponte's text, a quatrain comprising two sentences (in the libretto,

6. Allanbrook (*Rhythmic Gesture in Mozart*, 100) makes much of the distance here from Mozart's *seria* figures: "she shuns the exalted style almost entirely: her music is slow and contemplative, *di mezzo carattere*." True enough, and yet the *nobiltà* of her character is everywhere evident in this music. Still, we need to be reminded that the Countess, in Beaumarchais, is not of noble stock. On this, see, among others, Hildesheimer, *Mozart*, 185.

7. In the memorable production of Giorgio Strehler recently revived (September 2012) in Paris at the Opéra Bastille, the curtain is kept down for much of this music (as it is for the ritornello at the opening of the initial duet in act 1), finally revealing a troubled Countess, pacing, back to the audience. Even in this brilliant dramaturgical moment, her character is drawn before she turns to us, before she sings a note.

Ex. 8.2. Mozart, *Le nozze di Figaro*, act 1, scene 5: from "Non so più," mm. 25–36.

two complete clauses separated by a colon), is sung through in music that finds its way to a close in the key of the dominant at measure 34, at once returned to a local dominant seventh at the fermata at measure 36. And here something unforeseen happens. The Countess sings again her quatrain, now more urgently, in music whose accents throb in a diction less measured, and slightly unhinged. These final sixteen bars have a simple formal function: to sustain and finally to resolve that dominant seventh.

But beneath the formalities, the music touches something deeper. As the Countess lets the mask slip, Mozart finds the precise moment at which to gaze, with us, into her inner sorrow. Here, in ex. 8.3, is how the music unfolds from the fermata.

It's the *verso tronco* of the second line — "a miei duolo, a miei sospir" — that provokes the striking downbeat at measure 38: the A♮ which inflects the end of the phrase. This is not how composers commonly think to represent the sighs of which the Countess complains. Mozart is after something more personal: mimesis, not as the pictorial imitation of some *thing*, or an abstraction of classical gesture, but as the probing representation of human experience. It is not the figure of the sigh that is wanted here, but rather the felt emotion, the underlying cause of her sorrow. The first bassoon, silent for the past few bars, finds a high G♭ — a flatted ninth above the root F, an extreme dissonance, and pointedly unprepared, as though out of thin air — at just this moment, coincident with the Countess's A♮.[8] Its timing is perfect, setting loose those great sweeps with which the Countess makes her impassioned appeal to this figurative Amor to whom her cavatina is addressed. It is the nasal, double-reed burr of this G♭ that sticks in the ear, the tone that penetrates to her inner being.[9] Here, she becomes human.

8. Mozart loves to use the bassoon this way, its slightly pinched high register a locus for just such an entry. One thinks inevitably of the bassoon entrance on an anguished flatted ninth, again unprepared, in measure 4 of Pamina's "Ach, ich fühl's" in act 2 of *Die Zauberflöte*.

9. A copyist's score of acts 1 and 2 used for a performance in Potsdam in 1790, and which Karl-Heinz Köhler believes to have been prepared from the autograph after the Prague performances of 1787, displays a variant in the bassoon part, its rhythm at measure 35 made to agree with the voice: dotted quarter, two sixteenths. Claiming that this constitutes a "reinterpretation . . . by means of which the voice part is not only rhythmically supported, but the bassoon entrance justified as an imitation of the voice part," Köhler seems to me to miss the essential and for Mozart characteristic independence of voicing in the obbligato winds to enhance texture and articulation. See his "Figaro-Miscellen: einige

Ex. 8.3. Mozart, *Le nozze di Figaro*, act 2, scene 1:
La Contessa, from the cavatina "Porgi amor," mm. 34–45.

And it is here that Mozart hints at an essential, if impossible, erotic relationship in the opera.[10] For as the Countess invokes Amor, it is the very real figure of this "Cherubin d'amore" (as Basilio names him in the bantering before the Terzetto in act 1) who is subliminally conjured in the music. Cherubino has often enough been explained away as a Cupid (cupido [Lat.] = desire), as Eros, as Amor. And if these mythic allusions are not entirely beside the point, and even somewhat confused in what they suggest, they must cede to the actuality of the stage, and to Mozart's music. Eb major may mean many things to the ear of the 1780s. Schubart's *Charakteristik der Töne*, too commonly taken as gospel, speaks of it as "der Ton der *Liebe*, der *Andacht*, des *traulichen Gesprächs* mit *Gott*, durch seine drei b die heilige Trias ausdrückend" [the key of love, of devotion, of the intimate conversation with God, the Holy Trinity expressed through its three flats].[11] But there is a more modest claim to be made of its significance in Cherubino's "Non so più" and the Countess's "Porgi amor." Quite apart from the function of Eb in the unfolding of the tonal spectrum of the opera, the key establishes itself as a pitch-world inhabited, if ironically, by these two implausible lovers.[12] When the bassoon reaches for its Gb, it is *as though* the Countess, singing of her "sospir," has somehow intuited that very moment at which Cherubino, with the help of a similarly placed Gb, finds his way to the source of his "desio."

If that high Gb means to insinuate Cherubino into the *Empfindungs-Welt* of the Countess, it succeeds. The unwitting focus of much of the action of act 2, Cherubino is made the plaything of both the Countess and Susanna.

---

dramaturgische Mitteilungen zur Quellensituation," in *Mozart-Jahrbuch 1968/70* (Salzburg, 1970), 119–31, esp. 122.

10. Impossible within the confines of the opera, but not in the imagination of Beaumarchais. In *La mère coupable* (1792), sequel to *Le mariage de Figaro*, it is revealed to the Count that Léon is not really his son, but rather the product of a seduction performed by Chérubin with an apparently not unwilling Countess.

11. Christian Friedrich Daniel Schubart, *Ideen zu einer Aesthetik der Tonkunst*, written in 1784 but published only much later in an edition by Ludwig Schubart (Vienna: J. V. Degen, 1806; repr. Hildesheim: Olms, 1969). 377.

12. For Charles Rosen, the key has an even bolder mission: "it plays a role throughout the work that expresses emotional anguish or disquiet, and this strengthens the idea that Mozart thought of D major as somehow basic to the whole work *in a dissonant polar relation to Eb*" (emphasis mine). See his *The Classical Style*, xxv.

His ingratiating canzonetta, which he'd given to Susanna in act 1 — to be read to the Countess, to herself, and to Barbarina and Marcellina — is now put back in his hands: a command performance before the Countess. "Voi che sapete" begins as a set piece, its phrases balanced in perfect decorum. Soon enough the inner Cherubino sings through. The music has gotten itself to Ab major, a fleeting moment of stability in this faintly distant region. But now the poem turns inward, Cherubino searching for meaning in the contradictory signs of his behavior:

Ricerco un bene	I'm searching for affection
Fuori di me,	outside of myself.
Non so ch'il tiene,	I don't know how to hold it.
Non so cos'e.	nor even what it is!
Sospiro e gemo	I sigh and lament
senza voler,	without wanting to,
Palpito e tremo	I twitter and tremble
senza saper.	without knowing why.
Non trovo pace	I find peace
notte ne di,	neither night nor day,
Ma pur mi piace	But still I rather enjoy
languir cosi.[13]	languishing this way.

The music (shown in ex. 8.4) takes up the search, inflecting the Ab as an upper neighbor above the dominant in C minor, then contradicted at once by a cadence in G minor. Fever rising, the music climbs chromatically to the high Eb at the penetrating insight: "ma pur mi piace languir così." Here again, the double reeds seize the moment. The oboe touches the dissonant passing Gb in homage to those earlier Gbs, and in the same harmonic disposition; the bassoon sings again its "Porgi" phrase, transposed now to Db, here doubled by the flute two octaves above (again, a characteristic Mozart doubling), both doubling Cherubino's "languir così." Beneath the sensuous ambivalence of Da Ponte's couplet, Cherubino's music enacts the erotic climax and collapse.

13. I follow the stanzaic format in the libretto published for the first performance of the opera in Vienna, 1 May 1786, shown in facsimile in Wolfgang Amadeus Mozart, *Le nozze di Figaro, K. 492. Facsimile of the Autograph Score* (Los Altos, CA: Packard Humanities Institute, 2007), vol. 3, 61.

Ex. 8.4. Mozart, *Le nozze di Figaro*, act 2, scene 2:
Cherubino, from the arietta "Voi che sapete," mm. 52–62.

III

Finally, there is the edgy *"duettino"* (as Mozart titles it). In the company of the Countess in her rooms, and hearing the Count knocking from outside, Cherubino locks himself in the closet. The Count, hearing noises from within, smells a rat. Susanna, having reentered unnoticed and now hiding in an alcove, joins (*a parte*) the Count and the Countess in a *terzetto* that reflects on the confusion. Taking the Countess with him, the Count rushes off to fetch the tools to take the door apart, locking both the door to Susanna's adjoining room and the door behind him. Susanna and Cherubino are trapped. Anxiety is high.

This, too, is Cherubino music: skittish, unpredictable, almost improvised, enacted under great tension, without the studied impediments of reason. But it is also revelatory. Here is Cherubino thrust into the action. Discovery by the Count, in a matter of moments, will lead (warns Susanna) to his death. A window, the only apparent egress, is a good distance from the ground outside, and a terrified Susanna holds him back from a fateful plunge — for Cherubino, a leap into the unknown.

Hermann Abert, in the midst of a penetrating study of the opera, puts it this way: "For all its brevity, this is one of the most original numbers in the entire score, full of breathtaking, tingling excitement and animated by all manner of tensions on a larger and smaller scale." And Abert senses the significance of its final bars: "Only once, at Cherubino's words 'pria di nuocerle nel foco volerei' [rather than harm her, I'd leap into the fire], toward the end, is there a hint of stronger emotion that suddenly grants a fleeting insight into Cherubino's soul."[14]

A fleeting insight, indeed! But it is his final words — "Abbraccio te per lei. Addio: Così si fa" — that inspire music to plumb the internal convolutions of this Cherubino *in extremis*. (These final bars are shown in ex. 8.5.)

---

14. Hermann Abert, *W. A. Mozart*, newly revised and expanded edition of Otto Jahn's *Mozart* (Leipzig: Breitkopf & Härtel, 7th ed., 1956), vol. 2, 268. ". . . nur einmal, gegen den Schluß, bei Cherubins Worten 'pria di nuocerle in foco volerei' etc. findet sich ein Anflug eines stärkeren Pathos (in g-Moll), der uns plötzlich wieder einen flüchtigen Einblick in Cherubins Seele verstattet. Bei aller Kürze ist das Stück eines der originellsten der ganzen Partitur, voll atemversetzender, prickelnder Erregung, durch allerhand kleinere und größere Spannungen belebt. . . ." I've slightly altered the translation in Abert, *W. A. Mozart*, tr. Stewart Spencer, ed. Cliff Eisen (New Haven, CT, and London: Yale University Press, 2007), 953.

Ex. 8.5. Mozart, *Le nozze di Figaro*, act 2, scene 4:
from the duettino "Aprite presto," mm. 43–54.

For an instant, the flat side, through the minor subdominant, opens into an expressive recess: the incessant, desperate patter finds release in this one moment of eros. Da Ponte's four words — "Abbraccio te per lei" — have a story to tell. With Susanna in his arms, delaying for a moment the precarious leap, Cherubino yet has the wit (and the libido) to conjure the Countess in her place. The part-writing at measures 48–49, now drenched in the chromatic, somehow manages to find its way to the high E♭ at "lei" — the pronoun that allows Cherubino to invoke the Countess without uttering her name. "Per lei": Cherubino's sigh at the high E♭, its droop to the C, is the one moment in this breathless piece where time might be stretched — *rubato*: a stolen moment — a savoring of the embrace with Susanna, and vicariously with the Countess, before the leap into a perilous unknown. "Ei va a perire" — he's going to perish — sings Susanna, in shock, as he leaps.

In performance, this final "Addio" is often done as a quick peck on the cheek, but Mozart and Da Ponte intimate more here. The sheer complexity of the music, the shift at measure 49 to a fresh prosody in both strings and voice, struggle against the mad dash toward escape and the unremitting rhythmic figure that drives it. Most striking of all is the leap in the first violins up to the high A♮, a phrased sixth coupled with its inversion in the second violin. In the density of the chromaticism and the convolutions of the part-writing, this note sings out. Now, in a spontaneous flash of illumination, Cherubino seizes the moment. Before his leap into the unknown, he holds Susanna in momentary embrace. It is precisely this act, the lingering embrace, that is choreographed in the subtle nuances, the singular phrasing in the strings. There is indeed a taste of irony in the act itself, another layer to be parsed, for Cherubino has just now broken free of Susanna's grip — an embrace of another kind — as she struggles to restrain him.

A year later, Mozart would invoke just this figure to convey an attempt to break free of an embrace rather more ominously charged. Following the great quartet in act 1 of Don Giovanni, Donna Anna recognizes her seducer ("Don Ottavio, son morta!"). In the course of the *accompagnato*, we learn, in her telling, what transpired during those unseen moments — backstage, as it were — while Leporello paces back and forth at the opening of the opera. Donna Anna recalls the struggle to free herself from the grip of an intruder whose identity was concealed. Much else is concealed in this fraught narrative, where again Mozart's music probes beneath the diction of Da Ponte's lines. For while Donna Anna recounts her struggle — "a forza di svincolarmi, torcermi e piegarmi, da lui mi sciolsi" — the music (shown in ex. 8.6) is rather

Ex. 8.6. Mozart, *Don Giovanni*, act 1, scene 13:
from the recitativo "Don Ottavio, son morta!" mm. 47–52.

more assuasive. Those expressive sixths in the first violins, now ascending, the
A again on top, again in duo with the second violins as the bass moves into
chromatic territory, seem to touch some deeper sensibility in Anna's com-
posure.[15] In the much-discussed deceptive cadence and the nimbus-like triad
on F major — *piano*, suddenly — is captured a moment of sheer exhaustion, of
stasis, even of submission, or the imagining of it, before Anna can collect herself to continue that piece of the story that accords with what we witnessed
at her distraught entrance in the *Introduzione*, clinging to the arm of a Don
Giovanni in flight. But it is that momentary pause on the F-major triad that
is suggestive. Allanbrook is surely right to question whether Mozart would
have meant to engage in a kind of word-game with the deceptiveness of the
cadence, as a sign of Donna Anna's duplicity in the telling of the event.[16] Yet,
more than one recent performance takes the music to depict a deeper ambivalence in the struggle — *piegarsi*, after all, means to yield, to submit: Anna

15. In these three violent embraces, the music recalls the similarly phrased passage
in Claudio Monteverdi's *Combattimento di Tancredi e Clorinda*: "Tre volte il cavalier la
donna stringe con le robuste braccia" — the knight squeezes the woman three times with
his powerful arms. And it recalls another moment in the recognition of father and son in
Idomeneo, act 1, scene 10: Idamante: "Ah padre! . . . ah Numi! Dove son io? O qual tras-
porto" — though here the embrace is frustrated by the confused circumstances.

16. Allanbrook, *Rhythmic Gesture in Mozart*, 369 (fn. 11).

struggles with herself against submitting, but the cadence, more release than deception, suggests that she does not quite succeed.[17]

Cherubino's embrace of Susanna, and his freeing from her grip, has of course to do with neither the rapacious act of a Don Giovanni nor the ambivalent passion of a Donna Anna. And yet the moment, for Cherubino, is no less highly charged. Mozart's music takes Cherubino's adolescent passion no less seriously. Or, to put it differently, we take Cherubino seriously precisely because Mozart's music seems to touch some deeper string. The complexity of the moment is intensified in the imagining of the love-act — Cherubino in bed with the Countess — in this instant before a life-threatening defenestration.[18] It is all there in the overwrought music of measure 49, the finely wrought moment of desire prolonged for another instant in these final bars: love-death in a thimble.

IV

Implausible as it may seem, Mozart was evidently prepared to furnish a replacement for this irreplaceable duettino, perhaps in the run up to the first performance. In a number of copyist scores that date from as early as 1786, a setting in secco recitative of precisely the text "Aprite presto aprite" stands in for the duettino.[19] While nothing of this recitative has survived in Mozart's hand, its trace has been inferred from an evident gap in Mozart's autograph

17. Among the vast number of recorded performances, Renée Fleming's sensual swoon at "e piegarmi, da lui mi sciolsi" is especially telling. This was with James Levine and the Metropolitan Opera Orchestra, recorded in October 2000 and available as a DVD on Deutsche Grammophon. Anna Netrebko, singing at La Scala with Daniel Barenboim conducting (7 December 2011), doesn't swoon but rather turns subtly inward at these last words, and away from Ottavio, as though reflecting on a moment that she might like to have back.

18. The fantasy would be realized, finally, by Hofmannsthal and Strauss in the opening scene of *Der Rosenkavalier*.

19. Those scores were first described by Alan Tyson, in "Some Problems in the Text of *Le nozze di Figaro*: Did Mozart Have a Hand in Them?" in *Mozart: Studies of the Autograph Scores* (Cambridge, MA, and London: Harvard University Press, 1987), 290–327, esp. 292–97; and more recently and in greater detail in Wolfgang Amadeus Mozart, *Neue Ausgabe sämtlicher Werke* [= NMA]. Serie II, Werkgruppe 5, vol. 16: Le Nozze di Figaro (Ludwig Finscher) vorgelegt von Ulrich Leisinger, *Kritische Berichte* (Kassel: Bärenreiter-Verlag, 2007), 70–90.

score directly before the duettino, where the pagination runs from 215/216 (end of terzetto, recitative: "Dunque voi non aprite?") to 219/220 (duettino). Curiously, the thematic content of this alternative recitative has a good deal in common with the duettino, leading Karl-Heinz Köhler to assume that the latter was drawn from the former: that the duettino drew its material from the recitative.[20] For Alan Tyson, the wrongheadedness of this view of the thing was self-evident: these "melodic similarities . . . must surely represent an adaptation of the duettino as a recitative, not a conversion of the recitative into the duettino."[21] The case can be strengthened, for it stands against all common sense to imagine Mozart composing recitative with an ear toward thematic significance. That is not what *recitativo semplice* is about.

Some years earlier, Ludwig Finscher, similarly unconvinced by Köhler's account, was of the opinion that the recitative seemed "as though written by a musician who meant to replace the delicate stage business of the duettino with a more easily realized recitative, but who could not put the Duettino out of mind."[22] And he further noted that in its typography, the text of "Aprite presto aprite," as it goes in the printed libretto for the first performance, is clearly meant as a "geschlossene Nummer" — that is, as a complete formal number.[23] Finscher's point is further exemplified in the prosody of the text, in its rhymed trimeter. This alternative recitative, then, hints at other circumstances. The duettino is formidably difficult to perform, not least in that "delicate stage business" to which Finscher refers. Tyson, too, imagined the recitative having been written in response to performance difficulties. "Conductors and producers," he adds," still sometimes describe [the duettino] as a difficult number."[24] One can well imagine Mozart, in a crisis of desperation, seeking last-minute alternatives.

20. See Köhler, "Figaro-Miscellen," esp. 126–31, where the music of the recitative is badly garbled. The correct text is shown in NMA, *Kritische Berichte*, II, 5/16: 360–61.

21. Tyson further notes that the duettino is written on a paper whose watermark places it in the early stages of work on the opera. Alan Tyson, "Some Problems in the Text of *Le nozze di Figaro*," 302.

22. ". . . als sei es von einem Musiker geschrieben worden, der das technisch und szenisch heikle Duettino durch ein leichter zu realisierendes Rezitativ ersetzen sollte, bei seiner Arbeit aber das Duettino nicht vergessen konnte." NMA, Serie 2, Werkgruppe 5, vol. 16: *Le Nozze di Figaro*, Teilband 1: Akt I und II (Kassel: Bärenreiter, 1973), "Vorwort," xiv.

23. Ibid., xiv. A facsimile of this earliest libretto can be found in *Le Nozze di Figaro, K. 492. Facsimile of the Autograph Score*, vol. 3, esp. 63.

24. Tyson, "Some Problems in the Text of *Le nozze di Figaro*," 302.

Figure 8.1. Mozart, *Le nozze di Figaro*, act 2, scene 4: fragment, to have replaced
the duettino of Susanna and Cherubino. Facsimile of the manuscript at the Bibliotheca
Mozartiana der Internationalen Stiftung Mozarteum Salzburg. By kind permission.

And indeed, one such alternative has survived: a fragment in Mozart's
hand for the opening of a replacement for the duettino. (See fig. 8.1.) "Invece
del Duetto di Susanna e Cherubino," Mozart writes at the top of the page.
Instead of the duet! What we find here is the opening music of what seems to
have been conceived as a *recitativo accompagnato*. The second violin is given
a tremolo on D — *Allegro assai, pianissimo* — meant to set in motion the extreme anxiety of the moment. We are put in mind of another such opening,
tremolando in the middle strings: Donna Anna's recitative triggered by the
sight of her father's corpse ("Ma qual mai s'offre, oh Dei, spettacolo funesto
agli occhi miei!"). But of course such music always signals ahead, a gathering in the *accompagnato* of overwrought emotions toward the more formal
expression of aria. How, one must wonder, might that have played out in the
place of the duettino? Surely there is nothing in the text that suggests a par-
titioning into recitative and aria. And perhaps Mozart recognized this even

before setting the first word, and so the project was abandoned, evidently in favor of simple recitative.

V

When Gustav Mahler conducted *Figaro* at the Vienna Hofoper on 14 August 1897, Richard Heuberger, writing in the *Neue Freie Presse*, congratulated him "for having restored to Act II the dressing scene [Ankleideszene] between Cherubino and Susanna."[25] For a subsequent performance on 27 September, Robert Hirschfeld, writing in the *Wiener Abendpost*, was clearly moved by the duettino: "Leichtbeschwingt flogen die köstlichen Dinge, wie das Duett vor dem ersten Finale" [Exquisite things, like the duet before the first finale, flew by on the lightest wings].[26] And when Mahler conducted *Figaro* at the Metropolitan Opera in New York in 1909, Henry Krehbiel, the archly conservative critic for the *New York Tribune*, swallowing his avowed antipathy toward Mahler, wrote: "He first fired the enthusiasm of the audience (one that crowded the house) with the manner in which he invited Mme. Sembrich [Susanna] and Miss Farrar [Cherubino] to dash off the little duet accompanying the release of Cherubino from the cabinet. Here the spirit of haste and trepidation half extinguished the voices of singers and instruments. It was breathless."[27]

Something of this breathless rush can be felt in a recording of a remark-

25. Cited from Henry-Louis de La Grange, *Gustav Mahler*, vol. 2: *Vienna: The Years of Challenge (1897–1904)* (Oxford and New York: Oxford University Press, 1995), 47, where the translation misleadingly refers to "the short Susanna-Cherubino duet." By "Ankleideszene," Heuberger (whose authorship is only surmised by Mahler's response to the review) clearly meant Susanna's aria "Venite, inginocchiatevi," in which Cherubino is very much in the picture, though silently. The text may be found in the *Neue Freie Presse* for 15 August 1897, p. 6.

26. *Wiener Abendpost* (Beilage zur Wiener Zeitung) for 28 September 1897, p. 3. See La Grange, *Gustav Mahler*, vol. 2, 47, where the translation differs slightly.

27. La Grange, *Gustav Mahler*, vol. 4: *A New Life Cut Short (1907–1911)* (Oxford and New York: Oxford University Press, 2008), 339. Krehbiel's antipathy toward both Mahler's music and his interpretations of, especially, the symphonies of Beethoven, is amply documented in La Grange, vol. 4 (passim) and in his venomous obituary for the *New York Tribune*, La Grange, vol. 4, 1645–47. See also Joseph Horowitz, who writes of Krehbiel's "exceptional animus toward Mahler," in *Classical Music in America: A History of Its Rise and Fall* (New York: W. W. Norton, 2005), 194.

able performance conducted by Mahler's great protégé, Bruno Walter. This was Salzburg, 19 August 1937.[28] Much has been written about the highly charged political environment of that season, only months before the forced annexation (the *Anschluß*, as it was euphemistically named) of Austria by the Third Reich. Salzburg, some twelve miles from Hitler's compound at Berchtesgaden, was the frequent site of violence incited by Nazi agitators, and while Walter's apparent passivity even in the face of imminent catastrophe has been a topic of debate, it would be naive to believe him oblivious of the perilous situation.[29] Whether the political tensions of the moment and Walter's anxieties for his own future are to be heard in this performance is a matter of purest speculation. For it might just as plausibly be argued that in the midst of these sinister circumstances, Walter consumed himself in the fabrication of this other world: a *Nozze di Figaro*, this *folle journée*, whose internal challenges, political and otherwise, would have seemed blithely remote from the immediacy of the grim madness into which Walter and his family would be plunged in a matter of months.

That Walter knew Mahler's way with *Figaro* goes without question. At Mahler's invitation, Walter had come to Vienna in 1901 to serve as his assistant, a position that he retained until Mahler's departure from Vienna in 1908. During his years at the Hofoper in Vienna, between 1897 and 1908, Mahler conducted *Figaro* forty-nine times, more than any other opera.[30] It would be fatuous to claim that Walter's *Figaro* was merely a reheating of Mahler's. There is no evidence to support such a claim. Nor apparently was Walter ever given the opportunity to conduct *Figaro* at the Hofoper — "[Mahler] always conducted *Figaro* himself," recalled Alma Mahler[31] — though of course Walter conducted it often both before and after the Mahler years. Even in the performance of Mahler's music, Walter was very much his

28. The recording, made at the Festspielhaus in Salzburg on 19 August 1937, was produced for Andante Recordings by Ward Marston from the original Selenophone film and released by Andante in 2002.

29. A now-classic study of the political and ideological machinations in and around the Salzburg Festival is Michael P. Steinberg's *Austria as Theater and Ideology: The Meaning of the Salzburg Festival* (Ithaca, NY, and London: Cornell University Press, 2nd ed., 2000).

30. See, for one, Franz Willnauer, *Gustav Mahler und die Wiener Oper* (Vienna: Löcker, 1993), esp. 231–35.

31. Alma Mahler, *Gustav Mahler: Memories and Letters*, tr. Basil Creighton (Seattle and London: University of Washington Press, 1968), 102.

own man.[32] And yet, to hear this Salzburg *Figaro* unmindful of the highly charged atmosphere within which it was staged, to imagine it untouched by the complex years of collaboration with Mahler, is to divest the occasion of its aura, of the politics simmering beneath its elegant surface.

From the outset, Walter's tempi are brisk, bordering on the extreme. The *presto* of the Overture—a breakneck *prestissimo*, rather—establishes the larger rhythm, at once light-footed and urgent. Here, for the first time in Salzburg, was a *Figaro* sung in Da Ponte's language (Walter had performed it in Florence a month earlier), and it is tempting to think that the restoration of the opera in Italian, a rediscovery of this perfect marriage of word and tone, inspired the freedom of pace, even a sense of liberation. So how does it go with the duettino? The opening bars are indeed breathtaking. The half note is taken at roughly 108—but not for long. Esther Réthy (Susanna) and Jarmila Novotná (Cherubino), superb everywhere else in this *Figaro*, can't quite keep up. Things seem about to fall apart at several points, and the final bars convey the chaos of the moment, if not quite as Mozart had imagined it: so much for a lingering embrace! Walter's brave effort to capture the extremity of the moment seems, in spite of itself, to conjure something of the perilous ledge to which Mozart must have felt he'd driven his singers.

In Salzburg 2006, close upon a seventieth anniversary of the Walter performance, Nikolaus Harnoncourt takes a very different view, making of the duettino an elegant dance in slow motion—the half note at roughly 72!—the search for an exit more deliberately exploratory than the mad scramble that the circumstances otherwise dictate. Yet even here, time is not stretched for the embrace. Indeed, there is no embrace, as Cherubino (Christine Schäfer) breaks free of Susanna (Anna Netrebko), aided by a ubiquitous alter ego, a winged (and mute) Cupid who assists Cherubino at the window. The slower tempo allows that fleeting moment of eros to be heard even as it is lost to the business onstage.

32. "That Walter would not conduct Mahler's Sixth Symphony, and gave only two performances of the Seventh Symphony during all of his career, is symptomatic of a broader unease with the darker, fatalistic side of Mahler's music," writes Allan Keiler in a thoughtful reassessment of Walter's complex relationship to Mahler's music. See his "The Modest Maestro," a review of Erik Ryding and Rebecca Pechefsky, *Bruno Walter: A World Elsewhere* (New Haven, CT: Yale University Press, 2001), in *The New York Review of Books* 49(2) (14 February 2002).

THREE ADDENDA . . .

I

On a day in the midst of his early work on *Figaro*, Mozart depicted an encounter that, from our perspective, might seem a mirroring of Cherubino and the Countess viewed through a magnifying glass. In *Das Veilchen* (K. 476, on a poem by Goethe), perhaps the best known of Mozart's lieder, a lovesick violet aches, Cherubino-like, to be plucked by a distant shepherdess and pressed to her bosom.[33] In the unfolding of this little *scena*, the disconsolate violet sings its pathetic cavatina in G minor. At the longed-for moment, the oblivious maiden tramples the violet: "Es sank und starb und freut' sich noch . . ." In Goethe's eight syllables, the moment of transfiguration, of an actual love-death, is captured. Tinged in the chromatic, Mozart's pitch-perfect mutation of the augmented sixth on E♭ to a purer dominant of the dominant — E♭ becomes E♮ — enacts the internal mutation from "starb" to "freut."[34] In the ecstasy of its death throes, the violet sings an envoi to his unwitting lover — or rather, to the act itself, for she is addressed only in the third person: "Und sterb' ich denn, so sterb' ich doch/Durch sie, durch sie, zu ihren Füßen doch!" Goethe's poem ends here. Mozart, however, pays a final tribute to the violet, and in doing so, modulates the timbre from the tragic to the melodramatic: "Das arme Veilchen! Es war ein herzigs Veilchen." We can understand why Mozart felt it obligatory to add these mawkish words: the music wanted closure, a final cadenza-like moment before a

33. The autograph of the song, dated 8 June 1785, is now at the British Library, the Stefan Zweig Collection, Zweig MS. 56; see Arthur Searle, *The British Library Stefan Zweig Collection: Catalogue of the Music Manuscripts* (London: British Library, 1999), 73–74, and plate 62. It was written on paper that Mozart used for "the first two numbers in [*Figaro*] and their associated recitatives . . . as well as the first-act chorus and its preceding recitative," paper that was acquired "no later than the middle of 1785," as Dexter Edge writes. And he concludes that "Mozart may have begun work on the opera as early as the summer of 1785, or perhaps even in the late spring of that year, shortly after Leopold's departure from Vienna on 25 April." See Wolfgang Amadeus Mozart, *Le Nozze di Figaro, K. 492, Facsimile of the Autograph Score*, vol. 3, 15.

34. Carl Schachter draws attention to precisely this moment in the song: "In a magical way, Mozart captures the sudden change of mood and tone at the words 'und freut' sich.' The expected resolution of bass E♭ to D never materializes." See John Arthur and Carl Schachter, "Mozart's 'Das Veilchen,'" in *Musical Times* 130(1753) (March 1989): 149–55 and 163–64, esp. 154.

cadence that would in effect enclose the entire *scena*, even quoting something from the opening ritornello. But the poem, in its perfect locution, is diminished.[35]

II

In the absurdity of this impossible love is a bolder conceit that examines the theater of sensibility—of passion bordering on madness against the unforgiving calculus of reason. Such themes are central to Goethe's *Die Leiden des jungen Werther*, the epistolary novella of 1774 (his "Ein Veilchen auf der Wiese stand" dates from the same year). Its readers will recall the circumstances. Charlotte is engaged to the noble Albert, a respectable man of disciplined mind and high moral fiber. Werther (whose letters constitute the text of the novella), arriving in town, heart on sleeve, falls madly in love with Charlotte during Albert's long absence. The three then exist in what seems a suspended state of dissonance that continues even after the marriage of Albert and Charlotte. And yet, her feelings for Albert are perceptibly different in kind from those—well hidden until the very end—that she harbors for Werther.

Two weeks after Albert's return, Werther engages him in a lengthy dialogue that turns on the issue of suicide. It is much too early in the chronicle of his mental decline for Werther to entertain such notions in earnest, and so the discussion is rather in the abstract. When Werther impetuously places the mouth of an unloaded pistol against his own forehead, an appalled Albert exclaims: "What's the meaning of that? I cannot imagine how a man can be so foolish as to shoot himself; the very thought is repugnant to me." "Why is it," Werther asks, "that when people speak of things they must promptly pronounce them foolish or clever, or wicked or good! Whatever does it all mean? Have you really grasped the true and inmost nature of an action? Can you really give a definite account of the reasons why it happened, and why it had to happen? If you had, you might not be so ready to judge." The spontaneous actions of the man of passion, if they are to be understood, must be examined through a scrutiny that is situated in reason. At the end of this long dispute, Werther cries out: "My friend, man is only human [*der Mensch*

---

35. See, for one, Abert, *W. A. Mozart*, vol. 2, 215: "Ob Goethe trotz aller Sympathie für Mozart diese ganz unberlinerische Komposition seines Liedes innerlich gebilligt hat? Wohl kaum!" [In spite of all his sympathy for Mozart, could Goethe have accepted this thoroughly un-Berlin-like composition of his poem? Hardly!]

ist Mensch] and that jot of rational sense that one may possess is of little or no avail when passion rages and the limits of human nature constrict him." "We parted," Werther reflects, "without either having understood the other. But then, it is never easy for men to understand each other in this world."

The last page of the novella — the confused scene at the site of the suicide — tells us much. "*Emilia Galotti* lay open on his desk," Goethe's witness reports. In the penultimate scene of Lessing's tragedy (completed and published in 1772, only two years earlier than Goethe's novella), the eponymous heroine, deprived of her lover on their wedding day and forced to consort with the devious Prince Gonzaga, is about to take her own life, at which point her doting father, driven to madness by the circumstance, seizes the dagger and completes the act. The frantic, excruciating final dialogue between daughter and father only intensifies the effect. It might be inferred that Werther had been reading in search of inspiration for his own suicide — that behind the text, Goethe felt the need to justify Werther's act on the moral grounds implicit in Lessing's tragedy. But the specificity with which *Emilia Galotti* is placed at the scene insinuates something more subtle: that Goethe wants us to sort through the dramatic complexity that governs the human condition — wants us to read in these two works an interaction of character and plot.[36]

III

Neutered by the imperative of German diminutives, Goethe's *Veilchen* is linguistically neither masculine nor feminine — "*Es* sank und starb," Goethe must write. Even as we read past the grammatical rule to a sense of identity, it is yet unclear whether *this* violet wears men's clothes.[37] In Goethe's microcosmic *scena*, the world is observed through the passionately dispassionate lens of Enlightenment irony. Behind its androgynous mask, this timid creature plays out a sexual ambivalence that returns us to Cherubino's stage. "Timide a l'excès devant la Comtesse," Beaumarchais wrote of his Chérubin:

36. It is well known that Goethe's Werther was inspired by the suicide of Karl Wilhelm Jerusalem (1747 [or 1742?]–72), the author of several philosophical essays that were published in 1776 with a "Vorrede" by Lessing. At Jerusalem's death, a copy of *Emilia Galotti* was found opened at his desk. But the location of Lessing's *Trauerspiel* as stage prop in Goethe's novella has nothing to do with the circumstances of Jerusalem's suicide.

37. In Franz von Schober's *Viola*, known only because Schubert set it to exquisite music (D 786), the violet is unequivocally feminine, and one wonders whether Schober chose his title precisely to avoid the ambivalence latent in Goethe's poem.

"Il s'élance à la puberté, mais sans project, sans connaissance." He may as well have been writing of Goethe's *Veilchen*. And yet, the differences between the two are worth noting. In the figural world of Goethe's poem, the violet is a personification whose song is unheard by the shepherdess: unheard because, in a tweaking of conventional apostrophe, this flower, unable to articulate its lines, can only *think* its little aria: "Ach! *denkt* das Veilchen." In its mute isolation, the expression is yet more poignant, the metaphor enhanced and complicated in Mozart's music. Cherubino is, however, human through and through, and in Mozart's opera his behavior, his actions, have consequences.

. . . AND AN EPILOGUE

From Mozart and the lamentable sacrifice of this fragile duettino to the exigencies of performance, through Mahler, Bruno Walter, and Harnoncourt (and beyond) engaging the challenges of restoration, this brief excursion in and around performances of *Figaro* means only to weave the threads of a convoluted tapestry against which one might hear those few bars with which Cherubino signs himself before his impetuous leap. How, indeed, ought one to hear those bars? How to perform them? How to grasp them? The here and now of performance, the urgency to get us from one moment to the next, *allegro assai* (if not Walter's *prestissimo*), has somehow to accommodate the seemingly impossible acrobatics of a Cherubino who must negotiate this treacherous phrase while managing to hold Suzanna in a fleeting but meaningful embrace. The phrase is treacherous not because the notes are hard to sing—they're not, especially—but because the music at measures 47–49 turns suddenly introspective in its minor-mode chromatics, its texture approaching the nuanced complexity of the string quartet. If this were a stage play, Cherubino, now freed of a music that controls thought and embodies feeling, would enjoy some brief pleasure in the embrace, timing the accents of his delivery. The theatergoer might indeed think here of Beaumarchais, whose Chérubin has these more expansive words: "Dans un gouffre allumé, Suzon! oui, je m'y jetterais plutôt que de lui nuire . . . Et ce baiser va me porter bonheur" [I'd sooner throw myself into a flaming abyss—yes, Suzon!—than do her harm. And this kiss will bring me good luck]. He speaks in an elevated tone—"exalté," in the stage direction—and then embraces her before the leap: "Il l'embrasse et court sauter par la fenêtre." But this is opera, and the tempo of the music strictly regulates the action.

Here is the nub. Mozart and Da Ponte, quills in hand; a Cherubino onstage; a Mahler in the pit; the scholar, nose in score, pulling the texture apart at the keyboard of the mind; the violist, staking his claim to the notes — all converge at these few bars of music, not at crossed swords, but with a singularity of purpose: to find a balanced voicing and an easing of tempo sufficient to the moment; to achieve an equilibrium true to the ironic wit of a Beaumarchais. When the strings dig into their passionate chromatics behind Cherubino's embrace, this is no omniscient commentary from outside. Rather, we are plunged once again into the pulsing heart of this *Empfindungs-Geschöpf,* this creature of sensibility. These are his strings, singing with every fiber what his words can only suggest.

9

KONSTANZE'S TEARS

"These weeping Eyes, those seeing Tears"[1]

I

"Immer noch traurig, geliebte Konstanze? Immer in Tränen?" — Always sad, dear Konstanze? Always in tears? With these solicitous questions late in act 1 of Mozart's *Die Entführung aus dem Serail*, the Pasha Selim probes the *empfindsame* core of this woman who may be said to embody the moral compass of an opera whose moralities are obfuscated in the comic intrigues of *Singspiel* and in the bluster of the brutish Osmin.

Answers to these questions — reflections, rather, on a state of mind — come finally in Konstanze's deeply felt soliloquy early in act 2. (Believing that she is alone, she sings only to herself.) "Traurigkeit ward mir zum Loose," she begins. "*Traurigkeit* has become my fate." *Traurigkeit*: there's a word with which to open an aria! Setting declamatory traps as though to take the measure of the word, its three syllables do not make for a simple entry into Konstanze's lament. "Sorrow," it is often translated, or "sadness." These merely scratch the surface of a word whose root resonates deeply with, for one, *Trauer* (mourning) and *Trauerspiel*, and even by alliterative extension with *Tränen* (tears). Mozart's *Entführung* is, of course, no *Trauerspiel* — neither tragedy (as the word is most commonly translated) nor "mourning play," a distinction profoundly explored in Walter Benjamin's *Habilitationsschrift* of 1925.[2] Still, the word itself draws forth a music marked in tragedy,

---

1. Andrew Marvell, *Eyes and Tears*. From *Miscellaneous Poems*, 1681. A fine recent edition is *The Poems of Andrew Marvell*, ed. Nigel Smith (London and New York: Routledge, rev. 2013), 50–53, with copious notes and commentary. I have retained the original capitalization.

2. *Ursprung des deutschen Trauerspiels*, first published in Berlin (Ernst Rowohlt, 1928), now in Benjamin, *Gesammelte Schriften*, Unter Mitwirkung von Theodor W. Adorno and Gershom Scholem, ed. Rolf Tiedemann and Hermann Schweppenhäuser, vol. 1, part 1 (Frankfurt am Main: Suhrkamp Verlag, 1974), 203–430; in English as Walter Benjamin, *The Origin of German Tragic Drama*, tr. John Osborne (London and New York: Verso, 1998).

seeming to emanate from the depths of an Iphigénie, an Ilia. The opening bars formulate its phonemes before they are sung, the gritty sonorities of Mozart's wind band suggesting a commentary from outside, an emblem of the word before its meaning can be apprehended. When Konstanze utters its syllables, the strings now appropriate the motto an octave lower, its voicing slightly different, the rough edges of its dissonances softened as though the word itself were internalized, made human. (Recitative and aria are given in reduced score at the end of this chapter.)

"... weil ich dir entrissen bin," she continues — since I was torn away from you — sung first to a loving phrase in the relative major. But then the unexpected happens: silence, for a full half measure, followed by a knell, a mordant, empty octave D in the winds, *forte* and *tenuto*. Konstanze tries the phrase again, and now the music, wrenched back to G minor, does all that it can to tear the words out of her: "ent-ris-sen" — the word itself is torn apart. Silence again. Octave D. The phrase is tried once more, and the strings interpolate their own plaintive echo, set off by silence prolonged by fermatas on either side: Konstanze, listening to herself.

II

In the midst of a remarkable exchange of letters with Friedrich Nicolai and Moses Mendelssohn on the nature of *Trauerspiel* (the letters date from 1756), Gotthold Lessing seeks an explanation for the involuntary effluence of *Tränen*. For Lessing, "all sorrow accompanied by tears is a sorrow over something good that has been lost; no other suffering, no other unpleasant feeling will be accompanied by tears."[3] Whose tears? one might well ask. For Lessing and friends, the argument hangs on the question whether and how a *Leidenschaft* (a passion), an *Empfindung* (a sentiment, a feeling), might be conveyed from the actor to the *Zuschauer* (the observer, the spectator). "I ask not," writes Lessing, "whether the poet is able to bring the spectator to the point of sanctioning these passions that he observes in the actor, but whether the poet is able to bring the spectator to the point that he himself *feels* these passions, and does not merely feel that another feels

3. "alle Betrübnis welche von Tränen begleitet wird, ist eine Betrübnis über ein verlornes Gut; kein anderer Schmerz, keine andre unangenehme Empfindung wird von Tränen begleitet." "Briefwechsel über das Trauerspiel," in *Gotthold Ephraim Lessing: Werke*, vol. 4, Dramaturgische Schriften, ed. Karl Eibl (Munich: Hanser Verlag, 1973), 166.

them. In brief," he concludes, "I find that *Trauerspiel* excites in the spectator no passion other than *Mitleiden* [pity, compassion, sympathy]."[4] This compassion, this sympathy for these tragic characters, is itself marked in tears. "I hate the French tragedy," confesses Lessing, "which squeezes a few tears from me, but not before the end of the fifth act. The true poet disperses compassion through his entire *Trauerspiel*, everywhere bringing forth places in which the perfection and the flaws of his hero are displayed in a touching union — that is, he arouses tears."[5]

Whose tears? In these letters, Lessing is at pains to clarify a distinction between *Leidenschaften* felt, or at any rate, performed, by the actor, on the one hand, and the feeling aroused in us by these displays of emotion. Late in the correspondence, Lessing advances an analogy with the sympathetic vibration of two strings with one another. "Let us give these strings *Empfindung* [feeling]," he proposes. While the vibrations [*Bebung*] set in motion by the touching of the first string may yield a "schmerzliche" feeling, the very same *Erbebung* in the second string has, in Lessing's quaint description, an "angenehme Empfindung" [an agreeable sensation], for it has not been set in motion by touch (or at least not directly so).[6] "It's the same in *Trauerspiel*," writes Lessing. "The performing actor falls into an unpleasant *Affekt*, and I with him. But why is this *Affekt* agreeable in me? Because I am not the performing actor himself, upon whom this unpleasant idea has immedi-

---

4. "Ich frage nicht, ob ihn der Poet so weit bringt daß er diese Leidenschaften in der spielenden Person billiget, sondern ob er ihn so weit bringt, daß er diese Leidenschaften selbst *fühlt*, und nicht bloß fühlt, ein anderer fühle sie? Kurz, ich finde keine einzige Leidenschaft, die das Trauerspiel in dem Zuschauer rege macht, als das Mitleiden." Lessing, *Werke*, vol. 4, 161.

5. "Aber ich hasse die französischen Trauerspiele, welche mir nicht eher, als am Ende des fünften Aufzugs, einige Tränen auspressen. Der wahre Dichter verteilt das Mitleiden durch sein ganzes Trauerspiel; er bringt überall Stellen an, wo er die Vollkommenheiten und Unglücksfälle seines Helden in einer rührenden Verbindung zeigt, das ist, Tränen erweckt." Lessing, *Werke*, vol. 4, 187.

6. Lessing, *Werke*, vol. 4, 203. Letter of 2 February 1757, Lessing to Mendelssohn. We are reminded here of Diderot's vision of the sympathetic vibrations set off in his philosopher's clavichord, invoked as a model for the process of thought itself. See his "Conversation Between D'Alembert and Diderot," in Denis Diderot, *Rameau's Nephew and D'Alembert's Dream*, tr. with an Introduction by Leonard Tancock (Harmondsworth and New York: Penguin Books, 1966), 156–57.

ate effect, because I feel the *Affekt* purely as *Affekt*," without having been touched by the object that sets it in motion.[7]

There is yet a further complication—a paradox, we might call it—that Lessing does not address. The tears that we shed, in sympathy with what we witness onstage, are genuine—the real thing, produced by true feeling—while the *Leidenschaften* that provoke them, with which we vibrate only sympathetically, are the staged work of mimesis.

III

Back to Konstanze, ever in tears (as the Pasha observes). If Mozart's *Entführung* is no *Trauerspiel*, you'd have a tough time convincing Konstanze of that. Her passion for Belmonte is consuming, while her life, she senses, withers away, "gleich der wurmzernagten Rose, gleich dem Gras im Wintermoose"—like the rose eaten away by the worm, like the grass covered by winter moss—in Bretzner's bleak conceit.[8] "Zuletzt befreit mich doch der Tod," she will sing—death finally will free me—in reply to the Pasha's threat of "Martern aller Arten" [tortures of every kind].

When Mozart and Stephanie came to adopt Bretzner's libretto, a *recitativo accompagnato* was put before Konstanze's "Traurigkeit," its opening bars establishing the tone of a *scena* in *seria* mode. The upper strings then enact a weeping phrase, a sequence of slurred dyads in thirds—tears, we are meant to imagine, each run ending in some bitter, unexpected harmonic twist. But

7. "Die spielende Person gerät in einen unangenehmen Affekt, und ich mit ihr. Aber warum ist dieser Affekt bei mir angenehm? Weil ich nicht die spielende Person selbst bin, auf welche die unangenehme Idee unmittelbar wirkt, weil ich den Affekt nur als Affekt empfinde, ohne einen gewissen unangenehmen Gegenstand dabei zu denken." Lessing, *Werke*, vol. 4, 203–4.

8. The libretto is a reworking by Gottlieb Stephanie the Younger of Christoph Friedrich Bretzner's *Belmont und Constanze, oder Die Entführung aus dem Serail*, which had been performed in Berlin early in 1781 with music by Johann André. See Thomas Bauman, "Coming of Age in Vienna: *Die Entführung aus dem Serail*," in Daniel Heartz, *Mozart's Operas*, ed., with contributing essays, by Thomas Bauman (Berkeley, Los Angeles, Oxford: University of California Press, 1990), 67. The libretto for the premiere of the opera in Vienna on 16 July 1782 is shown in facsimile in Wolfgang Amadeus Mozart, *Die Entführung aus dem Serail, K. 384. Facsimile of the Autograph Score*, with introductory essays by Hendrik Birus and Ulrich Konrad (Los Altos, CA: Packard Humanities Institute, 2008), vol. 2, 47–63.

it is the incipit of each run that challenges the mind. Each will be heard as a dissonance suspended from some implicit dominant. But the final run, at measure 15, is yet more extreme. "Banger Sehnsucht Leiden," Konstanze sings — fearful torment of yearning — and the violins strike an unprepared (and unpreparable) dissonant dyad G–F over E♭–D♭, where the ear wants something more in tune with the F-minor harmony beneath it. The G/E♭ leaning on F/D♭, oblivious of the harmonic underpinning, infiltrates the poet's language: tears not in the pictorial sense, as some iconographic simile. These tears burn. Konstanze sings "banger Sehnsucht Leiden" once more, and now the strings draw forth a poignant chromatic echo of her phrase, their opening aggregate a sharp dissonance, marked *sforzando* — after the opening *piano*, the only dynamic marking in the entire recitative.

Whose tears? For the "metaphysical" poets of the seventeenth century, it is the tear observed, the lover reflected in this perfect orb, itself an image of the eye that creates it: "Fruits of much griefe they are, emblemes of more," in John Donne's remarkable conceit.[9] For Mozart, the inaudible tear must yet be *heard* — not the tear itself, but the expression of an inner sorrow from which it issues. In a letter of 26 September 1781, Mozart describes to his father what he is after in Belmonte's "O wie ängstlich, o wie feurig." "Would you like to know how I have expressed it," he writes, "and even indicated the throbbing heart? By the two violins playing octaves. . . . You feel the trembling — the faltering — you see how his throbbing breast begins to swell; this I have expressed by a crescendo. You hear the whispering and the sighing — which I have indicated by the first violins with mutes and a flute playing in unison."[10] A similar letter, had Mozart thought to write one months later on the composition of Konstanze's *scena*, is difficult to conjure in the mind. Here, the music moves beyond the depiction of the literal, beyond the figural throbbing and trembling incurred by Belmonte's *Ängstlichkeit*. The symptoms of Konstanze's *Traurigkeit* run deeper. The music has to probe internally, into her psyche, to find a source for its mimesis. The matter of agency is problematized.

The process is, in some measure, a linguistic one. This comes clear in the

9. John Donne, *A Valediction: of Weeping*; in, for one, *The Elegies and the Songs and Sonnets*, ed. Helen Gardner (Oxford: Oxford University Press, 1965), 69–70.

10. Anderson, *The Letters of Mozart and His Family*, 769; *Mozart. Briefe und Aufzeichnungen. Gesamtausgabe*, ed. Internationalen Stiftung Mozarteum Salzburg, vol. 3, 162–63.

second half of the aria, formulated in a single, shrewdly convoluted sentence:

> Even to the breeze I cannot tell
> my soul's bitter anguish,
> for, unwilling to carry it,
> it would breathe all my laments
> back into my poor heart.

But it is the German, with its end rhymes on *Schmerz* and *Herz*, that does the linguistic work.

> Selbst der Luft darf ich nicht sagen
> Meiner Seele bittern Schmerz:
> Denn, unwillig ihn zu tragen,
> Haucht sie alle meine Klagen
> Wieder in mein armes Herz.

Now in the relative major, the winds, in *concertante* mode, offer a conciliatory music, hinting at the breeze that Konstanze must refuse, even as she participates in its gentle speech. But when she utters the word *Schmerz*, the winds shudder with her. The word itself, stretched over two full bars, is stung by two adjacent diminished-seventh chords, and a third in the following measure. In the harmonic language of *Die Entführung*, this is extreme, both in its syntactical bending of the word and in the exhaustion of the total chromatic. But it is to the very end of the strophe, to the rhyming *Herz*, that the poem is driven, in Konstanze's breathless flight to a high A♭. The staging of this difficult note is daring, not least for the harmony that greets it: yet another diminished seventh, now muted and *piano* in the acoustical warmth of the strings. Here, again, the internalizing, the embodiment of feeling—literally so, for this is what Konstanze fears: that the breeze will only breathe her lament back to its source. This is not the throbbing heart— "o wie ängstlich"—of which Belmonte sings, a metonymic figure that invites the simile-inducing music that Mozart describes. Konstanze's heart is rather the vascular center of her feeling: the wounded vessel of her sorrow. And when she has finished, the old question returns, but now it is Blonde, who had been listening unobserved, who asks: "Ach mein bestes Fräulein! Noch immer so traurig?"

IV

In a brief unpublished essay of 1916, titled "Die Bedeutung der Sprache in *Trauerspiel* und *Tragödie*" [on the significance of language in Trauerspiel and Tragedy], Walter Benjamin asks "how the feeling of sadness can gain entry into the linguistic order of art" [wie Trauer als Gefühl in die Sprachordnung der Kunst den Eintritt findet]. "Words," he continues, "have a pure emotional life cycle [*Gefühlsleben*] in which they purify themselves by developing from natural sound to the pure sound of feeling. For such words, language is merely a transitional phase within the entire life cycle, and in them the *Trauerspiel* finds its voice. It describes the path from natural sound via lament to music."[11] The profound subtlety of Benjamin's often impenetrable language only points up the futility of translation. Still, this notion of the transformative nature of the word whose meaning is to be sought in its *Gefühlsleben*, in a life process that moves from pure sound through lament to this state that Benjamin identifies as *Musik*—whatever he means by that word—this notion that would insinuate the transfiguration of word into music is powerfully suggestive of what actually happens when Konstanze, alone in her voice, reaches for that high A♭. The word is made over into something other than the meaning that its linguistic credentials have assigned to the sum of its letters.

If Benjamin's conjuring of a *Gefühlsleben* of word may be understood to theorize language in an abstract, generalized sense, the image comes to life in the playing out of Konstanze's aria. As happens here, and in other arias of a certain poetic cast, the poem will be repeated in its entirety. In sonata terminology, this repetition is coordinate—or nearly so—with a reprise in which the second part of the exposition, here in B♭ major, must now be repositioned in the tonic minor. No simple transposition, the music has literally to be transfigured, a challenge that often inspires Mozart to unimaginable leaps of imagination. In "Traurigkeit," we are witness to a metamorphosis affecting every phrase of the second strophe. At "Selbst der Luft darf' ich nicht sagen," where the winds earlier offered some relief (in B♭ major), the

11. "Es gibt ein reines Gefühlsleben des Wortes, in dem es sich vom Laute der Natur zum reinen Laute des Gefühls läutert. Diesem Wort ist die Sprache nur ein Durchgangsstadium im Zyklus seiner Verwandlung und in diesem Worte spricht das Trauerspiel. Es beschreibt den Weg vom Naturlaut über die Klage zur Musik." "The Role of Language in *Trauerspiel* and Tragedy," in Walter Benjamin, *Selected Writings*, vol. 1, 60 (tr. Rodney Livingstone); Walter Benjamin, *Gesammelte Schriften*, vol. 2, part 1, 137–40, esp. 137.

music now languishes in plangent despair. Konstanze's first phrase sinks to a G that chokes off any hope of continuity. A Konstanze in greater control might instead have turned those last notes up to B♭.

Her second phrase is yet more remarkable, here deflecting that low G and finding in its place those very pitches with their diminished sevenths that earlier established a resonant "Schmerz." Context is everything, and now the *Musik* which, in the Benjaminian sense, is the final stage in the *Gefühls-leben* of this fraught word, embeds its chromatic complaint in mournful descent from a high G. And then there is the final couplet: "haucht sie alle meine Klagen wieder in mein armes Herz." It's as though Konstanze, hearing these words a second time — forced now to *sing* them in G minor — feels more acutely the betrayal of the "Luft" to whom she would not sing. That bold escape to the high A♭ at "Herz" is here turned on its head. Now in descent, the phrase traverses the diminished seventh, punctuated with a difficult diminished third: A♭, G, F♯, with, yet again, a diminished seventh in the strings waiting to envelop the word.[12] The inclination to explain these two phrases — the ascent to A♭; the descent to F♯ — as modeling some inversional trajectory signifying aspiration and defeat (or what you will) is, I think, to miss the deeper engagement here with Benjamin's notion of a process in which linguistic expression *becomes* music. Singing these words a second time, Konstanze *hears* herself. The implausibility of Bretzner's conceit — as though one could sing past the air — is unmasked. This second singing pierces to the heart.

V

Roughly a year earlier, in December 1780, Mozart had composed another aria in G minor, for another suffering woman. Ilia's "Padre, germani, addio!" is the music with which *Idomeneo* opens. Ilia's aria and Konstanze's,

---

12. Illuminating precisely this passage, Mozart's autograph records a first intention to repeat measures 116–20 followed by a repetition of measures 109–15. These bars (116–27) are then crossed through. Curiously, the entire autograph score of recitative and aria, with the exception of its final page, was removed at some point from the complete score of the opera and replaced by a score in the hand of a copyist, taking account of the deletion of those twelve bars of repetition. A facsimile of that missing autograph, today in private hands, is given in the commentary volume to the facsimile of the autograph of the complete opera in Wolfgang Amadeus Mozart, *Die Entführung aus dem Serail, K. 384. Facsimile of the Autograph Score*, vol. 2, 67–82.

for all their differences, have a good deal in common, in their formal conception and even in some shared phrases. But much had happened between the staging of *Idomeneo* in Munich and the composition of *Die Entführung*. We are in the depths of the season 1781–82, Mozart's first in Vienna. Work on the Stephanie libretto, begun in late September 1781, is interrupted because the court theater will be occupied with several major works by Gluck. On 24 October, Mozart writes to his father: "The first performance of Iphigenie took place yesterday," reminding us of the *Iphigenie auf Tauris*, in the Alxinger translation, that was our topic in an earlier chapter. "I tried to get a reserved seat in the third circle six days beforehand, but they were all gone. However, I was at nearly all the rehearsals."[13] Iphigenie's touching G-minor cavatina in act 3, "D'une image, hélas" (now "O sein Bild, zu fest gebunden"), brings once more to mind Pamina's "Ach, ich fühl's (ten years later): the clean, washed diction, the immediacy of expression, an unnerving epilogue in the orchestra.

Did the lean, sinewy prose of Gluck's music infiltrate into Mozart's "Traurigkeit" in some ineffable way? The sheer density of Mozart's music in 1781, the richness of its harmonic language, its lavish display of the voice, argue against such a notion. "In an opera," he wrote, in a letter of 13 October 1781, again in the midst of work on *Die Entführung*, "the poetry must be altogether the obedient daughter of the music. [In opera, Italian or French,] the music reigns supreme and when one listens to it all else is forgotten."[14] Gluck construed this eternal tension between word and tone rather differently. In a letter to the *Mercure de France* in 1773, the aging composer wrote of a proposed collaboration with Rousseau, with whom he would seek "a noble, moving and natural melody with a declamation in keeping with the prosody of each language and the character of each people."[15] That Mozart thought it worth his while to attend all those rehearsals of *Iphigenie*, marking time before the composition of act 2 of *Entführung*, might lead us to suspect that something of Gluck's parsimonious *Sprachgefühl* would find its way into the language of Konstanze's aria. At this propitious moment in his young career, Mozart's ear was turned elsewhere. Gluck, holding the stage that Mozart sought, was the problem, not the solution.

13. Anderson, *Letters*, 775. *Briefe und Aufzeichnungen*, vol. 3, 170–71.
14. Anderson, *Letters*, 773. *Briefe und Aufzeichnungen*, vol. 3, 167.
15. *The Collected Correspondence and Papers of Christoph Willibald Gluck*, ed. Hedwig and E. H. Mueller von Asow, 31; Howard, *An Eighteenth-Century Portrait*, 106.

There was of course another Constanze in Mozart's life. After a complicated courtship during this *Entführung* season, Mozart and Constanze Weber were married on 4 August 1782, only weeks after the first performance of the opera. To suggest that Bretzner's Konstanze and wife Constanze shared anything more than a name would be an affront to good sense. And yet, it would seem obdurate to dismiss as irrelevant the actuality of this lived experience: of a Mozart at once pursuing the hand of Constanze, fighting off a sordid imbroglio that involved her mother, seeking the grudging approval of a scolding father, and at the same time struggling to gain the stage for an opera that was stalled in the middle of act 2. To read such deeply felt music as Konstanze's "Traurigkeit" as tinged in autobiography is to play a dangerous game. Still, this fictional Konstanze did not materialize out of thin air. Perhaps it helps to conjure an autobiographical trace, the creative process as an *Augenblick* in which these shards of disparate experience recognize themselves in the mimetic mirror.

G minor. More than a key, it suggests rather an aura inhabited by Mozart's troubled women, inflecting even that momentary embrace, in G minor, with which Cherubino bids Susanna (and the Countess) farewell. I'm tempted to invoke once more that androgynous figure of Goethe's little ballad.[16] In the company of Konstanze, Ilia, Pamina, and Gluck's Iphigénie, Mozart's delusional *Veilchen*—"gebückt in sich und unbekannt"—is thoroughly outclassed. Still, its doleful cavatina, arrogating G minor to its purpose, touches a familiar nerve. The figure of the violet, powerless to break through the con-

16. "Mißvergnügen [displeasure], Unbehaglichkeit [uneasiness], Zerren an einem verunglückten Plane [worry about a failed plan]; mißmuthiges Nagen am Gebiß [ill-tempered gnawing at the bit]; mit einem Wort, Groll und Unlust [anger and disgust or repugnance]." This is how Daniel Schubart, writing in 1784 under the rubric "Charakteristik der Töne," thought to define G minor, later published in *Ideen zu einer Aesthetik der Tonkunst*, ed. Ludwig Schubart (Vienna: J. V. Degen, 1806; repr. Hildesheim: Olms, 1969), 377–78. But of course none of these epithets has anything to do with the music that expresses a *Charakteristik* of Konstanze or Pamina. Perhaps one might suggest something like "*Klage der unglücklichen Liebe.*—Jedes Schmachten, Sehnen, Seufzen der liebestrunknen Seele, liegt in diesem Tone." [Complaint of unhappy love.—This languishing, yearning, suffering of the love-drunk soul lies in this key.] These are Schubart's words, but they come in a portrayal of C minor. If a congeries of works in C minor, from Haydn, Mozart, and Beethoven, share qualities that might be expressed in common language, the longings of the suffering lover are nowhere to be found among them.

straints that define the natural world, yet possesses a sensibility that mimics the core of human feeling. Recognizing Lessing's *Mitleid* in ourselves, we weep only slightly less compassionately with Mozart's *Veilchen* than with those lofty heroines on their grand stage.

In its tropes of suffering and tears, Mozart's music sings across the boundaries of genre. *Singspiel, dramma per musica, opera seria, buffa*, ballad: each seeks to envelop its characters in a music delimited by convention. Mozart's women resist. When they sing, deep within themselves, the protocols of convention dissolve. Tinged in *Trauerspiel*, each conjures a world figured in tears. Mozart takes us with them, their music probing beyond a linguistic *Gefühlsleben*, beyond pathos to some inner moment of self-awareness, to the root of being.

Ex. 9.1. (pages 199 through 204) Mozart, *Die Entführung aus dem Serail*, act 2, scene 2: Konstanze, recitative and aria, complete, in piano reduction.

WORKS CITED

DOCUMENTS AND BIBLIOGRAPHIES

Albrecht, Theodore, ed. and trans. *Letters to Beethoven and Other Correspondence.* Lincoln and London: University of Nebraska Press, 1996.

Anderson, Emily, ed. and trans. *The Letters of Beethoven.* London: Macmillan & Co.; New York: St. Martin's Press, 1961.

———. *The Letters of Mozart and His Family.* New York: St. Martin's Press, 1966.

Bach, Carl Philipp Emanuel. *Autobiography. Verzeichniß des musikalischen Nachlasses.* Annotations in English and German by William S. Newman. Buren, The Netherlands: Frits Knuf, 1991.

———. *Briefe und Dokumente: Kritische Gesamtausgabe.* Edited by Ernst Suchalla. Göttingen: Vandenhoeck & Ruprecht, 1994.

———. *Carl Philipp Emanuel Bach. Portrait Collection,* 2 vols. Edited by Annette Richards, appendices edited by Paul Corneilson (*Complete Works,* series 8, vol. 4.1). Los Altos, CA: Packard Humanities Institute, 2012.

———. *The Catalog of Carl Philipp Emanuel Bach's Estate.* A Facsimile of the Edition by Schniebes, Hamburg, 1790. Annotated, with a Preface, by Rachel W. Wade. New York & London: Garland Publishing, 1981.

Bartlitz, Eveline. *Die Beethoven-Sammlung in der Musikabteilung der Deutschen Staatsbibliothek: Verzeichnis.* Berlin: Deutsche Staatsbibliothek, 1970.

Beethoven, Ludwig van. *Briefwechsel Gesamtausgabe,* 7 vols. Edited by Sieghard Brandenburg "im Auftrag des Beethoven-Hauses Bonn." Munich: G. Henle, 1996.

———. *Ludwig van Beethovens Konversationshefte,* vol. 4 (1968), edited by Karl-Heinz Köhler and Grita Herre, with the assistance of Ignaz Weinmann; vol. 5 (1970), edited by Karl-Heinz Köhler and Grita Herre, with the assistance of Peter Pötschner; vol. 10 (1993), edited by Dagmar Beck, with the assistance of Günter Brosche. Leipzig: VEB Deutscher Verlag für Musik.

Clark, Stephen L., ed. and trans. *The Letters of C. P. E. Bach.* Oxford: Clarendon Press, 1997.

Deutsch, Otto Erich. *Mozart und seine Welt in zeitgenössischen Bildern/Mozart and his World in Contemporary Pictures,* initiated by Maximilian Zenger, presented by Otto Erich Deutsch, in Wolfgang Amadeus Mozart, *Neue Ausgabe sämtlicher Werke,* Serie 10, Werkgruppe 32. Kassel: Bärenreiter, 1961.

Friedlaender, Max. *Das deutsche Lied im 18. Jahrhundert: Quellen und Studien.* Stuttgart and Berlin: Cotta'schen Buchhandlung, 1902; repr. Hildesheim: Georg Olms, 1962.

Frimmel, Theodor. *Beethoven Handbuch.* Leipzig: Breitkopf & Härtel, 1926.

Gluck, Christoph Willibald. *The Collected Correspondence and Papers of Christoph Willibald Gluck.* Edited by Hedwig and E. H. Mueller von Asow, translated by Stewart Thomson. New York: St. Martin's Press, 1962.

Helm, E. Eugene. *Thematic Catalogue of the*

Works of Carl Philipp Emanuel Bach.
New Haven, CT, and London: Yale
University Press, 1989.

Hoboken, Anthony van. *Joseph Haydn:
Thematisch-bibliographisches
Werkverzeichnis*, vol. 1. Mainz: B. Schott's
Söhne, 1957.

Howard, Patricia. *Gluck: An Eighteenth-
Century Portrait in Letters and
Documents*. Oxford: Oxford University
Press, 1995.

Jäger-Sunstenau, Hanns. "Beethoven-Akten
im Wiener Landesarchiv." In *Beethoven-
Studien: Festgabe der Österreichischen
Akademie der Wissenschaften zum 200.
Geburtstag von Ludwig van Beethoven*, ed.
Erich Schenk, 11–36. Vienna: Hermann
Böhlaus, 1970.

Kalischer, Alfred Christlieb. "Die
Beethoven-Autographe der Königl.
Bibliothek zu Berlin." In *Monatshefte für
Musikgeschichte* 27 (1895): 145–50, 153–
61, 163–70; 28 (1896): 1–7, 9–14, 17–22,
25–38, 41–53, 57–67, 73–80.

Kinsky, Georg. *Manuskripte, Briefe,
Dokumente von Scarlatti bis Stravinsky.
Katalog der Musikautographen-Sammlung
Louis Koch*. Stuttgart: Hoffmannsche
Buchdruckerei Felix Krais, 1953.

La Mara. *Musikerbriefe aus fünf
Jahrhunderten*, 2 vols. Leipzig: Breitkopf
& Härtel, [1886].

Landon, H. C. Robbins. *Haydn:
A Documentary Study*. New York:
Rizzoli, 1981.

Lappenberg, Johann Martin, ed. *Briefe
von und an Klopstock: Ein Beitrag zur
Literaturgeschichte seiner Zeit*. Brunswick:
Westermann, 1867; repr. Bern: Herbert
Lang, 1970.

Leisinger, Ulrich, and Peter Wollny. *Die
Bach Quellen der Bibliotheken in Brüssel.*

Katalog. Hildesheim, Zürich, New York:
Georg Olms, 1997.

Leitzmann, Albert. *Ludwig van Beethoven:
Berichte der Zeitgenossen, Briefe und
persönliche Aufzeichnungen*. Leipzig:
Insel-Verlag, 1921.

Mahler, Alma. *Gustav Mahler: Memories and
Letters*. Translated by Basil Creighton.
Seattle and London: University of
Washington Press, 1968.

Mozart, Wolfgang Amadeus. *Mozart:
Briefe und Aufzeichnungen*. Edited by
Wilhelm A. Bauer, Otto Erich Deutsch,
and Joseph Heinz Eibl. Erweiterte
Ausgabe, edited by Ulrich Konrad.
Kassel: Bärenreiter, Gemeinsame
Ausgabe, 2005.

———. *Mozart's Thematic Catalogue: A
Facsimile*, introduction and transcription
by Albi Rosenthal and Alan Tyson.
Ithaca, NY: Cornell University Press,
1990.

Nohl, Ludwig. *Musiker-Briefe*. Leipzig:
Duncker und Humblot, [1867].

Searle, Arthur. *The British Library Stefan
Zweig Collection: Catalogue of the Music
Manuscripts*. London: British Library,
1999.

Somfai, László. *Joseph Haydn: His Life
in Contemporary Pictures*. New York:
Taplinger, 1969.

Turner, J. Rigbie. *Four Centuries of Opera:
Manuscripts and Printed Editions in the
Pierpont Morgan Library*. New York:
Pierpont Morgan Library in association
with Dover Publications, 1983.

PRIMARY TEXTS AND
ORIGINAL SOURCES

Aristotle. *Poetics*. Edited and translated
by Stephen Halliwell. Loeb Classical
Library. Cambridge, MA: Harvard

University Press, 1995, corrected ed., 1999.

Bach, Carl Philipp Emanuel. *Versuch über die wahre Art, das Clavier zu spielen. Erster und zweiter Teil*. Faksimile-Nachdruck der I. Auflage, Berlin 1753 und 1762. Edited by Lothar Hoffmann-Erbrecht. Leipzig: Breitkopf & Härtel, 1969.

———. *Versuch über die wahre Art, das Clavier zu spielen*. In *Carl Philipp Emanuel Bach: The Complete Works*, series 7, vol. 1, nos. 1–3. Edited by Tobias Plebuch. Los Altos, CA: Packard Humanities Institute, 2011.

Beaumarchais, Pierre-Augustin Caron de. *The Figaro Plays*. Translated by John Wells, edited by John Leigh. London: J. M. Dent, 1997.

———. *Le Mariage de Figaro*. Edited with an introduction by Pol Gaillard. Paris: Les éditions Bordas, 1969.

Benjamin, Walter. "Die Bedeutung der Sprache in Trauerspiel und Tragödie," in Walter Benjamin, *Gesammelte Schriften*, vol. 2, part 1, 137–40. Edited by Rolf Tiedemann and Hermann Schweppenhäuser. Frankfurt am Main: Suhrkamp, 1977. Translated by Rodney Livingstone as "The Role of Language in *Trauerspiel* and Tragedy." In Benjamin, *Selected Writings*, vol. 1: 1913–26, 59–61. Edited by Marcus Bullock and Michael W. Jennings. Cambridge, MA, and London: Belknap Press of Harvard University Press, 1997.

———. *The Origin of German Tragic Drama*. Translated by John Osborne. London and New York: Verso, 1998.

———. *Ursprung des deutschen Trauerspiels*. Berlin: Ernst Rowohlt Verlag, 1928. Frankfurt am Main: Suhrkamp Verlag, 1963. Benjamin, *Gesammelte Schriften*,

Unter Mitwirkung von Theodor W. Adorno and Gershom Scholem, edited by Rolf Tiedemann and Hermann Schweppenhäuser, vol. 1, part 1, 203–430. Frankfurt am Main: Suhrkamp Verlag, 1974.

Berlioz, Hector. *The Memoirs of Hector Berlioz*. Translated and edited by David Cairns. New York and London: Alfred A. Knopf, 2002 [1969].

Burney, Charles. *An Eighteenth-Century Musical Tour in Central Europe and the Netherlands*. (Dr. Burney's Musical Tours in Europe. Vol. 2.) Edited by Percy A. Scholes. London: Oxford University Press, 1959.

Cramer, Carl Friedrich. *Klopstock (In Fragmenten aus Briefen von Tellow an Elisa)*. Hamburg: Schniebes, 1777. *Fortsetzung*. Hamburg: Schniebes, 1778.

———. *Klopstock. Er; und über ihn. Zweiter Theil. 1748–50*. Dessau: in der Gelehrten Buchhandlung, 1781; Leipzig and Altona: Kavenschen Buchhandlung, 1790.

———. *Magazin der Musik*. Hamburg: "in der Musicalischen Niederlage," 1783–86; repr. Hildesheim and New York: Georg Olms, 1971.

Diderot, Denis. "Conversation Between D'Alembert and Diderot." In Denis Diderot, *Rameau's Nephew and D'Alembert's Dream*. Translated with an Introduction by Leonard Tancock. Harmondsworth and New York: Penguin Books, 1966.

———. *Diderot on Art, II: The Salon of 1767*. Edited and translated by John Goodman. New Haven, CT, and London: Yale University Press, 1995.

———. "Regrets sur ma vieille robe de chambre." In *Diderot: Oeuvres complètes*, vol. 18: Arts et lettres (1767–70), 41–60.

Edited by Jochen Scholbach with Jeanne
Carriat et al. Paris: Hermann, 1984.
———. *Salons, III: 1767.* Edited by Jean
Seznec. London: Oxford University
Press, 2nd ed., 1983.
Donne, John. *The Elegies and the Songs
and Sonnets.* Edited by Helen Gardner.
Oxford: Oxford University Press, 1965.
Euripides. *Iphigenia in Tauris.* Translated by
Witter Bynner. In *Greek Tragedies,* vol. 2.
Edited by David Grene and Richmond
Lattimore. Chicago and London:
University of Chicago Press, 1960.
Forkel, Johann Nikolaus. *Allgemeine
Geschichte der Music.* Leipzig: Schwickert,
1788; repr. Graz: Akademische Druck-u.
Verlagsanstalt, 1967.
———. *Musikalisch-kritische Bibliothek,*
vol. 1. Gotha, 1778; repr. Hildesheim:
Olms, 1964.
———. "Ueber eine Sonate aus Carl Phil.
Emanuel Bachs dritter Sonatensammlung
für Kenner und Liebhaber, in F moll . . . :
Ein Sendschreiben an Hrn von ***" [On
a sonata in F minor from Carl Philipp
Emanuel Bach's third sonata collection
"für Kenner und Liebhaber": an open
letter to Mr. ***]. In Forkel, *Musikalischer
Almanach für Deutschland auf das Jahr
1784.* Leipzig: im Schwickertschen Verlag,
[n.d.]; repr. Hildesheim and New York:
Georg Olms, 1974.
Goethe, Johann Wolfgang von. *Die Leiden
des jungen Werther* [1774]. In *Der junge
Goethe,* Neu bearbeitete Ausgabe in fünf
Bänden, vol. 4, 105–87. Edited by Hanna
Fischer-Lamberg. Berlin: Walter de
Gruyter & Co., 1968.
———. *Die Leiden des jungen Werther.*
In Goethe, *Werke,* vol. 6: *Romane und
Novellen* I. Edited by Erich Trunz.
Munich: C. H. Beck, 1981.

———. *Italian Journey (1786–1788).*
Translated by W. H. Auden and
Elizabeth Mayer. New York: Schocken
Books, 1968.
———. "On the *Laocoon* Group." *Goethe:
The Collected Works,* vol. 3, pp. 15–23.
Essays on Art and Literature. Edited by
John Gearey; translated by Ellen von
Nardroff and Ernest H. von Nardroff.
Princeton, NJ: Princeton University
Press, 1994.
———. *The Sorrows of Young Werther.*
Translated by Victor Lange. *Goethe:
The Collected Works,* vol. 11. Edited
by David E. Wellbery. Princeton, NJ:
Princeton University Press, 1988.
———. *The Sorrows of Young Werther.*
Translated by Michael Hulse. London:
Penguin Books, 1989.
———. "Über Laokoon." In Goethe, *Werke.
Hamburger Ausgabe in 14 Bänden,* vol.
12: *Schriften zur Kunst,* 56–66. Edited by
Erich Trunz, commentary Herbert von
Einem. Munich: C. H. Beck, 1981.
———. *Werke. Hamburger Ausgabe in 14
Bänden,* vol. 1: *Gedichte und Epen,* vol. 1.
Edited by Erich Trunz. Munich: C. H.
Beck, 1981.
Herder, Johann Gottfried. *Abhandlung über
den Ursprung der Sprache* (1772). In
Herder, *Sämtliche Werke,* vol. 5, 1–154.
Edited by Bernhard Suphan. Berlin:
Weidmann, 1891; repr. Hildesheim:
Georg Olms, 1967.
———. "Fragmente einer Abhandlung über
die Ode." In Johann Gottfried Herder,
Sämtliche Werke, vol. 32, 61–63. Edited
by Bernhard Suphan. Berlin: Weidmann,
1899; repr. Hildesheim: Georg Olms,
1968.
———. *Selected Early Works 1764–1767.*
Edited by Ernest A. Menze and Karl

Menges; translated by Menze with Michael Palma. University Park: Pennsylvania State University Press, 1992.

———. *Essay on the Origin of Language.* In *On the Origin of Language (Jean-Jacques Rousseau, "Essay on the Origin of Languages"; Johann Gottfried Herder, "Essay on the Origin of Language").* Translated by John H. Moran and Alexander Gode. Chicago and London: University of Chicago Press, 1966.

Hölty, Ludwig Christoph Heinrich. *Werke und Briefe.* With a *Vorwort* by Uwe Berger. Berlin and Weimar: Aufbau-Verlag, 1966.

Kierkegaard, Søren. *Either/Or.* Translated by David F. Swenson and Lillian Marvin Swenson, with revisions and a foreword by Howard A. Johnson. Princeton, NJ: Princeton University Press, rev. 1959.

Kirnberger, Johann Philipp. *Die wahren Grundsätze zum Gebrauch der Harmonie . . . als ein Zusatz zu der Kunst des reinen Satzes in der Musik.* Berlin and Königsberg: G. J. Decker and G. L. Hartung, 1773; repr. Hildesheim and New York: Georg Olms, 1970.

Klopstock, Friedrich Gottlieb. *Ausgewählte Werke.* Edited by Karl August Schleiden, with a *Nachwort* by Friedrich Georg Jünger. Munich: Carl Hanser Verlag, 1962.

———. "Eine Beurteilung der Winckelmannischen Gedanken über die Nachahmung der griechischen Werke in den schönen Künsten" (1760), repr. in Klopstock, *Ausgewählte Werke,* 1049–1052.

———. *Klopstocks sämmtliche Werke.* Leipzig: Georg Joachim Göschen, 1823.

———. *Oden.* Edited by Franz Muncker

and Jaro Pawel. Stuttgart: G. J. Göschen, 1889.

———. "Von der Nachahmung des griechischen Silbenmaßes im Deutschen" (1755), repr. Klopstock, *Ausgewählte Werk,* 1038–1048.

———. *Werke und Briefe. Historisch-kritische Ausgabe: Briefe,* vol. 6, no. 2: 1773–75, Apparat/Kommentar. Edited by Annette Lüchow, with Sabine Tauchert. Berlin and New York: de Gruyter, 2001. *Briefe,* vol. 7, no. 2: 1776–82, Apparat/Kommentar. Edited by Helmut Riege Berlin and New York: de Gruyter, 1982.

Lessing, Gotthold Ephraim. *Briefwechsel über das Trauerspiel,* in Gotthold Ephraim Lessing, *Werke,* vol. 4: *Dramaturgische Schriften.* Munich: Carl Hanser Verlag, 1973.

———. *Laokoon: oder über die Grenzen der Mahlerey und Poesie. Mit beyläufigen Erläuterungen verschiedener Punkte der alten Kunstgeschichte.* Berlin: Bey Christian Friedrich Voß, 1766.

———. *Laocoön: An Essay on the Limits of Painting and Poetry.* Translated by Edward Allen McCormick. Indianapolis and New York: Bobbs-Merrill, 1962.

———. *Laocoon: An Essay upon the Limits of Painting and Poetry.* Translated by Ellen Frothingham. Boston: Roberts Brothers, 1874; repr. New York: Noonday Press, 1969.

———. *Laokoon: oder über die Grenzen der Mahlerei und Poesie.* In Lessing, *Werke,* vol. 6, *Kunsttheoretische und kunsthistorische Schriften.* Munich: Carl Hanser Verlag, 1974.

[Lessing, Moses Mendelssohn, Nicolai]. *Briefe, die Neueste Literatur betreffend,* 17. Theil. Berlin: Bey Friedrich Nicolai, 1764.

Longinus. *On the Sublime.* Translated by.

W. R. Roberts. In *Critical Theory Since Plato*. Edited by Hazard Adams, 76–102. New York: Harcourt Brace Jovanovich, 1971.

Marvell, Andrew. *The Poems of Andrew Marvell*. Edited by Nigel Smith. London and New York: Routledge, rev. 2013.

Mendelssohn, Moses. "Gedanken von dem Wesen der Ode. Zergliederung einiger sogenannten Oden der Fr. Karschin." In *Briefe, die Neueste Literatur betreffend*, 17. Theil, 274. Brief (Berlin: Bey Friedrich Nicolai, 1764), 150.

———. *Philosophical Writings*. Translated and edited by Daniel O. Dahlstrom. Cambridge: Cambridge University Press, 1997.

———. *Philosophische Schriften*, verbesserte Auflage, erster Theil. Berlin: Bey Christian Friedrich Voß, 1771. In Mendelssohn, *Schriften zur Philosophie und Äesthetik*, vol. 1 (in *Gesammelte Schriften: Jubiläumsausgabe . . . erster Band*). Edited by Fritz Bamberger. Berlin: Akademie-Verlag Berlin, 1929.

Reichardt, Johann Friedrich. *Briefe eines aufmerksam Reisenden die Musik betreffend*, vol. 2. Frankfurt and Breslau, 1776.

———. "Bruchstücke aus Reichardts Autobiographie," *Allgemeine musikalische Zeitung* 15 (1813), cols. 601–616, 633–42, 665–74.

———. "Ueber Klopstocks komponirte Oden," 22–23, 62–63 (music: 13–21, 56–61). *Musikalisches Kunstmagazin*, vol. 1. Berlin: Im Verlage des Verfassers, 1782; repr. Hildesheim: Georg Olms, 1969.

Rousseau, Jean-Jacques. *Dictionnaire de Musique*. Paris: Duchesne, 1768. Facsimile repr. with preface by Jean-Jacques Eigeldinger. Geneva: Editions Minkoff, 1998.

Schubart, Christian Friedrich Daniel. *Ideen zu einer Aesthetik der Tonkunst*. Edited by Ludwig Schubart. Vienna: J. V. Degan, 1806; repr. Hildesheim: Georg Olms, 1969.

Sulzer, Georg. *Aesthetics and the Art of Musical Composition in the German Enlightenment: Selected Writings of Johann Georg Sulzer and Heinrich Christoph Koch*. Edited by Nancy Kovaleff Baker and Thomas Christensen. Cambridge: Cambridge University Press, 1995.

———. *Allgemeine Theorie der Schönen Künste*. Neue vermehrte zweite Auflage. Leipzig: Weidmann, 1792–94; repr. Hildesheim: Georg Olms, 1970.

Triest, J. K. F. "Bemerkungen über die Ausbildung der Tonkunst in Deutschland im achtzehnten Jahrhundert." *Allgemeine musikalische Zeitung* 3 (1800–1801), col. 300 ff.

Winckelmann, Johann Joachim. *Gedancken über die Nachahmung der Griechischen Wercke in Mahlerey und Bildhauer-Kunst* (1755). Reprinted with translation in *Reflections on the Imitation of Greek Works in Painting and Sculpture*, trans. and ed. Elfriede Heyer and Roger C. Norton. La Salle, IL: Open Court, 1987.

STUDIES

Abbate, Carolyn. *Unsung Voices: Opera and Musical Narrative in the Nineteenth Century*. Princeton, NJ: Princeton University Press, 1991.

Abert, Hermann. *W. A. Mozart*. Newly revised and expanded edition of Otto Jahn's *Mozart*. Leipzig: Breitkopf & Härtel, 7th ed., 1956.

————. *W. A. Mozart*. Translated by Stewart Spencer. Edited by Cliff Eisen. New Haven, CT, and London: Yale University Press, 2007.

Alewyn, Richard. "'Klopstock!'" *Euphorion* 73 (1979): 357–64.

Allanbrook, Wye. *Rhythmic Gesture in Mozart*: Le Nozze di Figaro *and* Don Giovanni. Chicago and London: University of Chicago Press, 1983.

Arthur, John, and Carl Schachter. "Mozart's 'Das Veilchen.'" *Musical Times* 130 (March 1989): 149–55 and 163–64.

Bauman, Thomas. "Coming of Age in Vienna: *Die Entführung aus dem Serail*." In Daniel Heartz, *Mozart's Operas*, edited, with contributing essays, by Thomas Bauman, 65–87. Berkeley, Los Angeles, Oxford: University of California Press, 1990.

Boettcher, Hans. *Beethoven als Liederkomponist*. Augsburg: Dr. Benno Filser Verlag, 1928.

Bohm, Arnd. "'Klopstock!' Once More: Intertextuality in *Werther*." *Seminar: A Journal of Germanic Studies* 38(2) (2002): 116–33.

Bonds, Mark Evan. "The Sincerest Form of Flattery? Mozart's 'Haydn' Quartets and the Question of Influence." *Studi Musicali* 22 (1993): 365–409.

Brandenburg, Sieghard. "Beethovens politische Erfahrungen in Bonn." In *Beethoven: Zwischen Revolution und Restauration*, edited by Helga Lühning and Sieghard Brandenburg, 3–50. Bonn: Beethoven-Haus, 1989.

Buchholz, Ernst. *Der Konrektor von Einem und seine Tochter Charlotte*. Münden: W. Klugkist, 1899.

Busch, Gudrun. *C. Ph. E. Bach und seine Lieder*. Regensburg: Gustav Bosse, 1957.

Catterson, Lynn. "Michelangelo's *Laocoön*?" *Artibus et Historiae* 26(52) (2005): 29–56.

Churgin, Bathia. "Beethoven and Mozart's Requiem: A New Connection." *Journal of Musicology* 5 (Fall 1987): 457–77.

Cook, Nicholas. "The Editor and the Virtuoso, or Schenker versus Bülow." In Cook, *Music, Performance, Meaning: Selected Essays*, 83–99. Aldershot, Hampshire, UK; Burlington, VT: Ashgate, 2007.

Cooper, Barry. *Beethoven's Folksong Settings: Chronology, Sources, Style*. Oxford: Clarendon Press, 1994.

Cumming, Julie. "Gluck's Iphigenia Operas: Sources and Strategies." In *Opera and the Enlightenment*, edited by Thomas Bauman and Marita Petzoldt McClymonds, 217–40. Cambridge: Cambridge University Press, 1995.

Dahlhaus, Carl. "Ethos und Pathos in Glucks Iphigenie auf Tauris." *Die Musikforschung* 27 (1974): 289–300. Reprint in Dahlhaus, *Gesammelte Schriften*, vol. 5, 441–53. Laaber: Laaber Verlag, 2003.

Dieckmann, Herbert. "Description of Portait." *Diderot Studies* 2 (1952): 6–8.

Dubowy, Norbert (after Mell). "Lolli, Antonio." In *Die Musik in Geschichte und Gegenwart*. 2nd, newly revised edition, edited by Ludwig Finscher. Personenteil, vol. 11. Kassel: Bärenreiter; Stuttgart: J. B. Metzler, 2001.

Grigat, Friederike. "Christian Gottlob Neefe und seine Verleger," in *Christian Gottlob Neefe (1748–1798)*, edited by Helmut Loos, 191–226.

Gruber, Gernot. "Gluck und Mozart." *Hamburger Jahrbuch für Musikwissenschaft* 5 (1981): 169–86.

Hadlock, Heather. "The Career of Cherubino, or the Trouser Role Grows

Up." In *Siren Songs: Representations of Gender and Sexuality in Opera*, edited by Mary Ann Smart, 67–92. Princeton, NJ, and Oxford: Princeton University Press, 2000.

Hildesheimer, Wolfgang. *Mozart*. Frankfurt am Main: Suhrkamp Verlag, 1977. English as *Mozart*, translated by Marion Faber. New York: Farrar, Straus, Giroux, 1982.

Horowitz, Joseph. *Classical Music in America: A History of Its Rise and Fall*. New York: W. W. Norton, 2005.

Hortschansky, Klaus. *Parodie und Entlehnung im Schaffen Christoph Willibald Glucks* (*Analecta Musicologica* 13). Cologne: Arno Volk Verlag Hans Gerig KG, 1973.

Keiler, Allan. "The Modest Maestro." Review of *Bruno Walter: A World Elsewhere*, by Erik Ryding and Rebecca Pechefsky. *New York Review of Books* 49(2) (14 February 2002).

Kerman, Joseph. *The Beethoven Quartets*. New York: Alfred A. Knopf, 1967.

Köhler, Karl-Heinz. "Figaro-Miscellen: einige dramaturgische Mitteilungen zur Quellensituation." *Mozart-Jahrbuch 1968/70* (Salzburg, 1970), 119–31.

Krähe, Ludwig. *Carl Friedrich Cramer bis zu seiner Amtsenthebung*. Berlin: Mayer & Müller, 1907.

Kramer, Richard. "Cadenza Contra Text: Mozart in Beethoven's Hands." *19th Century Music* 15 (Fall 1991): 116–31, and, slightly revised, in *Unfinished Music*, 211–32.

———. "'*Das Organische der Fuge*': On the Autograph of Beethoven's Quartet in F Major, Opus 59 No. 1." In *The String Quartets of Haydn, Mozart, and Beethoven: Studies of the Autograph*

Manuscripts, edited by Christoph Wolff, 223–65. Cambridge, MA: Harvard University Department of Music, distr. Harvard University Press, 1980.

———. "Probing the *Versuch*." *Keyboard Perspectives* 5 (2012): 83–94.

———. *Unfinished Music*. New York: Oxford University Press, 2008, rev. ed. 2012.

Kropfinger, Klaus. "'Denn was schwer ist, ist auch schön, gut, gross.'" *Bonner Beethoven-Studien* 3 (2003): 81–100.

La Grange, Henry-Louis de. *Gustav Mahler*, vol. 2: *Vienna: The Years of Challenge (1897–1904)*. Oxford and New York: Oxford University Press, 1995.

———. *Gustav Mahler*, vol. 4: *A New Life Cut Short (1907–1911)*. Oxford and New York: Oxford University Press, 2008.

Lanham, Richard A. *Handlist of Rhetorical Terms*. Berkeley, Los Angeles, Oxford: University of California Press, 2nd ed., 1991.

Leux, Irmgard. *Christian Gottlob Neefe (1748–1798)*. Leipzig: Fr. Kistner & C. F. W. Siegel, 1925.

Lockwood, Lewis. "Beethoven's Sketches for *Sehnsucht* (WoO 146)." In *Beethoven Studies* [vol. 1], edited by Alan Tyson, 97–122. New York: W. W. Norton, 1973.

Loos, Helmut, ed. *Christian Gottlob Neefe (1748–1798): Eine eigenständige Künstlerpersönlichkeit. Tagesbericht Chemnitz 1998*. Chemnitz: Gudrun Schröder Verlag, 1999.

Lorenz, Michael. "Joseph Lange's Mozart Portrait." Blog post at Lorenz's website, 19 September 2012.

Lühning, Helga. "Die Cavatina in der italienischen Oper um 1800." *Analecta Musicologica* 21 (1982): 333–34.

Maierhofer, Waltraud. "Angelika Kauffmann

Reads Goethe: Illustration and Symbolic Representation in the Göschen Edition." *Sophie Journal* (online) 2(1) (2012): 1–34.

Mell, Albert. "Lolli, Antonio." In *The New Grove Dictionary of Music and Musicians*, edited by Stanley Sadie. Vol. 11, 137–39. London and New York: Macmillan, 1980. Revised, 2nd ed. Vol. 15, 82–85. UK: Macmillan; US: Grove's Dictionaries, 2001.

Michael, Wilhelm. *Überlieferung und Reihenfolge der Gedichte Höltys*. Halle: Max Niemeyer, 1909.

Möller, Eberhard. "Christian Gottlob Neefe und seine Klopstock-Oden." In *Christian Gottlob Neefe (1748–1798): Eine eigenständige Künstlerpersönlichkeit*, edited by Helmut Loos. 109–27. Chemnitz: Gudrun Schröder Verlag, 1999.

Muncker, Franz. *Friedrich Gottlieb Klopstock: Geschichte seines Lebens und seiner Schriften*. Stuttgart: Göschen, "Ausgabe in einem Bande," 1893.

Münster, Robert. "Die Mozart-Portraits des Joseph Lange." *Mozart Studien* 19 (2010): 281–95.

Noiray, Michel. "Der Brief Glucks an Guillard: Zum Parodieverfahren in zwei Arien der 'Iphigénie en Tauride.'" In *Christoph Willibald Gluck und die Opernreform*, edited by Klaus Hortschansky, 373–89. Wege der Forschung, 613. Darmstadt: Wissenschaftliche Buchgesellschaft, 1989.

Nottebohm, Gustav. *Beethovens Studien*. Leipzig and Winterthur: J. Rieter-Biedermann, 1873.

———. *Zweite Beethoveniana: Nachgelassene Aufsätze*. Leipzig: C. F. Peters, 1887.

Oppel, Reinhard. "Ueber Beziehungen Beethovens zu Mozart und zu Ph. Em. Bach." *Zeitschrift für Musikwissenschaft* 5 (1922–23): 30–39.

Ottenberg, Hans-Günter. *Carl Philipp Emanuel Bach*. Leipzig: Verlag Philipp Reclam jun., 1982. English as *C. P. E. Bach*, translated by Philip J. Whitmore. Oxford and New York: Oxford University Press, 1987.

Rapp, Regula. "'Soll ich nach dem Manne der Tagesmode forschen . . .': Die C.-P.-E.-Bach-Herausgeber Hans von Bülow und Johannes Brahms." In *Carl Philipp Emanuel Bach: Musik für Europa*, edited by Hans-Günter Ottenberg, 506–17. Frankfurt [Oder]: Konzerthalle "Carl Philipp Emanuel Bach," 1998.

Richards, Annette. "An Enduring Monument: C. P. E. Bach and the Musical Sublime." In *C. P. E. Bach Studies*, edited by Annette Richards, 149–72. Cambridge: Cambridge University Press, 2006.

Richter, Simon. *Laocoon's Body and the Aesthetics of Pain: Winckelmann, Lessing, Herder, Moritz, Goethe*. Detroit: Wayne State University Press, 1992.

———. "Sculpture, Music, Text: Winckelmann, Herder and Gluck's *Iphigénie en Tauride*." In *Goethe Yearbook* 8 (1996): 157–71.

Rosen, Charles. *The Classical Style: Haydn, Mozart, Beethoven*. New York: W. W. Norton, expanded ed., 1997.

Salzer, Felix. "Haydn's Fantasia from the String Quartet, Opus 76, No. 6." *The Music Forum*, vol. 4, edited by Felix Salzer, 161–94. New York: Columbia University Press, 1976.

Schachter, Carl. See Arthur, John.

Schenker, Heinrich. "A Contribution to the Study of Ornamentation," translated by

Hedi Siegel. *The Music Forum*, vol. 4, edited by Felix Salzer, 1–139. New York: Columbia University Press, 1976.

———. *Ein Beitrag zur Ornamentik als Einführung zu Ph. Em. Bachs Klavierwerken.* Vienna: Universal Edition, 1904, rev. 1908.

———. "Die Kunst der Improvisation." In Schenker, *Das Meisterwerk in der Musik* [vol. 1], 11–40. Munich, Vienna, Berlin: Drei Masken Verlag, 1925. English, as "The Art of Improvisation," translated by Richard Kramer, in *The Masterwork in Music*, vol. 1, 2–19, edited by William Drabkin. Cambridge and New York: Cambridge University Press, 1994; and repr. New York: Dover Publications, 2015.

Schiedermair, Ludwig. *Der junge Beethoven.* Leipzig: Quelle & Meyer, 1925.

Schmid, Ernst Fritz. *Carl Philipp Emanuel Bach und seine Kammermusik.* Kassel: Bärenreiter, 1931.

Schütt, Rüdiger. "Von Kiel nach Paris: Carl Friedrich Cramer in den Jahren 1775 bis 1805." In *Ein Mann von Feuer und Talenten: Leben und Werk von Carl Friedrich Cramer*, edited by Rüdiger Schütt, 13–46. Göttingen: Wallstein, 2005.

Solomon, Maynard. *Mozart: A Life.* New York: HarperCollins, 1995.

Somfai, László. "A Bold Enharmonic Modulatory Model in Joseph Haydn's String Quartets." In *Studies in Eighteenth-Century Music: A Tribute to Karl Geiringer on his Seventieth Birthday*, edited by H. C. Robbins Landon in collaboration with Roger E. Chapman, 370–81. London: George Allen and Unwin Ltd, 1970.

Steinberg, Michael P. *Austria as Theater and Ideology: The Meaning of the Salzburg Festival* Ithaca, NY, and London: Cornell University Press, 2nd ed., 2000.

Tyson, Alan. "The 'Razumovsky' Quartets: Some Aspects of the Sources." In *Beethoven Studies*, vol. 3, edited by Alan Tyson, 107–40. Cambridge: Cambridge University Press, 1982.

———. *Mozart: Studies of the Autograph Scores.* Cambridge, MA, and London: Harvard University Press, 1987.

Van der Zanden, Jos. "A Beethoven Sketchleaf in the Hague." *Bonner Beethoven-Studien* 3 (2003): 153–67.

Vrieslander, Otto. *Carl Philipp Emanuel Bach.* Munich: R. Piper & Co., 1923.

White, Hayden. *Metahistory: The Historical Imagination in Nineteenth-Century Europe.* Baltimore, and London: Johns Hopkins University Press, 1973.

Willnauer, Franz. *Gustav Mahler und die Wiener Oper.* 2nd ed. Vienna: Löcker, 1993.

Youngren, William H. *C. P. E. Bach and the Rebirth of the Strophic Song.* Lanham, MD, and Oxford: Scarecrow Press, 2003.

MUSIC EDITIONS AND FACSIMILES

Bach, Carl Philipp Emanuel. *Arias and Chamber Cantatas.* Edited by Bertil van Boer. *The Complete Works*, series 6, vol. 4. Los Altos, CA: Packard Humanities Institute, 2010.

———. *Ausgewählte Klavierkompositionen.* Mit Fingersatz und Phrasierungsbezeichnung von Dr. Hugo Riemann. Leipzig: Steingräber-Verlag, n.d., plate number 501.

———. *Clavier-Sonaten nebst einigen Rondos fürs Forte-Piano für Kenner und Liebhaber.* Dritte Sammlung. Leipzig: "im Verlage des Autors," 1781. Facsimile in *The Collected Works for Solo Keyboard by Carl Philipp Emanuel Bach*, vol. 2. Edited by Darrell Berg. New York and London: Garland Publishing, 1985.

———. *"Kenner und Liebhaber" Collections I.* Edited by Christopher Hogwood. Carl Philipp Emanuel Bach, *The Complete Works*, series 1, vol. 4.1. Los Altos, CA: Packard Humanities Institute, 2009.

———. *Klavierwerke*, 2 vols. Edited by Heinrich Schenker. Vienna: Universal Edition [preface: 1902].

———. *Lieder und Gesänge.* Edited by Otto Vrieslander. Munich: Drei Masken Verlag, 1922.

———. *Miscellaneous Songs.* Edited by Christoph Wolff. Carl Philipp Emanuel Bach, *The Complete Works*, series 6, vol. 3. Los Altos, CA: Packard Humanities Institute, 2014.

———. *The Polyhymnia Portfolio.* Edited by Christoph Wolff. Carl Philipp Emanuel Bach, *The Complete Works*, series 8, vol. 2. Los Altos, CA: Packard Humanities Institute, 2014.

———. *Sechs Sonaten für Klavier allein von C. Ph. Em. Bach*, bearbeitet u. mit einem Vorwort herausgegeben von Hans von Bülow. Leipzig: C. F. Peters, [preface: 1862].

Beethoven, Ludwig van. *Beethoven's "Eroica" Sketchbook: A Critical Edition.* Transcribed, edited, and with a commentary by Lewis Lockwood and Alan Gosman. Urbana, Chicago, and Springfield: University of Illinois Press, 2013.

———. *Ludwig van Beethoven: Ein Skizzenbuch aus dem Jahre 1809 (Landsberg 5).* Edited by Clemens Brenneis. Bonn: Beethoven-Haus, 1993.

———. *Beethoven: String Quartet Opus 59 No. 1 (First "Razumovsky" Quartet, in F major)*, with an Introduction by Alan Tyson. London: Scolar Press, 1980.

———. *Werke: Gesamtausgabe.* Abteilung 12, vol. 1: *Lieder und Gesänge mit Klavierbegleitung.* Edited by Helga Lühning. Munich: G. Henle Verlag, 1990.

———. *Werke: Gesamtausgabe.* Abteilung 11, vol. 1: *Schottische und walisische Lieder.* Edited by Petra Weber-Bockholdt. Munich: G. Henle Verlag, 1999.

Gluck, Christoph Willibald. *Iphigénie en Tauride.* Edited by F. Pelletan and B. Damcke. Paris: Simon Richault, [1874].

———. *Iphigenie auf Tauris.* Edited by Gerhard Croll. In Gluck, *Sämtliche Werke*, Serie 1, vol. 11. Kassel: Bärenreiter Verlag, 1965.

———. *Iphigénie en Tauride.* Edited by Gerhard Croll. In Gluck, *Sämtliche Werke*, Serie 1, vol. 9. Kassel: Bärenreiter Verlag, 1973.

———. *Iphigénie en Tauride.* Edited by Hermann Abert. German translation by Peter Cornelius. London, Zurich, New York: Edition Eulenburg, [n.d.].

———. *Oden und Lieder auf Texte von Friedrich Gottlieb Klopstock und Lorenz Leopold Haschka.* Edited by Daniela Philippi and Heinrich W. Schwab. In Gluck, *Sämtliche Werke*, Abteilung 6: Vokalmusik, vol. 2. Kassel, Basel, etc.: Bärenreiter Verlag, 2011.

———. *Lieder und Arien von Chr. W. Gluck.* Edited by Max Friedlaender. Leipzig: Peters, [n.d.].

Mozart, Wolfgang Amadeus. *Die Entführung aus dem Serail, K. 384. Facsimile of the Autograph Score.* Introductory Essay by Hendrik Birus. Musicological Introduction by Ulrich Konrad. Los Altos, CA: Packard Humanities Institute, 2008.

————. *Idomeneo, K. 366, with Ballet K. 367. Facsimile of the Autograph Score.* Introductory Essay by Hans Joachim Kreutzer. Musicological Introduction by Bruce Alan Brown. Los Altos, CA: Packard Humanities Institute, 2006.

————. *Le nozze di Figaro, K. 492. Facsimile of the Autograph Score.* Introductory Essay by Norbert Miller. Musicological Introduction by Dexter Edge. Los Altos, CA: Packard Humanities Institute, 2007.

————. *Neue Ausgabe sämtlicher Werke.* Serie 2, Werkgruppe 5, vol. 16. *Kritische Berichte.* Le Nozze di Figaro (Ludwig Finscher) vorgelegt von Ulrich Leisinger. Kassel: Bärenreiter-Verlag, 2007.

Neefe, Christian Gottlob. *Lieder mit Klaviermelodien.* Glogau: Christian Friedrich Günthen, 1776.

————. *Oden von Klopstock, mit Melodien von Christian Gottlob Neefe.* Flensburg and Leipzig: in der Kortenschen Buchhandlung, 1776. Facsimile reprint as Christian Gottlob Neefe, *Oden von Klopstock,* in *Dokumentation zur Geschichte des deutschen Liedes,* vol. 9, ed. Siegfried Kross. Hildesheim, Zurich, New York: Georg Olms, 2003. A newly revised edition is *Oden von Klopstock in Musik gesezt von Neefe.* Neuwied: Johann Ludwig Gehra ["In Bosslers Notenoffizin zu Speier gedrukt"], 1785.

INDEX

Page numbers in italic indicate illustrations or musical examples.